Laptops & Tablets For Seniors

FOR

DUMMIES®

2ND EDITION

Laptops & Tablets For Seniors

FOR DUMMIES®

2ND EDITION

by Nancy Muir

WILEY

John Wiley & Sons, Inc.

Laptops & Tablets For Seniors For Dummies®, 2nd Edition

Published by
John Wiley & Sons, Inc.
111 River Street
Hoboken, NJ 07030-5774
www.wiley.com

Copyright © 2011 by John Wiley & Sons, Inc., Indianapolis, Indiana

Published by John Wiley & Sons, Inc., Indianapolis, Indiana

Published simultaneously in Canada

WILEY

About the Author

Nancy Muir is the author of over 60 books on technology and business topics. In addition to her writing work, Nancy runs a website on technology for seniors called TechSmartSenior.com and a companion website for her iPad books in the *For Dummies* series, iPadMadeClear.com. She writes a regular column on computers and the Internet on Retirenet. com. Prior to her writing career Nancy was a manager at several publishing companies, and a training manager at Symantec.

Dedication

To my wonderful husband, Earl, who puts up with book after book and has even co-authored a few of them. Thanks, honey — you're the best!

Author's Acknowledgments

I was lucky enough to have Blair Pottenger, the absolute best editor in the world, assigned to lead the team on this book. Thanks also to Sharon Mealka for her able work as technical editor, and to Barry Childs-Hleton, the book's copy editor. Last but never least, thanks to Katie Mohr, Acquisitions Editor, for hiring me to write this book.

Publisher's Acknowledgments

We're proud of this book; please send us your comments at http://dummies.custhelp.com. For other comments, please contact our Customer Care Department within the U.S. at 877-762-2974, outside the U.S. at 317-572-3993, or fax 317-572-4002.

Some of the people who helped bring this book to market include the following:

Acquisitions and Editorial

Project Editor: Blair J. Pottenger

Acquisitions Editor: Katie Mohr

Senior Copy Editor: Barry Childs-Helton

Technical Editor: Sharon Mealka

Editorial Manager: Kevin Kirschner

Editorial Assistant: Amanda Graham

Sr. Editorial Assistant: Cherie Case

Cover Photo: ©istockphoto.com / Jacob Wackerhausen

Cartoons: Rich Tennant (www.the5thwave.com)

Composition Services

Senior Project Coordinator: Kristie Rees

Layout and Graphics: Carrie A. Cesavice, Joyce Haughey, Sennett Vaughan Johnson, Corrie Socolovitch

Proofreader: Toni Settle

Indexer: Glassman Indexing Services

Special Help: Kim Holtman

Publishing and Editorial for Technology Dummies

Richard Swadley, Vice President and Executive Group Publisher

Andy Cummings, Vice President and Publisher

Mary Bednarek, Executive Acquisitions Director

Mary C. Corder, Editorial Director

Publishing for Consumer Dummies

Kathy Nebenhaus, Vice President and Executive Publisher

Composition Services

Debbie Stailey, Director of Composition Services

Contents at a Glance

Table of Contents

Chapter 7: Setting Up Your Display 99

Chapter 8: Getting Help with Vision, Hearing, and Dexterity Challenges... 113

Chapter 9: Setting Up Printers and Scanners.................. 133

Computers for consumers have come a long way in just 20 years or so. They're now at the heart of the way many people communicate, shop, and learn. They provide useful tools for tracking information, organizing finances, and being creative.

During the rapid growth of the personal computer, you might have been too busy to jump in and learn the ropes, but you now realize how useful and fun working with a computer can be — and you've decided to opt for a laptop.

This book helps you get going with your laptop quickly and painlessly.

About This Book

This book is specifically written for mature people like you, folks who are relatively new to using a computer and want to discover the basics of buying a laptop, working with software, and getting on the Internet. In writing this book, I've tried to take into account the types of activities that might interest a 50+-year-old citizen discovering computers for the first time.

Foolish Assumptions

This book is organized by sets of tasks. These tasks start from the very beginning, assume you know little about computers, and guide you through from the most basic steps in easy-to-understand language. Because I assume you're new to laptops, the book provides explanations or definitions of technical terms to help you out.

Introduction

Conventions used in this book

This book uses certain conventions to help you find your way around:

➡ When you have to type something in a text box, I put it in **bold** type. Whenever I mention a web site address, I put it in another font, `like this`. Figure references are also in bold, to help you find them.

➡ For menu commands, I use the ⇨ symbol to separate menu choices. For example, choose Tools⇨Internet Options. The ⇨ symbol is just my way of saying "Open the Tools menu and then click Internet Options."

➡ Callouts for figures draw your attention to an action you need to perform. In some cases, points of interest in a figure might be circled. The text tells you what to look for; the circle makes it easy to find.

 Tip icons point out insights or helpful suggestions related to tasks in the step list.

All computers are run by software called an *operating system*, such as Windows. Because Microsoft Windows—based personal computers (PCs) are the most common type, the book focuses on Windows 7 functionality.

Why You Need This Book

Working with computers can be a daunting prospect to people who are coming to them later in life. Your grandchildren may run rings around you when it comes to technology, but fear not: recent research refutes the adage that you can't teach an old dog new tricks. With the simple step-by-step approach of this book, even the technophobic can get up to speed with a laptop.

You can work through this book from beginning to end or simply open up a chapter to solve a problem or help you learn a new skill whenever you need it. The steps in each task get you where you want to go quickly, without a lot of technical explanation. In no time, you'll start picking up the skills you need to become a confident laptop user.

How This Book Is Organized

This book is conveniently divided into several handy parts to help you find what you need.

➡ **Part I: First Steps with Your Laptop:** If you need to buy a laptop or get started with the basics of using a computer, this part is for you. These chapters help you understand how a laptop differs from a desktop computer, and what features differentiate netbooks and tablets from a laptop. You get to explore the different specifications, styles, and price ranges for laptops, and discover how to set up your laptop out of the box, including hooking it up to a printer. There's even a chapter on the important topic of power management so you can maximize the battery life of your laptop. Chapter 5 is dedicated to those who want to jump into the tablet computer world, with a quick overview of how tablets work and a comparison of some of the models available today.

➡ **Part II: Exploring Windows:** These chapters provide information for exploring the Windows desktop when you first turn on your computer and customizing Windows to work the way you want it to. Finally, I provide information on using the Help system that's part of Windows.

➡ **Part III: Having Fun and Getting Things Done with Software:** Here's where you start working with that new laptop. First, I cover how to work with applications and the files you create with them. Then, using the popular and inexpensive (or often free) Microsoft Works software, discover how to create documents in the Works Word Processor and work with numbers in the Spreadsheet application. Chapters in this part also introduce you to built-in Windows applications you can use to work with digital photos, listen to music, and play games (including online games).

➡ **Part IV: Exploring the Internet:** It's time to get online! The chapters in this part help you understand what the Internet is and what tools and functions it makes available to you. Find out how to explore the Internet with a web browser; how to stay in touch with people via e-mail, instant messaging, chat, blogs; and even how to make Internet phone calls. I also introduce you to the social web, provide an overview of social networking sites such as Facebook, introduce microblogging with such services as Twitter, look at sharing videos, and even offer guidelines for dating online.

➡ **Part V: Taking Care of Your Laptop:** Now that you have a laptop, you have certain responsibilities toward it (just like having a child or puppy!). In this case, you need to protect your laptop from theft and protect the data on your computer, which you can do using Windows and Internet Explorer tools. In addition, you need to perform some routine maintenance tasks to keep your hard drive uncluttered and virus-free.

Get Going!

Whether you need to start from square one and buy yourself a laptop or you're ready to just start enjoying the tools and toys your current laptop makes available, it's time to get going, get online, and get laptop-savvy.

Part I

First Steps with Your Laptop

Discovering the Laptop Advantage

*L*aptop computers started as very expensive options for those who travelled on business and were willing to carry almost ten pounds of machine to be able to use a computer on the road.

Move forward in time, and you'll find that laptops have become a much more affordable, portable, and ubiquitous option that many are choosing as their only computer, whether they travel much or not. If you're thinking about joining the laptop revolution, it's time you understand the advantages a laptop can offer.

In this chapter, I introduce you to the key differences between a desktop computer and a laptop, the computing opportunities your laptop offers, and the different styles of laptops available. In addition, I provide an overview of two laptop options: the netbook and extremely portable tablet format that hit the big time with the introduction of the Apple iPad in 2010.

Understand the Difference between a Desktop and Laptop

The fact is that when it comes to performing computing tasks, a desktop and laptop are pretty much identical. They both have an operating system such as Windows 7 or Mac OS X. They both contain a hard drive where you store data and computer chips that process data, and they both run software and access the Internet.

Where a desktop and laptop differ is their physical appearance, size, and weight. Here's a rundown of the key differences:

➡ **Appearance:** A desktop computer is typically encased in a tower, into which you plug a separate monitor, keyboard, and mouse. (Though some newer models have the brains of the computer incorporated into a monitor base.) A laptop has all its parts in one unit, as shown in **Figure 1-1.** The central processing unit (CPU) — chips, monitor, keyboard, and touchpad (a laptop version of a mouse) — all fit in one compact package that includes ports for plugging in peripherals such as a transmitter for a wireless mouse or printer.

Figure 1-1

➠ **Power source:** A desktop computer is powered by plugging it into a wall outlet. A laptop contains a battery; you can run the laptop off of a charged battery, or plug the laptop into a wall outlet.

➠ **Portability:** Having a battery and coming in a more compact package makes a laptop more portable (though some larger models are a bit hefty to tote around); a desktop stays put on a desktop as a rule.

➠ **Extras:** Very small laptops might not include a CD/DVD drive and therefore require an external drive, like the one shown in **Figure 1-2,** to be attached.

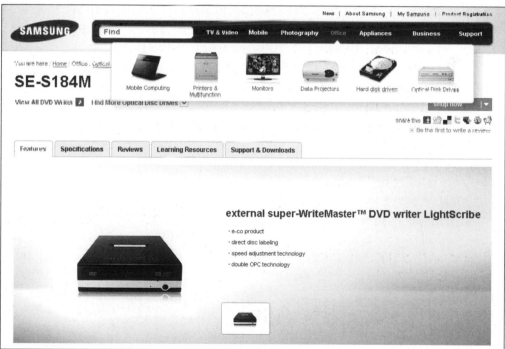

Figure 1-2

Get a Feel for Super Portable Netbooks and Tablets

There's a lot of hype in the media today that may have left you confused about the difference among laptops, netbooks, and tablets. Here's an overview.

Netbooks are a very lightweight type of laptop first introduced in 2007. Where laptops usually weigh in at about 4 to 7 pounds, netbooks weigh a mere 2-or-so pounds and their screens come in at around 9 to 12 inches. Of course, their light weight has tradeoffs, mainly in the form of a much smaller keyboard and, in their early years, limitations on their ability to use the most up-to-date operating systems (the software that runs your computer); early netbooks used Windows XP rather than Windows Vista because Vista used up so much of their relatively small data-storage capability. By 2009, netbooks had grown to become essentially small laptops, using the Windows 7 Starter operating system (still a bit limited compared to the full Windows 7). Netbooks offer a lower price point than laptops at about $250–$400 and have pretty good battery life, but some seniors are a bit challenged by their tiny keyboards.

The next big variation on a portable computer came in 2010 when Apple launched iPad. Though tablet PCs had been around for some years, it took Apple to make the format, which sports a touchscreen and onscreen keyboard, catch on. Since the iPad, companies such as Dell, Acer, Hewlett-Packard, Samsung, and Motorola have brought out their own tablets.

Tablets, also called *slates*, are more like a hefty pad than a computer. There is no keyboard and no mouse. Instead, you tap the screen to make choices and enter text. The onscreen keyboard is still smaller than a laptop keyboard, but there are physical keyboard accessories that you can use with tablets to make input easier. Tablets also have super battery life at 10 hours — almost a month in standby mode (when you're not actually using them). Tablets connect to the Internet using either Wi-Fi or 3G technologies (3G is what your cellphone uses to connect virtually anywhere). 3G models require that you pay for your connection time.

Tablets, which are coming out from many manufacturers to compete with iPad as of this writing, weigh about 1.5 pounds (more or less), and were first planned as devices for consuming media. Whether used to read eBooks, play games such as Scrabble, browse the Internet, play music, or watch movies, these devices have proven incredibly popular. The big surprise since the launch of the iPad has been how big a hit tablets are with business and educational groups. Applications (called *apps*) range from credit card readers for retail businesses to eReaders such as Kindle, and reasonably robust productivity tools such as word processors and spreadsheets.

 Tablets are a very popular choice for many seniors because they are pretty easy to get the hang of, they're very portable, and great for many activities seniors use computers for, such as e-mailing, browsing the web, and playing games, music, or movies. If you decide to buy a tablet and choose an iPad, you might want to check out my book, *iPad For Seniors For Dummies, 2nd Edition* (John Wiley & Sons, Inc.).

Explore All You Can Do with Your Laptop

Your laptop is a computer in a smaller package, so you can perform all the typical computing tasks with it. If you've never owned a computer of any type, your laptop purchase will open up a world of activities. Even if you're buying your laptop just to do e-mail (I hear this a lot from seniors!), do yourself a favor and explore a few other computing tasks that your laptop will allow you to do, such as these:

➡ **Run software programs to accomplish everyday tasks.** Utilize word processors to write letters or create flyers, spreadsheet software to organize your finances or household inventory, or photo-imaging software to work with your snapshots.

➡ **Work with financial activities.** From keeping your checkbook and credit card records in software databases and doing your taxes to investing, banking, and shopping online, these types of activities can be very safe to perform online, and they are incredibly convenient, with your accounts available 24/7.

➡ **Keep in touch with friends and family.** The Internet makes it possible to communicate with other people via e-mail; share video images using *webcams* (tiny, inexpensive video cameras that capture and send your images to another computer); and make phone calls using a technology called VoIP (Voice over Internet Protocol) that uses your laptop and Internet connection to place calls. You can also chat with others by typing and sending messages using a technology called *instant messaging*. These messages are exchanged in real time so that you and your grandchild, for example, can see and reply to text immediately. Part V of this book explains these topics in more detail.

➡ **Research any topic from the comfort of your home.** Online, you can find many reputable web sites that give you information on anything from expert medical advice to the best travel deals. You can read news from around the corner or around the world. You can visit government web sites to find out information about your taxes, Social Security, and more, or even go to entertainment sites to look up your local television listings.

➡ **Create greeting cards, letters, or home inventories.** Whether you're organizing your holiday card list or figuring out a monthly budget, computer programs can help. For example, **Figure 1-3** shows a graph that the Excel program creates from data in a spreadsheet.

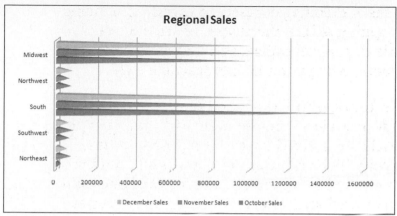

Figure 1-3

⮕ **Pursue hobbies such as genealogy or sports.** You can research your favorite teams online or connect with people who have the same interests. The online world is full of special-interest chat groups where you can discuss these interests with others.

⮕ **Play interactive games with others over the Internet.** You can play everything from shuffleboard to poker or action games in virtual worlds.

⮕ **Share and create photos, drawings, and videos.** If you have a digital camera, you can transfer photos to your laptop (doing this is called *uploading*) or copy photos off the Internet and share them in e-mails or use them to create your own greeting cards. If you're artistically inclined, you can create digital drawings. Many popular web sites make sharing digital movies easy, too. If you have a digital video camera and editing software, you can use editing tools to make a movie and share it with others. Steven Spielberg, look out!

➠ **Shop online and compare products easily, day or night.** You can shop for anything from a garden shed to travel deals or a new camera. Using handy online features, you can easily compare prices from several stores or read customer product reviews. Web sites such as www.nextag.com list product prices from a variety of vendors on one web page, so you can find the best deals. Beyond the convenience, all this information can help you save money.

Appreciate the Portability Factor

Because your laptop is portable, you can move it around your house or around town with relative ease. What does this portability allow you to do?

➠ You can access your e-mail account from anywhere to stay in touch with others or get work done away from home or the office. You can also store documents online so that you can access them from anywhere.

➠ Use public *hotspots* — locations that provide access to the Internet, such as airports and Internet cafés — to go online. For example, some hotels today provide Wi-Fi access free of charge, so you can work on your laptop from the lobby or your room.

➠ Even if you're staying in town, it might be fun to take your laptop to a local café and putter while sipping a latte.

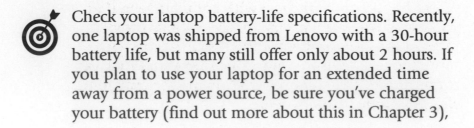 Check your laptop battery-life specifications. Recently, one laptop was shipped from Lenovo with a 30-hour battery life, but many still offer only about 2 hours. If you plan to use your laptop for an extended time away from a power source, be sure you've charged your battery (find out more about this in Chapter 3),

and keep an eye on it. You could lose some work if you haven't saved it and the battery power runs out.

Understand Types of Laptops and Tablets

Today, there are several types of laptop that vary by size and weight, functionality, and the way you enter information into them. Here are some options available to you:

➡ The garden-variety laptop (also referred to as a *note-book computer*) runs around 5–8 pounds and has a monitor size ranging from about 13 inches to 16 or so. It's portable and can handle most computing tasks. *Multimedia/gaming laptops* are laptops that have more sophisticated graphics and sound cards.

➡ *Desktop replacements* are laptops with more heft. They might weigh more than 10 pounds and have larger monitors (perhaps 18 inches). Their keyboards are roomier as well. However, though they aren't too difficult to move around your home, they aren't meant to be as portable as other types of laptops.

➡ *Netbooks* (see **Figure 1-4**) were first introduced for those who mainly wanted to use a computer to access the Internet. They lack CD/DVD drives and weigh only about 2–3 pounds. They have less-powerful and slower processors, and less *memory* (space to store documents). Still, if you mainly want to check e-mail from anywhere, a netbook might fit the bill.

➡ *Tablets* (see **Figure 1-5**) are smaller devices (any-where from 7 to 10 inches) with a touchscreen that you use to interact with the device. Tablets provide most of the bells and whistles of your laptop with more processing power than a netbook, and they can connect to the Internet using Wi-Fi or (in some models) cellphone 3G networks.

Figure 1-4

Figure 1-5

➡ *Mobile Internet Devices* (MIDs) are the latest addition to the laptop lineup. A MID falls somewhere between your cellphone and a netbook in size. It's super-portable, but for all but the most eager cellphone texters, a MID probably sports too small a keyboard for everyday computing tasks.

Buying a Laptop

*I*f you've never owned a laptop and now face purchasing one for the first time, deciding what model to get can be a somewhat daunting experience. There are lots of technical terms to figure out, various pieces of *hardware* (the physical pieces of your laptop, such as the monitor and keyboard) to become familiar with, and *software* (the programs that serve as the brains of the computer, helping you create documents and play games, for example) that you need to understand.

In this chapter, I introduce you to the world of activities your new laptop makes available to you, and I provide the information you need to choose just the right laptop for you. I also provide some advice about making the choice between a laptop or tablet and the advantages of each. Remember as you read through this chapter that figuring out what you want to do with your laptop is an important step in determining which laptop you should buy. You have to consider how much money you want to spend, how you'll connect your laptop to the Internet, and how much power and performance you'll require from your laptop.

Get ready to . . .

Understand Hardware and Software

Your computing experience is made up of interactions with hardware and software. The *hardware* is all the tangible computer equipment, such as the body of your laptop containing the hard drive, keyboard, and touchpad for pointing at and clicking on items onscreen. The *software* is what makes the hardware work or lets you get things done, such as writing documents with Microsoft Word or playing a Solitaire game. Think of the hardware as being like your television set, and think of the software as being like the shows that you watch on it.

The hardware on your laptop consists of

➡ **A central processing unit (CPU),** which is the very small, very high-tech semiconductor *chip* (integrated circuit) that acts as the brains of your computer. The CPU is stored in your laptop along with the other nuts and bolts of your computer.

➡ **A monitor,** which displays images on its screen similar to the way your TV screen displays programs. Your computer monitor shows you, for example, the Microsoft Windows 7 desktop or a document in a software program.

➡ **A keyboard,** which is similar to a typewriter keyboard. In addition to typing words and numbers, you can use a keyboard to give the computer commands.

➡ **A touchpad,** which you also use to give your computer commands, but this little device is more tactile. You move your laptop cursor on the screen by using a built-in pointing device, which might be in the form of a touchpad or a small button. Slide your fingertip around the touchpad. This moves a pointer around onscreen. You position this pointer on an onscreen button or menu name, for example, and then click a left or right button on your touchpad that causes an action. You can also tap and drag your fingertip to select text or an object to perform an action on it (such as deleting a file or making a line of text bold).

➡ **A webcam and speakers, and probably a microphone,** are likely to be built in to your laptop. A webcam allows you to produce video images you can share during video phone calls and instant messaging sessions. Speakers play back sounds, and a built-in microphone allows you to record audio files.

➡ **Ports to attach peripherals,** such as a printer or scanner. Your laptop comes with slots (called *ports*) where you plug in various peripherals. The type of port you'll use most often is called a USB port; it's a small slot useful for plugging in small sticks called *flash drives* on which you can store data, or devices that typically today sport a USB connector (such as digital cameras and smartphones).

Software (also known as *programs* or *applications*) is installed on your laptop hard drive, which resides in the laptop casing. Here are a few basics about software:

➡ **You use software to get your work done, run entertainment programs, and browse the Internet.** For example, Quicken is a financial-management program you can use to balance your checkbook or keep track of your home inventory for insurance purposes.

➡ **Some programs come preinstalled on your laptop; you can buy and install other programs as you need them.** Computers have to have an operating system installed to be of any use at all, because that software runs all the other programs. Also, some programs are included with your operating system — such as Solitaire, an electronic version of the old favorite card game, which comes with Windows 7. But you're not limited to pre-installed software. You can purchase other software or download free software programs from the Internet. For example you can find Skype (a program that enables you to make online phone calls using your laptop) on the Internet and install it on your laptop yourself.

➡ **You can uninstall programs you no longer need.** Uninstalling unwanted programs helps to free up some space on your laptop, which helps it perform better.

➡ **Some software programs called** *utilities* **exist to keep your laptop in shape.** An antivirus program is an example of a utility used to spot and erase computer viruses from your system. Your *operating system* (such as Windows 7 Home Premium, which you hear more about in the task "Choose a Version of Windows," later in this chapter) also includes some utilities, such as Disk Cleanup to free up wasted space on your hard drive or the Windows Defender program. Windows Defender protects your laptop from unwanted intrusion by malicious programs called *spyware*. See Part V for details about using utilities.

Select a Type of Laptop

Just as there are many styles of shoes or mobile phones, you can find several styles of laptops. Some are smaller and more portable, while others are essentially desktop replacements with large screens and a bit of heft. Some use different operating systems to make everything run, and some excel at certain functions such as working with graphics or playing games. This task explains some features you'll need to consider when choosing the type of laptop you should buy.

➡ **Operating system (OS):** An OS is the software that allows you to work with all the other software programs, manage files, and shut down your computer. Windows is probably the most common computer operating system, and this book focuses mainly on its features.

However, Mac laptops from Apple are also popular. These use Apple-specific software including the Mac operating system, and many software applications written for Windows are also available for the Mac. You can also set up your Mac to run the Windows operating system, which gives you the best of both worlds. Some computers run on a freely available operating system called Linux, which has similar functionality to Windows.

➡ **Computer design:** A *laptop* is a portable computer, weighing anywhere from two to ten pounds. The lightest ones (as light as two pounds) are called *netbooks*. A *tablet PC* is a kind of laptop that allows you to write on the screen with a special stylus, and its design is uniquely compact. The monitor, keyboard, and touchpad are built in to a laptop. Note that if the monitor is damaged, you have to pay quite a bit to have it repaired, or you can hook it up to an external monitor.

Figure 2-1 shows (from left to right) a laptop, netbook, and tablet PC. Laptops are perfect if you want to use your computer mainly away from home or you have little space in your home for a larger computer. Consider their design and weight when purchasing a laptop. (See the next task for more about the latest portable format, the tablet computer).

Figure 2-1

➡ **Pictures and sound:** If you work with a lot of *visual elements* (for example, photographs, home movies, or computer games), consider a laptop that has a good graphics card. Games often involve sound, so a high-end sound card might also be useful. Laptops with more sophisticated sound and image capabilities are often referred to as *gaming* or *multimedia* models, and they typically require a large-capacity hard drive to handle these functions. Because the capabilities of these cards change all the time, I don't give you exact specifications for what's considered high-end; instead, ask the person you're buying the laptop from whether the system can handle sophisticated sound and graphics.

One clue that the model has better support for higher-end graphics is if it has a *discrete* (that is, a card separate from the CPU) graphics card, versus one built in to the CPU (called *integrated graphics*).

Decide Whether a Tablet Would Work

As mentioned in Chapter 1, tablets such as iPad and BlackBerry PlayBook are an interesting variety of portable computing device. They differ from laptops in that they typically have mobile operating systems with unique interfaces. They don't have a keyboard or mouse or DVD drive. Some do have cameras for both still photos and video. **Remember:** Most of the advice in this chapter is for Windows-based laptops, not for tablets.

If you decide to buy an iPad, take a look at my book, *iPad For Seniors For Dummies, 2nd Edition* (John Wiley & Sons, Inc.), for more specific advice on iPad features.

That said, tablets do have laptop-like features you should consider when deciding whether you should opt for one over a laptop. If you want a super lightweight device to browse the Internet, send and receive e-mail, and peruse content like ebooks, music, or movies, a tablet might be just right. If you need more of a workhorse to do a good deal of word processing or spreadsheets, for example, a laptop is probably a better bet.

Tablets come in different sizes such as 7 inch or 10 inch and weigh far less than a laptop; as with a laptop, tablet screens have different resolutions, meaning that some have crisper-looking graphics than others; they have their own processors (different from those used in laptops), some being faster than others; their memory capacity will almost always be smaller than a laptop and can range from 8 GB to 64 GB; and their battery life is typically longer than most laptops.

Besides iPad, which has been available for over a year, most tablet models are relatively new to the market. Visit a site such as www. tabletpccomparison.net/ to read about the different features to help you make a choice if you decide a tablet is right for you.

Choose a Version of Windows

As mentioned in an earlier task, your laptop's operating system (software that runs all the programs and organizes the data on your computer) will be one of your first choices. This book focuses on computers running the current version of Windows, which is called Windows 7. Windows 7 comes in three different versions for home and business users. The three different versions of Windows 7 are

➡ **Home Premium:** If you consider yourself primarily a home user, you should consider the Home Premium version of Windows 7. This version includes entertainment tools such as Windows Media Center for playing music and movies. If you want to do more than look at photos, you'll find that this version of Windows 7 is good at working with design and image-manipulation programs such as Photoshop. Also be aware that Home Premium includes great features for managing the battery power of your laptop.

➡ **Windows 7 Professional:** Great for small businesses or working from home. This version of Windows has enhanced security features.

➡ **Windows 7 Ultimate:** Provides everything that Professional provides, plus a few more bells and whistles for protecting your laptop from thieves with BitLocker and handling languages other than English.

 Before Windows 7, there was Windows Vista, and before that, Windows XP. Many people still use computers that run Vista or XP and get along just fine. However, Windows XP doesn't come with as many security tools. If you decide to use Windows XP, find a friend or family member who's knowledgeable about laptops and can help you use XP features or other software programs that will help keep your laptop secure. Note that if you're using Vista or XP, some of the steps for common tasks are different than they are if you use Windows 7; however, you can still use this book to find out about many computer basics.

Determine a Price Range

You can buy a laptop for anywhere from US $299 to $5,000 or more, depending on your budget and computing needs. You may start with a base model, but extras such as a larger monitor or higher-end graphics card can soon add hundreds to the base price.

You can shop in a retail store for a laptop or shop online using a friend's computer (and perhaps get his or her help if you're brand new to using a computer). Consider researching different models and prices online and using that information to negotiate your purchase in the store if you prefer shopping at the mall. Be aware, however, that most retail stores have a small selection compared to all you can find online on a website such as NewEgg.com.

Buying a laptop can be confusing, but here are some guidelines to help you find a laptop at the price that's right for you:

➡ **Determine how often you will use your computer.** If you'll be working on it eight hours a day running

a home business, you will need a better-quality laptop to withstand the use. If you turn on the computer once or twice a week, it doesn't have to be the
priciest model in the shop.

➡ **Consider the features that you need.** Do you want
(or have room for) a heftier laptop with an 18-inch
monitor? Do you need the laptop to run very fast
and run several programs at once, or do you need to
store tons of data? (Computer speed and storage are
covered later in this chapter.) Understand what you
need before you buy. Each feature or upgrade adds
dollars to your laptop's price.

➡ **Shop wisely.** If you walk from store to store or do
your shopping online, you'll find that the price for the
same laptop model can vary by hundreds of dollars at
different stores. See if your memberships in organizations such as AAA, AARP, or Costco make you eligible
for better deals. Consider shipping costs if you buy
online, and keep in mind that many stores charge a
restocking fee if you return a laptop you aren't happy
with. Some stores offer only a short time period in
which you can return a laptop, such as 14 days.

➡ **Buying used or refurbished is an option, though new
laptops have reached such a low price point that this
might not save you much.** In addition, technology
goes out of date so quickly, you might be disappointed
with buying an older model. Instead, consider going to
a company that produces customized, non–name-
brand laptops at lower prices — perhaps even your
local computer repair shop. You might be surprised at
the bargains you can find (but make sure you're dealing with reputable people before buying).

➡ **Online auctions are a source of new or slightly
used laptops at a low price.** However, be sure you're
dealing with a reputable store or person by checking

reviews that others have posted about them or contacting the Better Business Bureau. Be careful not to pay by check (this gives a complete stranger your bank account number) but instead use the auction site's tools to have a third party handle the money until the goods are delivered in the condition promised. Check the auction site for guidance on staying safe when buying auctioned goods.

 Some web sites, such as Epinions.com, allow you to compare several models of laptops side by side, and others such as NexTag.com allow you to compare prices on a particular model from multiple stores. For helpful computer reviews, visit sites such as www. Cnet.com and www.Epinions.com.

Select a Monitor

Monitors are the window to your computer's contents. A good monitor (also known as a screen) can make your computing time easier on your eyes. The crisper the image, the more impressive the display of your vacation photos or that highly visual golf game.

Consider these factors when choosing your laptop:

➡ **Size:** Monitors for the average laptop user come in several sizes, from tiny 9-inch screens on smaller laptops to 18-inch screens on desktop replacement models. Laptops with larger screens are typically more expensive. A laptop with a larger monitor will take up more space on your desk than a laptop with a smaller monitor.

➡ **Image quality:** The quality can vary greatly. You will see terms such as LCD (liquid crystal display; also referred to as *flat panels*), flat screen, brightness, and resolution.

Look for a laptop with an LCD monitor, preferably with a screen (see **Figure** 2-2) that reduces glare.

Figure 2-2

➠ **Resolution:** A monitor's resolution represents the number of pixels that form the images you see on the screen. The higher the resolution, the crisper the image. You should look for a laptop that can provide at least a 1,024 × 768 pixel resolution.

Opt for Longer Battery Life

Because you're likely to use your laptop away from home now and then, the amount of time it retains a battery charge can be important. Though many laptops still only last a couple of hours on one charge, newer models are beginning to offer battery lives of six to ten hours.

 The most popular type of battery for laptops today is Lithium Ion (LiON). Nickel Metal Hydride (NiMH) is an older technology with much less capacity.

Check the battery life rating when looking at a laptop and decide if you might need more hours, for example, to use the laptop on a long airplane flight, if the power goes out for hours in your area during storms, or for other situations when power just won't be available.

Choose an Optical Drive

You've probably seen a DVD player used to play movies at home. Laptops can also read data from or play movies or music from DVDs or store data on them (called *burning*). Your laptop is likely to come with an *optical drive*, which is a small drawer that pops out, allowing you to place a DVD in a tray, push the drawer back into the laptop, and access the contents of the DVD. If you buy a software program, it will come on a CD or DVD, so you also need this drive to install software. However, very small laptops such as netbooks have no DVD drives, to save space. In that case, you can buy an external DVD drive and plug it into a port on your laptop.

When you buy a laptop with a built-in or an external DVD drive, keep these things in mind about optical drives:

➠ **DVDs versus CDs:** DVDs have virtually replaced CDs as the computer storage medium of choice, but you might still find a CD floating around with music or data on it that you need to read. For that reason, you might want a DVD/CD combo drive.

➠ **DVD drives:** DVD drives are rated as read (R), write (W), or read-writable (RW). A *readable* DVD drive only allows you to look at data on your discs, but not save data to them. A *writeable* DVD drive allows you to save data (or images, or music) to discs. A *read-writeable* DVD drive lets you both read and write to DVDs.

➠ **DVD standards:** In the earliest days of DVDs, there were two different standards, + and –. Some drives could play DVDs formatted + but not those formatted –, for example. Today, you should look for a DVD drive that is specified as +/– so that it can deal with any DVD you throw at it.

➠ **Blu-ray discs:** If you want to be able to play the latest optical discs, get a laptop with a Blu-ray player. Blu-ray is a great medium for storing and playing back feature length movies because it can store 50GB, which is the size of most movies.

 One of the first things you should do when you buy a laptop, if it doesn't come with recovery discs, is to burn recovery discs you can use if you have to restore the laptop to its factory settings. You might need to do this, for example, if a virus corrupts your settings. Your laptop should offer this as an option when you first start it, but if it doesn't, check your laptop help system or the manufacturer's web site to find out how to burn recovery discs, which will allow you to return your system to factory settings if you have a major crash.

Understand Processor Speed and Memory

Your laptop contains a processor stored on a computer chip. The speed at which your laptop runs programs or completes tasks is determined in great measure by your computer processor speed. Processor speed is measured in *gigahertz* (GHz). The higher this measurement, the faster the processor. I won't quote the speed you should look for because these chips are constantly getting smaller and more powerful. However, when you shop, you probably shouldn't consider anything lower than 2 GHz and know that the higher numbers give the best performance and factor that into your decision depending on your needs.

In addition, computers have a certain amount of storage capacity for running programs and storing data. You'll see specifications for RAM and hard-drive data storage capacity when you go laptop shopping. Again, the specific numbers will change, so the guideline is to look for higher RAM numbers if you feel you need more storage capacity.

➡ **RAM is the memory needed to simply access and run programs.** RAM chips come in different types, including DRAM, SDRAM, and the latest version, DDR2. Look for a minimum of 1 gigabyte (GB) of RAM for everyday computing.

➠ **RAM chips are rated by** *access speed*, **which relates to how quickly a request for data from your system can be completed.** You might see RAM speed measured in megahertz (MHz). Today, 800 MHz could be considered an acceptable access speed. Note that there are two common RAM types — SRAM and DRAM, with DRAM being the more efficient.

➠ **Your hard drive has a certain capacity for data storage measured in gigabytes (GB).** These days, you should probably look for a minimum of a 250GB hard drive, but hard drives can come with a range of huge capacities, with the largest being measured in *terabytes* (TB, measured in thousands of gigabytes).

➠ **Your laptop will require some RAM to run the operating system.** Windows 7 requires 1 gigabyte (GB) of main memory and 16GB of hard-drive space.

➠ **Your processor has multiple cores.** Most processors today are multiple-core processors, such as the i3, i5, and i7 processor lines from Intel. *Multiple core* means that two or more processors are involved in reading and executing software instructions as you use your laptop. Those with two processors are called *dual-core*, those with four processors are called *quad-core*, and processors with six cores are referred to as *hexa-core*. The bottom line with cores is that the more you have, the faster your laptop can process instructions because all the cores can be working at once, making multitasking possible. (*Multitasking* is when you're running several programs at once, as when you're playing music, downloading files from the Internet, running an antivirus scan, and working in a word processor — all at the same time.)

Determine How You'll Connect to the Internet

You have to decide how you'll connect to the Internet. You can use a dial-up connection over a standard phone line or pay a fee to get a broadband connection such as DSL. (Check with AARP to find out if they offer discounted connections in your area.) However, if you want a wireless connection that works like your cellphone to pick up a signal in certain hotspots, you have to be sure to buy a laptop with wireless capabilities (and luckily, most new model laptops have these). Here's how these connections work:

➡ **Dial-up:** If you intend to use a dial-up connection (that is, connect over your phone line), your laptop has to have a dial-up modem either built in or in an external model. Dial-up connections can be very slow, and while you're using them you can't use your phone to make or receive calls. I discourage using dial-up unless you absolutely have to.

➡ **Wireless:** Wireless connections require that you have a laptop equipped with wireless capability. You can access the Internet wirelessly when you're near a wireless *hotspot* (a place that offers wireless service), and many hotspots are appearing at public places such as hotels, airports, and restaurants. You can also subscribe to a Wireless Wide Area Network (WWAN) service from a mobile phone provider, to tap into its connection. Check laptop models to be sure they are wireless-enabled. There are various techy standards for wireless, such as 802.11a, b, or g. The very latest standard to look for is 802.11n, which delivers better wireless performance.

➡ **Broadband:** Broadband connections can be DSL (digital subscriber line) or cable. In both cases, you pay a fee to a provider, which might be your phone company or cable company. DSL works over your phone line but doesn't prohibit you from using the phone when you're online. Cable runs over your cable TV line and is a bit faster than DSL, though connections can be less dependable. Both are considered *always-on* connections, meaning that you don't have to wait to dial up to a phone connection or connect to a wireless network — you're always connected.

 See Chapter 19 for more about setting up your Internet connection.

Buy a Customized Laptop

You can buy prepackaged laptops online or in an electronics store. An alternative is to buy a customized laptop. Companies such as Dell (see **Figure 2-3**) and Gateway offer customized laptops. When you buy the laptop, you can pick and choose various features, and the provider will build the system for you.

Here are some of the variables you'll be asked about when you purchase a customized system, many of which are discussed in this chapter:

Figure 2-3

➡ Type and speed of processor

➡ Amount of RAM or hard drive capacity

➡ Installed software, such as a productivity suite like Microsoft Office or Microsoft Works, or a premium version of an operating system

➡ More sophisticated graphics or sound cards

➡ Peripherals such as a printer or the addition of a wireless mouse

➡ Larger or higher-end monitor

➡ Wireless capability

➡ Warranty and technical support

These all add to your final price, so be sure you need an option before you select it. Most of these companies provide explanations of each item to help you decide.

Get Accessories for Your Laptop

Laptop users might benefit from several types of accessories to protect their laptops or add functionality. Here are a few to consider:

➡ **A laptop case** will help you carry the laptop around and also protect it from damage. Some cases are soft-sided, some are hard-sided, and most provide space to store a cable or DVDs for your next road trip.

➡ **A fingerprint reader** comes built in to some laptops. These keep intruders from accessing your computer contents. A fingerprint reader authorizes you via your very unique fingerprint. You can also buy external fingerprint readers.

➠ You can buy **laptop locks,** which connect to your laptop. You can wrap the lock around a desk leg or chair arm (like a bicycle lock). This provides a measure of protection if you have to leave your laptop unattended for a few minutes in a public place.

➠ **External CD/DVD drives** are helpful if you buy a smaller laptop that has no such drive built in. These drives are useful for installing software programs or playing audio or video content.

➠ **Flash drives** are small storage devices that you slot into a USB drive on your laptop. Some flash drives have such a large storage capacity that you can use them as a second hard drive for storing files, and they offer the convenience of being easily moved from one computer to another.

Setting Up Your Laptop

Once you unpack your new laptop, you might need help getting it set up. Here I cover the basics: inserting and charging the battery, turning the computer on and off, logging on and off Windows 7, and mastering the basic use of your built-in mouse and function keys.

Next, you can set the date and time in your computer's internal clock so they match your time zone and apply Daylight Saving Time settings properly. Finally, you get to work with your user accounts. Windows allows you to create multiple user accounts; each account saves certain settings and allows you to control files and folders separately. When each user logs on with a particular user account, it's like accessing a unique personal computer.

Here, then, are the procedures that you can follow to get going with your laptop.

Install and Charge the Battery

Your laptop comes with a battery that you should insert and charge when you first take the laptop out of the box. The battery is a rectangular affair (similar to the one shown in **Figure 3-1)** that slips into the bottom of your laptop. Note that tablet models are typically sealed so that your battery is not accessible; if yours is one of those, you don't have to insert a battery; just plug the tablet in to charge the battery.

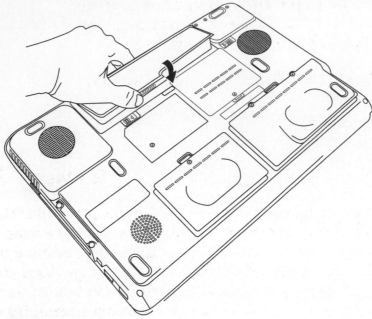

Figure 3-1

It's a good idea to charge your battery completely when you first plug it in, which could take several hours. Follow these instructions to do that:

1. Locate the plug in your laptop packaging. (It's usually a two-piece cable; one half of the cable has a large, boxy transformer on one end that plugs in to the other half.)

2. Plug one end of the cable into a wall outlet and the other into the round power connection port on your laptop. Your user's manual should indicate where this connection is located (usually on the back or near the back of the right or left side of the laptop).

3. When you turn your laptop on (see the next task), you'll find a small icon (usually called the Battery Meter icon) that looks like a standard battery with a plug next to it on the right side of your Windows taskbar. (The taskbar is the blue area at the very bottom of your screen.) Click this Battery Meter icon to see whether the battery is fully charged to 100-percent capacity. (If you aren't yet sure how to move around the screen and click, see the upcoming task, "Use the Touchpad, Your Laptop's Built-In Mouse".)

This icon changes to just a battery (no plug) when the computer isn't plugged in; this battery icon indicates visually how much charge your battery has left before it drains.

Turn On Your Laptop and Log On and Off Windows 7

When you turn on your laptop, it takes a few moments to load the files it needs to run your operating system. If this is the first time you've started up a brand new computer, you might be asked to make certain settings. If the computer has been used before (perhaps you bought it used, or the person in the store showed you how to start it up and make some settings), you won't see the setup screens; instead, you'll be taken to a user sign-in screen. At that point, if a password has been set for your account, you'll have to type it in; if not, you'll just click a user icon to sign on and go to the Windows desktop. Here are the steps to turn on your laptop and log on to Windows:

1. With your laptop's battery charged (see the previous task), you're ready to turn it on. Start by pressing the power button on your computer to begin the Windows 7 startup sequence. The power button might be somewhere toward the back of the keyboard or even on the monitor. Again, your users' manual will help you locate the power button on your particular laptop model.

2. In the resulting Windows 7 Welcome screen, use your keyboard to enter your password in the text box provided, if you've set one (see Chapter 25 for more about this). Then press the left side of your touchpad to click the arrow button or click Switch User and choose another user to log on as. (To move the onscreen cursor over one

of these selections you slide your fingertip on the touchpad below your keyboard. If you need help with using
the touchpad to make your selection, see the next task.)
Windows 7 verifies your password and displays the
Windows 7 desktop, as shown in **Figure 3-2**. The icons
on your desktop may vary, depending on what programs
your computer's manufacturer may have installed.

Note: If you haven't set up the password-protection feature or accounts for more than one user, you're taken
directly to the Windows 7 desktop. For more on adding
and changing passwords, see Chapter 25.

Figure 3-2

You can create different user accounts and log on to one account at a time. User accounts save documents and settings for that user so whoever uses the computer has a personal Windows environment to go back to. To create another user account, see the task "Create a New User Account" later in this chapter.

 After you set up more than one user account, before you get to the password screen, you have to click the icon for the user you wish to log on as.

Use the Touchpad, Your Laptop's Built-In Mouse

Unlike a typewriter, which uses only a keyboard to type text on paper, with a laptop you use both a keyboard and a pointing device to enter text and give commands to the computer. Though you might have used a keyboard of some type before, or a traditional mouse attached to a desktop computer, a laptop pointing device, called a *touchpad*, might be new to you. Frankly, a laptop touchpad takes a little getting used to.

A laptop's mouse can be one of two types, as shown in **Figure 3-3**: the touchpad and the pointing stick. The *touchpad*, by far the most common type, is a flat area located beneath your keyboard. A *pointing stick* is a small button located among your computer's keys. In effect, when you move your finger across the touchpad surface or place your finger on the pointing stick and move the stick slightly in any direction, a corresponding *mouse pointer* moves around your computer screen. With a touchpad — which I focus on here because it's what you're likely to have on your laptop — you perform clicking actions to open or select things on-screen by using the right and left buttons at the bottom edge of the touchpad. The left button is used for left-click actions, the right button for right-click actions. Left-clicking opens or selects items; right-clicking opens a shortcut menu from which you can choose commands to perform actions.

Some touchpads have extra bells and whistles, like allowing you to use actions in a certain area of the touchpad to scroll faster. Check your laptop user manual to see whether your device offers special features.

 With tablet computers, the touchscreen replaces the mouse; you touch the screen with your fingertip or a stylus to select or move things around. See Chapter 5 for more about working with tablets.

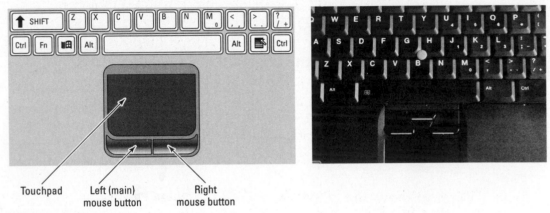

Touchpad   Left (main)   Right
mouse button   mouse button

Figure 3-3

Here are the main functions of a touchpad and how to control them:

→ **Clicking:** When people say "click," they mean "press and release the left mouse button." Clicking has a variety of uses. You can click while in a document to move the *insertion point*, a little vertical line that indicates where your next action will take place. For example, you might click in front of a word you already typed and then type another word to appear before it in a letter you're writing. Clicking is also used in various windows to select check boxes or radio buttons (also called *option buttons*) to turn features on or off, or to select objects such as a picture or table in your document. Double-clicking can also be used to open objects for editing or to quickly select whole words.

➡ **Right-clicking:** If you click the right touchpad button, Windows displays a shortcut menu that is specific to the item you clicked. For example, if you right-click a picture, the menu that appears gives you options for working with the picture. If you right-click the Windows desktop, the menu that appears lets you choose commands that display a different view or change desktop properties.

➡ **Clicking and dragging:** To click and drag, you press and continue to hold down the left mouse button and then move (drag) the mouse to another location. For instance, you can press the left touchpad button (keeping it held down) and drag your finger on a touchpad up, down, right, or left to highlight contents of your document. This highlighted text is *selected*, meaning that any action you perform, such as pressing the Delete key on your keyboard or clicking a button for Bold formatting, is performed on the selected text.

➡ **Scrolling:** Many touchpads and wireless mouse models have a way to scroll through a document or web site on your screen. Just roll the wheel on a mouse down (toward you) to move down through pages going forward in the document; scroll up to move backward in your document. With a touchpad, there is often an area marked on the right or left where you can run your fingertip up or down to scroll through a document.

 If you're used to a desktop computer mouse and can't get the hang of the built-in mouse on your laptop, consider buying a portable wireless mouse. By plugging a small transmitter into a USB port on your laptop, you can use this more standard mouse to point, click, and drag, just as you do with a desktop computer.

Use the Function Keys

On a laptop computer, you might find that in order to save space some shortcut functions, such as muting sound or brightening your screen, are accessible by using function keys. Here are the basics of function keys:

→ Function keys run across the top of your laptop keyboard, labeled F1, F2, and so on.

→ You'll find a key labeled Fn (for Function) near the bottom of your keyboard.

→ By pressing and holding down the Function key (Fn) and a numbered function key (F1, for example), you can perform actions such as controlling your built-in speaker's volume.

→ The functions assigned to your laptop's keys will vary, depending on the model and manufacturer. Check your user's manual to find out the specific functions assigned to your keyboard.

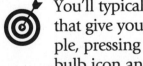 You'll typically find small icons on your function keys that give you a clue about what the keys do. For example, pressing both the function key that has a little light-bulb icon and the up arrow key will probably brighten your screen. Pressing a function key with double, right-pointing arrows (like those you see on a music player) may move you to the next track on an audio CD.

Set the Date and Time

1. The date and clock on your computer keep good time, but you might have to provide the correct date and time for your location. To get started, press the Windows key on your keyboard (the one with the Windows logo on it) to display the taskbar, if it isn't visible. (The taskbar is the blue area at the very bottom of your screen.)

2. Using the right button on your touchpad, right-click the Date/Time display on the far right end of the taskbar and then slide your finger on the touchpad till the cursor rests on the Adjust Date/Time from the shortcut menu that appears and click the left touchpad button to select it.

3. In the Date and Time dialog box that appears (see **Figure** 3-4), click the Change Date and Time button.

4. In the Date and Time Settings dialog box that appears, use your left mouse button to click in the Time field and enter a new time, or click the up and down arrows next to that field to change the time. If you wish, click a new date in the calendar display to set the date.

5. When you're finished with adjusting the settings, click OK.

6. To change the time zone, click the Change Time Zone button, choose an option from the Time Zone drop-down list, and click OK.

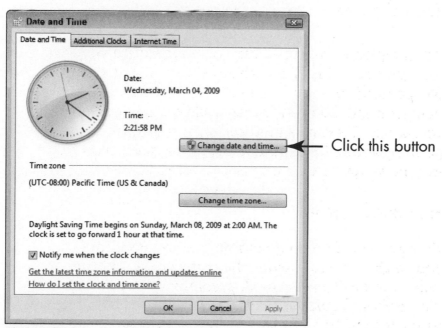

Figure 3-4

7. Click OK to apply the new settings and close the dialog box.

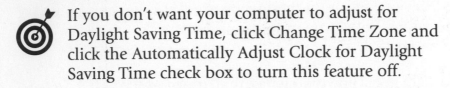

If you don't want your computer to adjust for Daylight Saving Time, click Change Time Zone and click the Automatically Adjust Clock for Daylight Saving Time check box to turn this feature off.

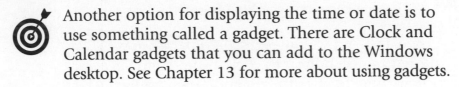

Another option for displaying the time or date is to use something called a gadget. There are Clock and Calendar gadgets that you can add to the Windows desktop. See Chapter 13 for more about using gadgets.

Create a New User Account

1. If you want to create a new user account that will save settings and documents for another person, choose Start⇨Control Panel.

2. In the resulting window, click the Add or Remove User Accounts link.

3. In the resulting Manage Accounts window, as shown in **Figure 3-5**, click the Create a New Account link. (Text links are typically blue; when you move your cursor over them, a small icon of a finger with pointing hand appears).

4. In the next window, shown in **Figure 3-6**, enter an account name, and then select the type of account you want to create. You can choose from these two:

- **Administrator,** who can do things like create and change accounts and install programs

- **Standard user,** who can't do the tasks an administrator can

5. Click the Create Account button and then close the Control Panel by clicking the X symbol in the upper-right corner of the window.

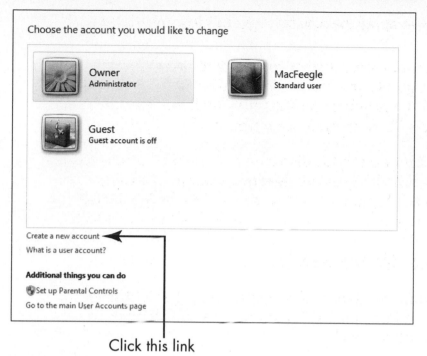

Click this link

Figure 3-5

Enter the account name here

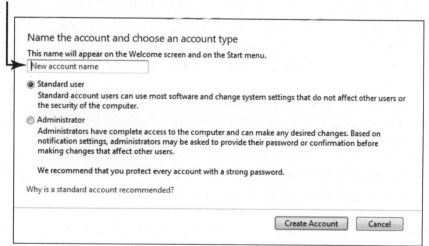

Figure 3-6

47

After you create an account, you can make changes to it, such as assigning a password or changing the account type, by double-clicking it in the Manage Accounts window you reached in Step 4 (in the preceding step list) and following the links listed there.

Switch User Accounts

1. Click Start and then click the arrow on the side of the Shut Down button. (See **Figure 3-7**.)

2. Choose Switch User from the pop-up menu that appears. In the resulting screen, click the user you want to log on as.

3. If the user account is password protected, a box appears for you to enter the password. Type the password and then click the arrow button to log on.

4. Windows logs you on with the specified user's settings.

If you forget your password and try to switch user accounts without entering one, Windows shows your password hint, which you can create when you assign a password to help you remember it. See the preceding task for instructions on creating and modifying a user account.

You can set up several user accounts for your laptop, which helps you save and access specific user settings and provide privacy for each user's files with passwords. Again, to find out about setting up user accounts and changing their settings, see the preceding task in this chapter.

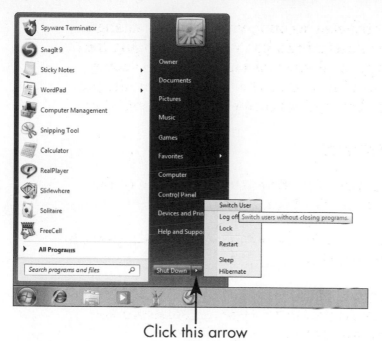

Click this arrow

Figure 3-7

Change Your User Account Picture

1. If you don't like the picture associated with your user account, you can change it. Choose Start⇨Control Panel⇨Add or Remove User Accounts.

2. In the resulting Manage Accounts window, click the account you want to change. (See **Figure 3-8**.)

3. In the resulting window, click the Change Picture button and click another picture (or browse to see more picture choices) to select it.

4. Click the Change Picture button; the window closes.

5. Click the Control Panel Close button to close it.

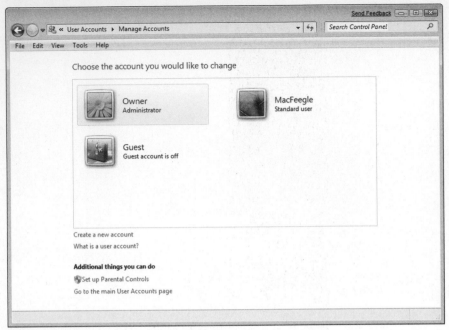

Figure 3-8

Shut Down Your Laptop

To turn off your laptop when you're done, you have to initiate a shut-down sequence in your operating system instead of simply turning off the power. Don't simply turn off your computer at the power source — unless you have to because of a computer malfunction. Windows might not start up properly the next time you turn it on if you don't follow the proper shutdown procedure.

To properly turn off your laptop, choose Start and then click the Shut Down button. (Simply press the power button later to turn it back on.) Or you can click the arrow to the right of the Shut Down button and choose one of the following from the menu shown in **Figure 3-9:**

➡ **Hibernate:** If you prefer to stop your laptop running but not turn the power off, choose this option (or simply close the lid of your laptop) to shut the laptop down. When you want to use it again, just open the lid.

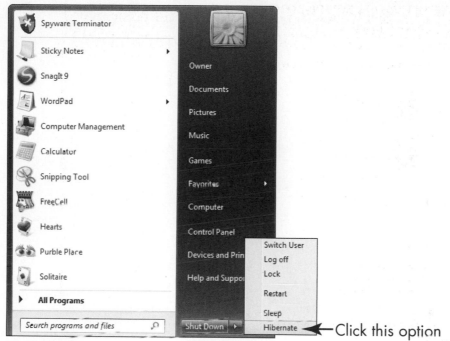

Figure 3-9

➠ **Sleep:** If you're going away for a while but don't want to have to go through the whole booting-up sequence (complete with Windows 7 music) when you return, you don't have to turn off your laptop. Just select the Sleep command instead to put your laptop into a kind of sleeping state where the screen goes black and the fan shuts down.

When you get back, just click your mouse button or press Enter — or, in some cases (especially on some laptops), press the Power button; your laptop springs to life, and whatever programs and documents you had open are still open.

➠ **Restart:** If you want to *reboot* (turn off and turn back on) your laptop, choose this option.

If your laptop freezes up for some reason, you can turn it off in a couple of ways. Press Ctrl+Alt+Delete twice in a row (the preferred method), or press the power button on your CPU and hold it until the laptop shuts down.

Managing Power

*O*ne of the big differences between a desktop computer and your laptop is that your laptop can run off of a battery. *Battery life,* or the length of time it takes your laptop battery to run out of juice, is getting better all the time — some recent laptop batteries get as much as 9 hours on one charge, and Lenovo recently launched a laptop that's supposed to offer 30 hours. Other laptop batteries get as little as a couple of hours of battery life.

For that reason, it's important that you understand some tools that Windows 7 provides to help you manage your laptop power, including these:

➠ Choosing a *power plan,* which has preset timings for actions such as dimming your screen or putting your computer to sleep.

➠ Creating a customized power plan by choosing settings you want.

➠ Adjusting settings for your display that deal with the screen brightness (a brighter screen uses more power), how frequently your screen automatically dims, and so on.

➠ Changing how much time lapses before your laptop automatically goes to sleep — a state that uses minimal power but keeps the currently open documents and programs active (and quickly available to you).

➠ Defining power button functions gives you some control over what happens when you press the laptop's power button or close the lid.

Choose a Power Plan

1. Choose Start➪Control Panel➪Hardware and Sound➪Power Options.

2. In the Power Options window that appears (see **Figure 4-1**), locate the Hide Additional Plans section. If this section isn't already displayed, click the downward arrow on the Show Additional Plans section; doing so changes the arrow's direction to upward and the Hide Additional Plans section displays.

The Power Saver plan

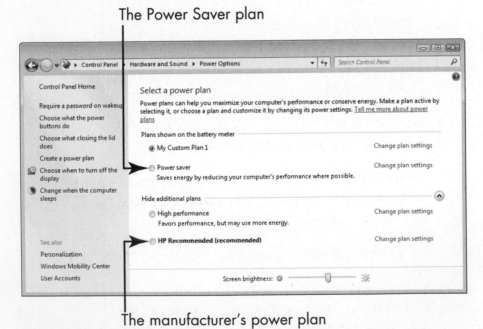

The manufacturer's power plan

Figure 4-1

3. Click the radio button next to a plan to select it. Note that there might be a laptop manufacturer's power plan among your selections. (In **Figure 4-1**, the manufacturer's power plan is the HP Recommended option.) The Power Saver plan (in **Figure 4-1**, this is listed in the Plans Shown on the Battery Meter section) causes your computer to go to sleep more frequently and dims the screen brightness. A higher-performance setting will never put the computer to sleep and will have a brighter screen setting. If you run your laptop on a battery frequently, the Power Saver plan is your best bet.

4. Click the Close button to close the window.

 There are several options you can use for shutting down or putting your laptop to sleep. See Chapter 3 for more about these.

Create a Customized Power Plan

1. If the preset power plans don't appeal to you, you can modify one and save it as your own customized power plan. Choose Start⇨Control Panel⇨Hardware and Sound⇨Power Options.

2. In the Power Options window that appears, click the Create A Power Plan link on the left side.

3. In the Create A Power Plan window that appears (shown in **Figure 4-2**), select the preset plan that is closest to what you want to create.

4. Enter a name for the plan in the Plan Name text box and click Next.

5. In the Edit Plan Settings window that appears (see **Figure 4-3**) make settings for how the laptop power functions when plugged in or running off the battery. (See the next two tasks in this chapter for information about changing display settings and changing how quickly the computer goes to sleep.)

Select a power plan to customize

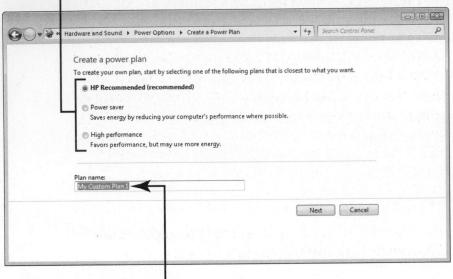

Enter a name for the customized plan

Figure 4-2

Make your plan settings here

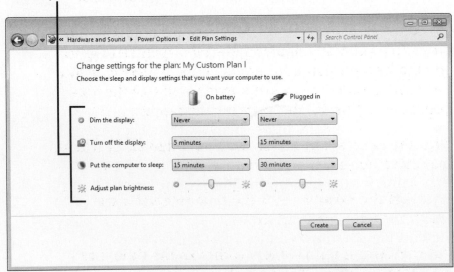

Figure 4-3

6. Click Create to create your new plan. Windows returns you to the Power Options window with your new plan added to the list of power plans.

 If you choose to run your laptop with the power cord plugged in, your laptop could get warm to the touch, even though it has an internal fan. Consider unplugging your laptop occasionally to run off of battery power, or buying a *laptop cooler*, a pad with a fan inside that dispels heat when you rest your laptop on it.

Adjust Display Settings

1. Choose Start➪Control Panel➪Hardware and Sound. The Hardware and Sound window appears.

2. Click the Power Options link.

3. Find the selected power plan. (There's a dot in the radio button next to it.) To the right of that selected option, click the Change Plan Settings link for the selected power plan.

4. In the Edit Plan Settings window that appears (shown in **Figure 4-4**), modify any of the following display settings to control the laptop when it's running on the battery and you haven't used it for a time — keeping in mind that the longer your screen stays on, the more power it uses:

- **Dim the Display:** Modifies the time intervals at which the screen automatically dims.

- **Turn Off the Display:** Sets the time interval after which the screen goes black.

- **Put the Computer to Sleep:** Indicates the time interval after which the computer sleeps. See the next task for more on this option.

- **Adjust Plan Brightness:** Adjusts the preset screen brightness; a less-bright screen saves power.

5. Click the Save Changes button to close the Edit Plan Settings window and save your new settings.

Modify your plan settings here

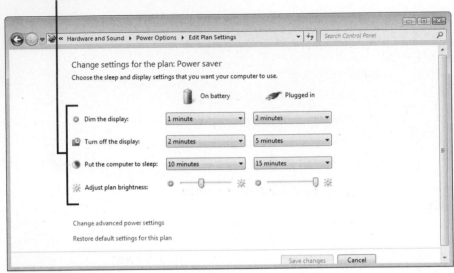

Figure 4-4

 You can adjust many settings for screen brightness and modify your power plan in the Mobility Center. Choose Start⇨Control Panel⇨Hardware and Sound, and then click the Windows Mobility Center link.

Change How Quickly the Computer Goes to Sleep

1. The third option in the Edit Plan Settings window you saw in the previous task deals with putting your computer to sleep. To change this setting, select Start⇨Control Panel⇨ Hardware and Sound. The window shown in **Figure 4-5** appears.

2. In the Power Options section, click the Change When the Computer Sleeps link.

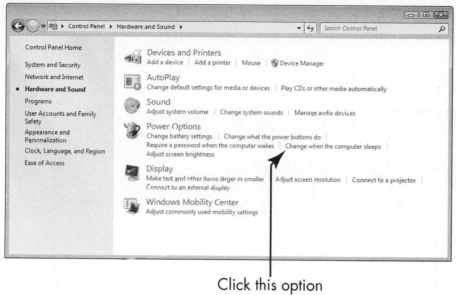

Click this option

Figure 4-5

3. In the Edit Plan Settings window that appears (see
Figure 4-6), find the Put the Computer to Sleep field
and click the arrow in the On Battery column.

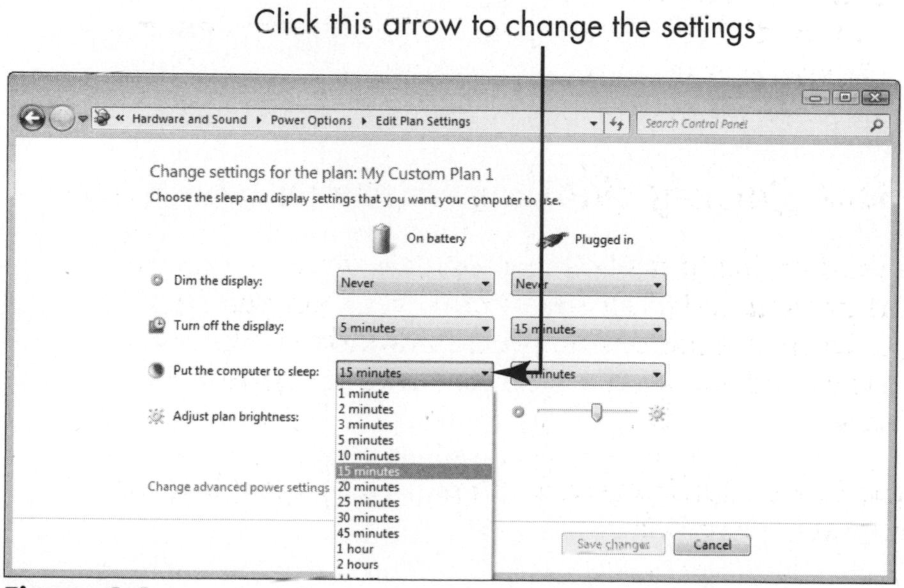

Click this arrow to change the settings

Figure 4-6

4. From the drop-down list, select another setting for when the computer automatically puts itself to sleep. A smaller interval saves battery power, but it might disrupt your work. So choose a setting according to your preferences.

5. Click the Save Changes button to save the new setting.

Define Power Button Functions

1. You can control what happens when you press the Power button, close the computer lid, or press the Sleep button (if your laptop offers one). Choose Start⇨Control Panel⇨ Hardware and Sound. The Hardware and Sound window appears.

2. In the Power Options section, click the Change What the Power Buttons Do link.

3. In the System Settings window that appears (see **Figure** 4-7), change the options in the On Battery column. The options (depending on the setting) include

- **Do Nothing:** Does nothing. You guessed that, right?

- **Sleep:** Essentially pauses your computer, leaving your open programs and documents intact, held in your computer memory. When you awaken your computer, it comes back almost immediately, ready for you to work. Sleep draws a small amount of power.

- **Hibernate:** Saves open programs and documents on your computer hard drive and then turns off your computer so you're not using any power. If you'll be away from your computer for a while but want to return to the items you had opened before quickly, Hibernate is a good choice. Hibernate is usually the default action when you close a laptop lid. Hibernate requires you to log on again when you revive your computer by pressing Enter, clicking the power button, or using your mouse.

- **Shut Down:** Closes any open programs and powers down your computer. You have to turn the power on again to use it — no programs or documents are open when you turn the laptop on again.

Choose your options here

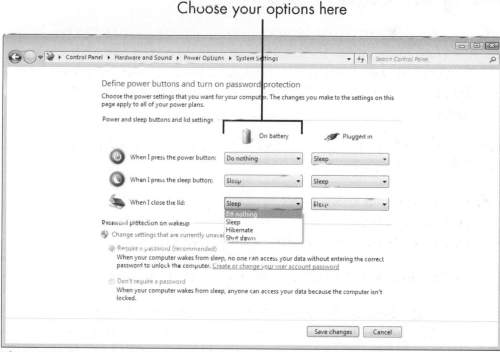

Figure 4-7

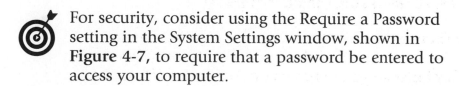 For security, consider using the Require a Password setting in the System Settings window, shown in **Figure 4-7,** to require that a password be entered to access your computer.

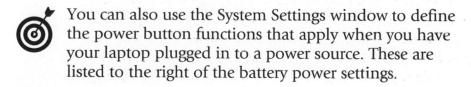 You can also use the System Settings window to define the power button functions that apply when you have your laptop plugged in to a power source. These are listed to the right of the battery power settings.

Opting for a Tablet Computer

*T*ablet computers such as the Apple iPad 2 and Motorola Xoom are the latest fad in portable computing. If you are thinking of going the tablet route rather than buying a traditional laptop, or want a tablet in addition to your laptop, this chapter helps you make some important choices.

First, I help you understand what a tablet is and how it differs from a laptop. Then I explore key features in common to tablets, including their size, weight, touchscreen interface, and onscreen keyboards. Along the way I sprinkle in some buying advice for some of the popular models on the market today, along with information about the world of applications (called *apps*) that help you have fun and get work done on a tablet.

Know the Advantages of a Tablet

The term *tablet* surfaced to the general public around 2000 when Microsoft promoted the release of Tablet PCs from several major manufacturers. These laptop-like, Windows-based devices sometimes had a physical keyboard and sometimes didn't, but their main distinction was a touchscreen you could use with a stylus (a penlike device minus the ink) to write or provide other input to the computer. Tablet PCs are still around, but never really took off.

In 2010, Apple hit a home run when it released iPad (see **Figure 5-1**), referred to as either a tablet or slate computer. iPads sold in the millions, and building on this success, at the Computer Electronics Show in January of 2011, approximately 80 manufacturers announced plans to produce their own tablet models. As of this writing, several models are on the market, including Motorola Xoom, Samsung Galaxy Tab, Fujitsu Stylista, and BlackBerry PlayBook.

Figure 5-1

A tablet (sometimes called simply a *tab*) lets you do most things you can do on a laptop such as reading e-mail and viewing pictures, but it is different from a laptop in several key ways:

➡ A tablet typically uses a mobile operating system such as Apple's iOS or BlackBerry's OS rather than a full-blown operating system.

➡ Battery life on tablets is often longer than the average laptop, coming in at around 10 hours or so.

➡ A tablet has a *touchscreen* that you use to provide input to your computer, either with your fingertip or a stylus.

➡ There is an onscreen keyboard on a tablet you can use to enter text (though many models have wireless capability, which you can also use to connect to a wireless or Bluetooth-enabled physical keyboard).

➡ Tablets are very light, weighing in at anywhere from slightly less than a pound to a couple of pounds. Tablets are also smaller than most laptops, anywhere from 7 inches to 10 inches or so in screen size.

➡ Most tablets are available in both wireless only and wireless and 3G models. Depending on the device you choose, you can connect through a wireless network or a cellphone network on a model that supports both.

➡ You can get free apps or purchase apps for your tablet that work on the mobile operating system and allow you to perform a wide range of functions, from video calling to playing games and playing digital musical instruments.

Understand Tablet Operating Systems

An operating system, such as Windows 7, runs processes and software applications on your computer and helps you store and organize files. Most tablets use a *mobile* operating system (OS) similar (or identical) to operating systems used on smartphones. Mobile operating systems don't require as much processing power as a desktop or laptop computer operating system, but they perform pretty much the same tasks.

Here's a rundown of some of the mobile OS's out there:

➡ iPad, the first of the recent generation of tablets, uses the Apple iOS that also drives the popular iPhone mobile phone and iPod Touch.

⟶ Android is the mobile OS promoted by Google. The Android 3.0 interface is optimized for tablets.

⟶ BlackBerry OS is the BlackBerry operating system, the same one used on BlackBerry phones for years.

⟶ The HP webOS (one of my personal favorites) was inherited with the company's acquisition of Palm Computing, and is available on their TouchPad tablets.

Whichever tablet you choose, you should play around with it and see how the interface provided by the operating system feels to you.

Compare Tablet Features and Prices

As of the writing of this book there are a handful of tablet models available, with more coming all the time. I suggest you visit a site such as www.tabletpccomparison.net shown in **Figure 5-2** when you're considering a purchase to see what's currently available.

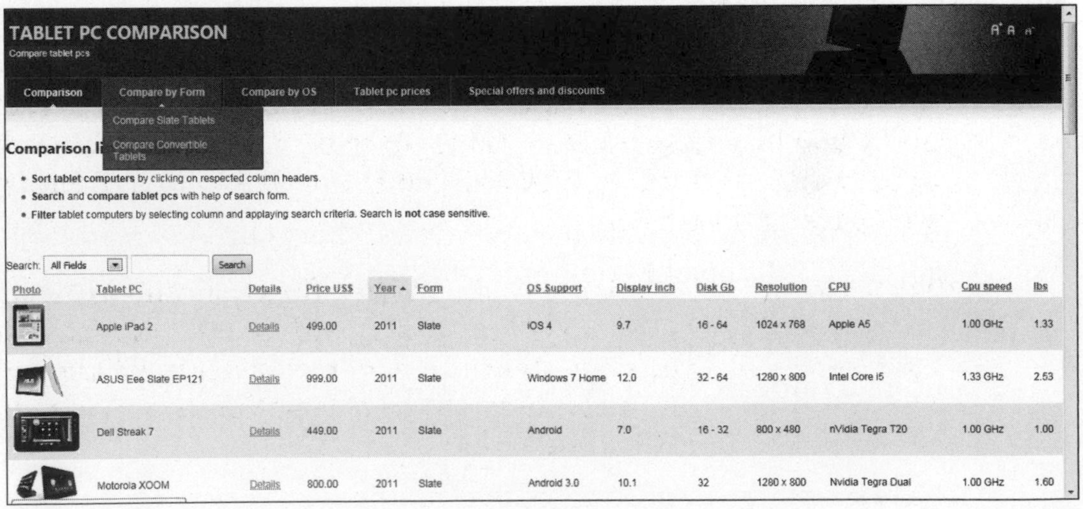

Photo	Tablet PC	Details	Price US$	Year ▲	Form	OS Support	Display inch	Disk Gb	Resolution	CPU	Cpu speed	lbs
	Apple iPad 2	Details	499.00	2011	Slate	iOS 4	9.7	16 - 64	1024 x 768	Apple A5	1.00 GHz	1.33
	ASUS Eee Slate EP121	Details	999.00	2011	Slate	Windows 7 Home	12.0	32 - 64	1280 x 800	Intel Core i5	1.33 GHz	2.53
	Dell Streak 7	Details	449.00	2011	Slate	Android	7.0	16 - 32	800 x 480	nVidia Tegra T20	1.00 GHz	1.00
	Motorola XOOM	Details	800.00	2011	Slate	Android 3.0	10.1	32	1280 x 800	Nvidia Tegra Dual	1.00 GHz	1.60

Figure 5-2

Table 5-1 provides a handy list of the features included in some of the most popular tablets today.

Table 5-1	Comparison of Tablet Models			
Tablet Name	**Price**	**Display Size**	**Resolution**	**Operating System**
Apple iPad	$499–$699	9.7"	1024×768	Apple iOS 4.0
Dell Streak	$449	7.0"	800×480	Android
Motorola Zoom	$800	10.1"	1280×800	Android
ASUS Eee Slate	$999	12.0"	1280×800	Windows 7 Home
BlackBerry PlayBook	$500	7.0"	1024×600	BlackBerry OS
Samsung Galaxy Tab	$600	7.0"	1024×600	Android

Explore Touchscreens

Touchscreens allow you to provide input to your tablet with your finger or a stylus rather than a mouse. Most tablets on the market today allow you to simply use your finger to select items, open apps, drag apps or objects, flick from one screen to another, or scroll through a web page or document.

The touchscreen experience is kind of like fingerpainting gone hi-tech. It's an intuitive way to select things, and with a little practice quite easy to master. **Figure 5-3** shows an easy maneuver involving pinching and spreading your fingers outward to enlarge (or inward to reduce) the screen on an iPad, for example.

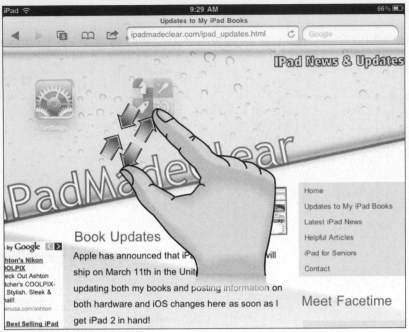

Figure 5-3

Use an Onscreen Keyboard

In addition to providing the touchscreen so you can select and maneu-ver items onscreen, tablets provide an onscreen keyboard for you to enter text and numbers. Typically the keyboard appears when you tap in a field or area where data entry makes sense, such as the Search field in a web browser (see **Figure 5-4**).

Onscreen keyboards typically have a few different keyboards built in. One might contain mostly letters, another numbers, and another, sym-bols. There is usually a key on the keyboard that you can tap to select a different keyboard. For example, you can tap the .?123 key (shown in **Figure 5-4**) to switch to the keyboard with numbers and symbols on it.

 Onscreen keyboards are pretty easy to use, but if you opt for a smaller tablet, for example one with a 7-inch screen, you might find using it challenging. In that case, you can connect your tablet to a wireless or Bluetooth physical keyboard — an optional accessory for which you'll have to pay a price.

Search field

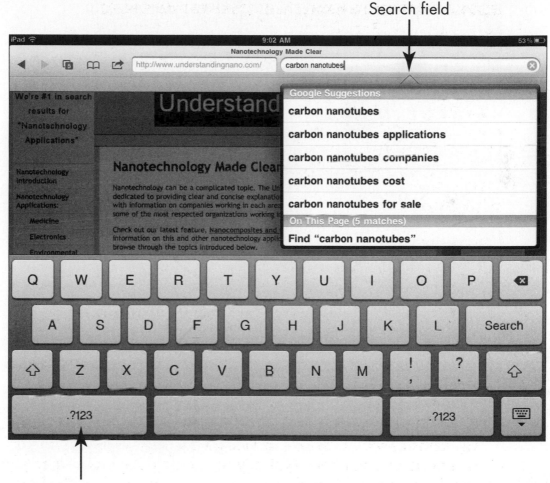

Tap this key to change to the numbers keyboard

Figure 5-4

Choose How to Connect to the Internet

Tablets offer two ways to go online. Some are wireless only models, which require a wireless network to connect to the Internet. That wireless network, called a *Wi-Fi hotspot,* might be your home network if you have one, or a public network such as you might find in a hotel, coffee shop, library, or airport.

Not every public hotspot is free; many hotels charge a fee for Internet access, and in my part of the world, the ferry system charges you to go online for the 30-minute trip across the water. Still, there are many public hotspots you can take advantage of — including some towns that provide free Wi-Fi throughout the area.

The second option for going online with a tablet is a wireless-plus-3G model. These devices can use a Wi-Fi network to connect to the Internet, but they can also connect through a cellphone provider's 3G network. You will have to pay a monthly fee to your phone provider for using this service, however it allows you to go online wherever your phone provider's network is available.

Discover the World of Apps

Consider traditional software such as Microsoft Excel. You would buy an application for a few hundred dollars and have a wealth of functionality. Apps are a bit different. You don't pay much for them — perhaps 99 cents to $14.99 or so, and some apps are even free — and each app provides a small bit of functionality. For example, following our Excel example, one app might provide a calculator for doing sums, another app might allow you to create charts, and still another would allow you to store and sort data. You build a set of apps that fits your needs by downloading them one at a time.

Today the world of apps has exploded as third parties build apps to fit certain mobile phone and tablet operating systems. iPad, for example, has the biggest world of apps. Android's choices are fewer as of this writing but growing. Other operating systems, such as BlackBerry and Windows, are playing catch-up.

Apps often provide fun features such as games (see **Figure** 5-5), apps for reading ebooks and ezines (electronic magazines), virtual musical instruments, or drawing programs.

My favorite iPad apps are Virtuoso, a virtual piano app, and Angry Birds, a highly addictive game that is fun to play in doctors' waiting rooms, while waiting for a train, or in competition with my husband at the dining table after dinner.

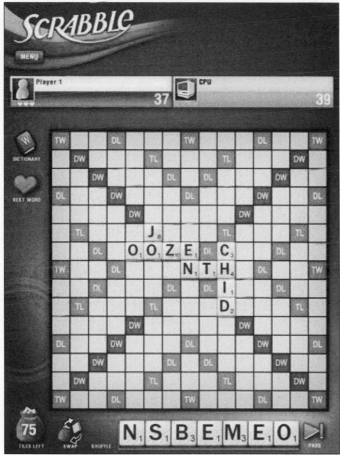

Figure 5-5

Part II
Exploring Windows

The 5th Wave   By Rich Tennant

JEEZ—YOU'D THINK THESE PEOPLE NEVER SAW A LAPTOP BEFORE!

GATE 9   ATE 8

Getting around the Windows 7 Desktop

The Windows 7 desktop is a command center for organizing your laptop work. The desktop appears when you log on to a Windows 7 laptop. The Start menu is located on the desktop; you use this menu to access your laptop settings, files, folders, and software. On the desktop, there is also a taskbar that offers settings, such as your laptop's date and time, as well as shortcuts to your most frequently accessed programs or files and to currently open but minimized windows.

This chapter is an introduction to all the things you can do via the desktop. Along the way, you discover the Recycle Bin, where you place deleted files and folders, and the Frequently Used Programs area, which allows quick access to commonly used programs. You also find out how to work with application windows, create a desktop shortcut, and shut down your laptop when you're done for the day.

Understand the Desktop

The Windows desktop is the place where you access various Windows functions and open and work with all the files and programs that you use to get your work done. The desktop appears when you first turn on your laptop. You can use various elements of the desktop to open or manage files, access settings for Windows, go online, and more. **Figure 6-1** shows the desktop and some of the elements on it, including the following:

➡️ **The taskbar** is home to the Start menu, which you open by clicking the Start button. Currently open programs are listed here, and you can click one to switch programs. Finally, you can work with various settings such as the volume control using icons displayed on the taskbar.

➡️ The right side of the taskbar, which is called the **Notifications area,** contains many commonly used functions such as the laptop date and time settings, the network connections icons, and the icon you click to safely remove hardware, such as a USB storage device, from your laptop. You can also quickly display the desktop using the Show Desktop button on the far right of the Notifications area.

➡️ **The Frequently Used Programs area** is a set of icons within the taskbar that you use to open frequently used programs. You can customize this area of the taskbar to contain any programs you want. See the task "Work with Frequently Used Programs" later in this chapter.

➡️ **The Recycle Bin** holds recently deleted items. It will empty itself when it reaches its maximum size (which you can modify by right-clicking the Recycle Bin and choosing Properties), or you can do so manually. Check out the task "Empty the Recycle Bin" later in this chapter for more about this.

➡️ **Desktop shortcuts** are icons that reside on the desktop and provide shortcuts to opening software programs or files. Your laptop usually comes with some shortcuts, such as the Recycle Bin and a browser shortcut, but you can also add or delete shortcuts. Click a desktop shortcut to open an associated file or folder. See the "Create a Shortcut to a File or Folder" task later in this chapter.

➡ **Gadgets** are handy little tools that can be placed on the desktop. Windows 7 includes stock ticker, clock, and calendar gadgets, but you can also download lots of other gadgets from the Windows web site. Chapter 13 explains how to get started with gadgets.

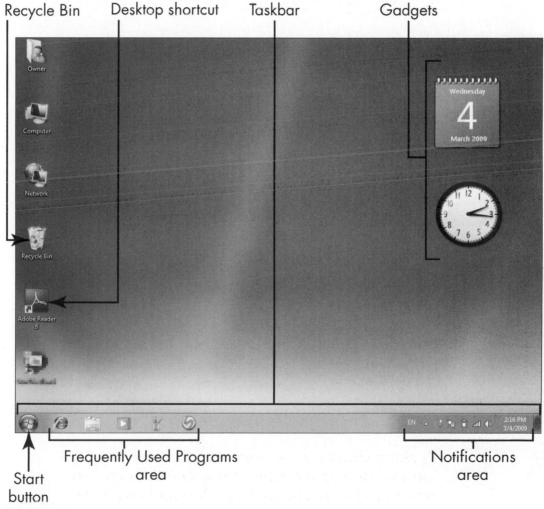

Figure 6-1

The desktop is always there as you open program windows to get your work done. If you make a program window as big as it can be (referred to as *maximizing* it), you won't see the desktop, but the desktop is still there. You can go back to it at any time by shrinking a window (minimizing it) or closing windows. You can also press Alt+Tab simultaneously and choose the desktop from the open programs icons in the window that appears, or click the Show Desktop button.

Work with the Start Menu

1. Press the Windows key on your keyboard or click the Start button on the desktop to display the Start menu. (See **Figure 6-2**.)

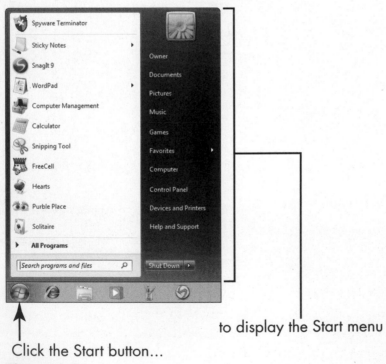

to display the Start menu

Click the Start button...

Figure 6-2

2. From the Start menu, you can do any of the following:

- Click All Programs to display a list of all programs on your laptop. You can click any program in the list to open it.

- Click any category on the right of the Start menu to display a Windows Explorer window with related folders and files. (See **Figure 6-3.**)

Files in the Pictures folder

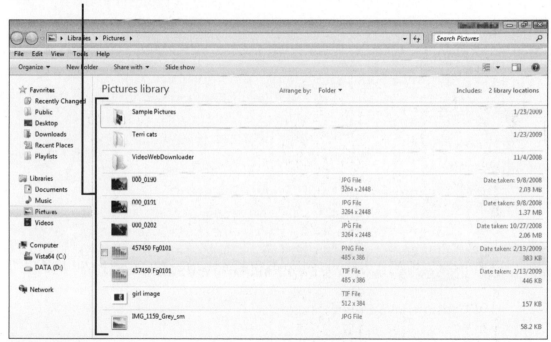

Figure 6-3

- Click either frequently used programs at the left of the Start menu or click the arrow to the right of an application to display a list of recently used files. Click a file to open it in that application.

- Click the Power button icon to close all programs and turn off Windows.

- Click the arrow next to the Power button to display a menu of choices for putting your laptop in Sleep or Hibernate mode (see the next tip for more about these settings); restarting your laptop; or for logging off or logging on as a different user.

3. When you move your cursor away from the Start menu, it disappears.

 Putting your laptop in Sleep mode is like pausing your laptop without closing open documents and programs. Sleep still uses a bit of power but allows you to quickly get back to work after only a few seconds. Hibernate mode is mainly for laptops because it saves your battery life. When you choose Hibernate (or simply shut your laptop's lid), open documents or program settings are saved to your hard drive and your laptop switches off. It takes a few seconds longer to start up your laptop from Hibernate and display the Windows desktop, but it saves more power than Sleep.

 Open the Start menu, right-click in a blank area, and click Properties to display the Taskbar and Start Menu Properties dialog box, where you can customize the Start menu behavior. For example, you can modify the functionality of the Power button and choose whether to list recently opened programs and files in the Start menu.

 If you open the Start menu and right-click in a blank area of the menu, a shortcut menu pops up. Choose Properties to display the Taskbar and Start Menu Properties dialog box, where you can customize the Start menu behavior. If you would rather use the look and feel of the Start menu in older versions of Windows, select Classic Start Menu in the Taskbar and Start Menu Properties dialog box and then click OK. (*Note:* This book deals only with the Windows 7 style Start menu features.)

Work with Frequently Used Programs

1. If you have programs you use often, you can pin them to the Frequently Used Programs area, which is the area of the taskbar just to the right of the Start button. (See **Figure 6-4**.) When you first open Windows, this area may include icons for programs such as Internet Explorer and Windows Media Player, or a shortcut to open Windows Explorer.

Frequently Used Programs area

Figure 6-4

2. To open one of these items, click its icon, and the window for that program opens. (See the Windows Media Player program in **Figure 6-5**.)

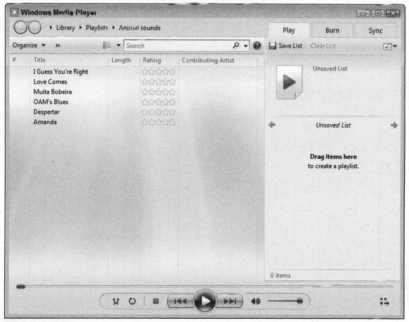

Figure 6-5

3. To close an item you've opened, click the Close button in the top-right corner of the window (the button with an X on it).

 To display additional items on the taskbar, right-click that application in the Start menu or on the Desktop and then choose Pin to Taskbar. You can also drag a desktop icon to the taskbar. (If you want help creating a desktop shortcut, see the task, "Create a Shortcut to a File or Folder," later in this chapter.)

 You can add other functions to the taskbar. Right-click a blank area of the taskbar and choose Properties. Click the Toolbars tab to display it. Click the check box for any of the additional items listed there, such as a browser Address bar, or Links.

Arrange Icons on the Desktop

1. Right-click the desktop and choose View in the resulting shortcut menu; be sure that Auto Arrange Icons isn't selected, as shown in **Figure 6-6**. (If it is selected, deselect it before proceeding to the next step.) Click the desktop, and the shortcut menu disappears.

Verify that Auto Arrange Icons isn't selected

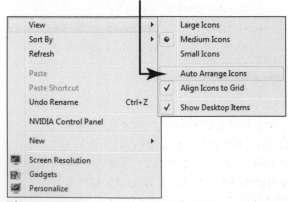

Figure 6-6

2. Right-click the Windows 7 desktop. In the resulting short-cut menu, choose Sort By, and then click the criteria for sorting your desktop shortcuts. (See **Figure 6-7**.)

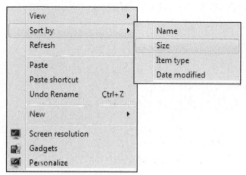

Figure 6-7

3. You can also click any icon and drag it to another location on the desktop — for example, to separate it from other desktop icons so you can find it easily.

If you've rearranged your desktop by moving items hither, thither, and yon and you want to arrange your icons into orderly rows along the left side of your desktop, snap them into place with the Auto Arrange feature. Right-click the desktop and then choose View⇨Auto Arrange Icons.

To change the size of the desktop icons, use the shortcut menu in Step 1 and choose Large Icons, Medium Icons, or Small Icons in the View submenu.

Empty the Recycle Bin

1. When you throw away junk mail, it's still in the house for a time — it's just in the trash bin instead of on your desk. That's the idea behind the Windows Recycle Bin. Your old files sit there, and you can retrieve them until you empty it or until it reaches its size limit and Windows dumps a few files. Right-click the Recycle Bin icon on the Windows 7 desktop and choose Empty Recycle Bin from the menu that appears. (See **Figure 6-8.**)

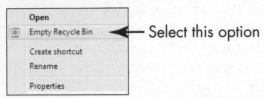

Select this option

Figure 6-8

2. In the confirmation dialog box that appears (see **Figure 6-9**), click Yes. A progress dialog box appears, indicating that the contents are being deleted. *Remember:* After you empty the Recycle Bin, all files in it are unavailable to you.

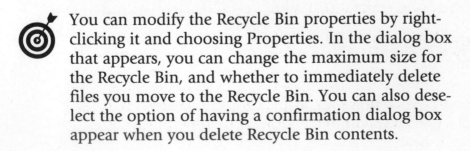

Figure 6-9

Up until the moment you permanently delete items by performing the preceding steps, you can retrieve items in the Recycle Bin by right-clicking the desktop icon and choosing Open. Select the item you want to retrieve and then click the Restore This Item link near the top of the Recycle Bin window.

You can modify the Recycle Bin properties by right-clicking it and choosing Properties. In the dialog box that appears, you can change the maximum size for the Recycle Bin, and whether to immediately delete files you move to the Recycle Bin. You can also deselect the option of having a confirmation dialog box appear when you delete Recycle Bin contents.

Find a File with Windows Explorer

1. Windows Explorer is a program you can use to find a file or folder by navigating through an outline of folders and subfolders. It's a great way to look for files on your laptop. Right-click the Start menu button and choose Open Windows Explorer, or click the Windows Explorer button on the taskbar. (It looks like a set of folders.)

2. In the resulting Windows Explorer window (shown in **Figure 6-10**), double-click a folder in the main window or the list along the left side to open the folder.

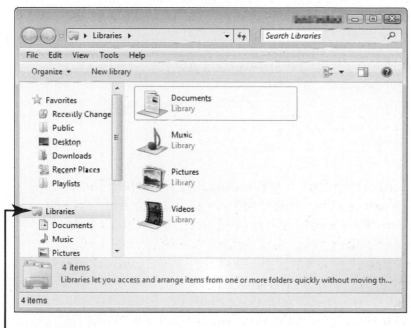

Double-click a folder to open it
Figure 6-10

3. The folder's contents are displayed. If necessary, open a series of folders in this manner until you locate the file you want.

4. When you find the file you want, double-click it to open it.

 To see different perspectives and information about files in Windows Explorer, click the arrow on the Views button (it looks like series of columns) and choose one of the following menu options: Extra Large Icons, Large Icons, Medium Icons, or Small Icons for graphical displays; Details to show details such as Date Modified and Size; Tiles to show the file/folder name, type, and size; and Content to display the date modified and file size only. If you are working with a folder containing graphics files, the graphics automatically display as *thumbnails* (tiny versions of the pictures) unless you choose Details.

 There are some shortcuts to commonly used folders in the Start menu, including Documents, Pictures, Music, and Games. Click one of these, and Windows Explorer opens that particular window.

Create a Shortcut to a File or Folder

1. Shortcuts are handy little icons you can put on the desktop for quick access to items you use frequently. This is especially useful for laptop users who may have to get to what they need quickly to save on battery power. (See this chapter's first task, "Understand the Desktop," for an introduction to shortcuts.) To create a new shortcut, first choose Start⇨All Programs and locate the program on the list of programs that appears.

2. Right-click an item, Freecell for example, and choose Send To⇨Desktop (Create Shortcut), as shown in **Figure 6-11**.

3. The shortcut appears on the desktop, as shown in **Figure 6-12**. Double-click the icon to open the application.

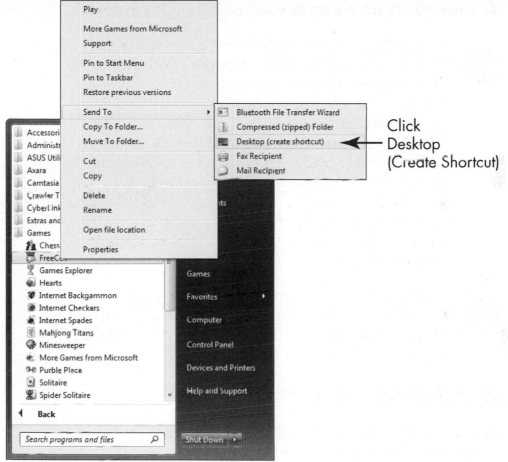

Figure 6-11

 Occasionally, Windows 7 offers to delete desktop icons that you haven't used in a long time. Let it. The desktop should be reserved for frequently used programs, files, and folders. You can always re-create shortcuts easily if you need them again.

 To clean up your desktop manually, right-click the desktop and choose Personalize. Click the Change Desktop Icons link to the left. In the Desktop Icon Setting dialog box that appears, click the Restore Default button, which returns to the original desktop shortcuts set up on your laptop.

Double-click to use the new shortcut

Figure 6-12

 You can create a shortcut for a brand-new item by right-clicking the desktop, choosing New, and then choosing an item to place there, such as a text document, bitmap image, or contact. Then double-click the shortcut that appears and begin working on the file in the associated application.

Start a Program

1. Before you can use a program, you have to start it (also called *launching* a program). Launch an application by using any of the following four methods:

- Choose Start➪All Programs. Locate the program name on the All Programs list that appears and click it. Clicking an item with a folder icon displays a list of programs within it; just click the program on that sublist to open it (as shown in **Figure 6-13**).

- Double-click a program shortcut icon on the desktop. (See **Figure 6-14**.)

- Click an item on the taskbar. The taskbar should display by default; if it doesn't, press the Windows key (on your keyboard) to display it, and then click an icon on the taskbar (refer to **Figure** 6-14), just to the right of the Start button.

- If you used the program recently and saved a document, choose it from the list of recently used programs displayed when you first open the Start menu. Then click a document created in that program from the list that displays.

Click a folder to display the programs within it

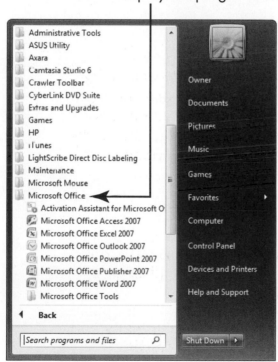

Figure 6-13

2. When the application opens, if it's a game, play it; if it's a spreadsheet, enter numbers into it; if it's your e-mail program, start deleting junk mail . . . You get the idea.

Double-click a program shortcut . . .

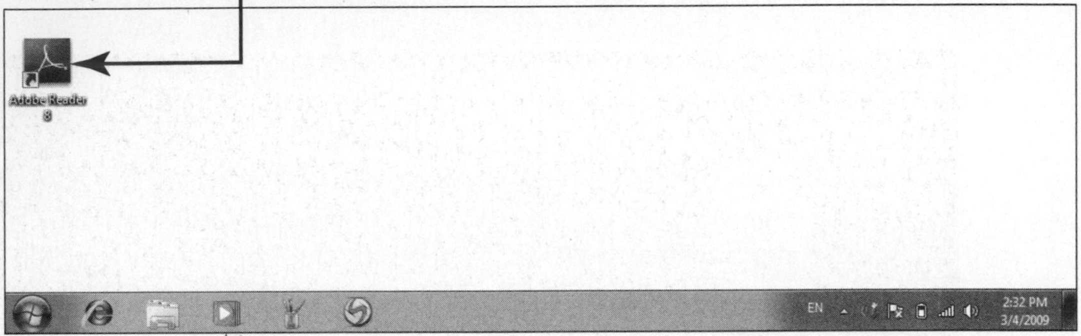

or click a program icon

Figure 6-14

 Not every program that's installed on your laptop appears as a desktop shortcut or taskbar icon. To add a program as a desktop shortcut, right-click the program name in the Windows Start menu and choose Send To⇨Desktop (Create Shortcut) from the menu that appears.

Resize Windows

1. When you open an application window, it can be maximized to fill the whole screen, restored down to a smaller window, or minimized to an icon on the taskbar. With an application open and maximized, click the Restore Down button (the icon showing two overlapping windows) in the top-right corner of the program window. (See **Figure 6-15.**) The window reduces in size.

2. To enlarge a window that has been restored down to again fill the screen, click the Maximize button. (***Note:*** This button is in the same location as the Restore Down button; this button changes its name to one or the other, depending on whether you have the screen reduced in size or maximized. A ScreenTip identifies the button when you rest your mouse pointer on it.)

The Restore Down button

Figure 6-15

3. Click the Minimize button (it's to the left of the Restore Down/Maximize button and looks like a small bar) to minimize the window to an icon on the taskbar. To open the window again, just click the taskbar icon.

 With a window maximized, you can't move the window. If you reduce a window in size, you can then click and hold the title bar to drag the window around the desktop, which is one way to view more than one window on your screen at the same time. You can also click and drag the corners of a reduced window to change it to any size you want.

Switch between Programs

1. Open two or more programs. The last program that you open is the active program.

2. Press Alt+Tab to move from one open application window to another.

3. Press and hold Alt+Tab to open a small box, as shown in **Figure 6-16**, revealing all opened programs.

Press the Tab key to select another
open program in this list

Figure 6-16

4. Release the Tab key but keep Alt pressed down. Press Tab to cycle through the icons representing open programs.

5. Release the Alt key, and Windows 7 switches to whichever program is selected. To switch back to the last program that was active, simply press Alt+Tab, and that program becomes the active program once again.

 All open programs also appear as items on the Windows 7 taskbar. Just click any running program on the taskbar to display that window and make it the active program. If the taskbar isn't visible, press the Windows key on your keyboard to display it.

Use the Shake Feature

1. The Shake feature lets you clear away open windows on your desktop by minimizing every open window except the one that you want to work with. With several

windows open, click the title bar of one you want to
stay maximized.

2. Drag the window back and forth rapidly (shake it) and
all other open windows minimize to the taskbar (see
Figure 6-17).

Figure 6-17

3. To restore all the windows to the desktop, repeat Step 2.

Use the Snap Feature

1. Snap is useful for displaying and aligning more than one
window on your screen at a time or quickly resizing windows. Snap is very handy for working on two documents
at once, copying text or files from one to the other by
clicking or selecting and dragging from one open window
to another. Click the title bar of an open window you
want to move and take either of the next two actions.

2. Drag the window to the left or right side of the desktop to make it align to that side.

3. To make a window fit the full height of the desktop, click its title bar and drag it to the top of the screen (see **Figure 6-18**).

Figure 6-18

 Use the Snap feature to expand a document window to fill the height of the screen to make scrolling through longer documents easier.

Use the Peek Feature

1. Peek is a feature that uses the Show Desktop button on the Windows taskbar to quickly display the desktop, and then go back to an open program or window. The ability to quickly peek at the desktop is useful for actions such as checking a weather gadget while working in a program or opening another program using a desktop shortcut. With a window open, click the Show Desktop button (see **Figure 6-19**).

Show Desktop button

Figure 6-19

2. To go back to the window, click the Show Desktop button again.

 Peek also displays thumbnails of open windows when you hold your mouse over one on the taskbar to allow you to preview window contents without opening them.

Close a Program

1. With an application open, first save any open documents (typically you can choose File➪Save to do this, though in recent Microsoft Office products, you click the Office button in the upper-left corner and choose Save As) and then close the application by using one of these methods:

- Click the Close button in the upper-right corner of the window.

- Press Alt+F4 to close an active open window.

- Choose File (or click the Office button)⇨Exit (as shown in **Figure 6-20**).

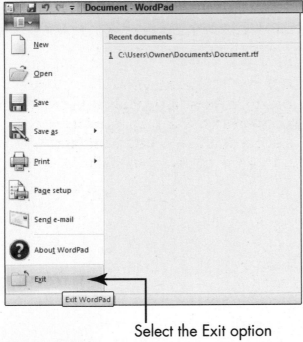

Select the Exit option

Figure 6-20

2. The application closes. If you haven't saved changes in any open documents before trying to close the application, you see a dialog box (before the application closes) asking whether you want to save the document(s). (See **Figure 6-21**.) Click Save, Don't Save, or Cancel depending on whether you want to save your changes.

 To save a document before closing an application, choose File⇨Save and use settings in the Save dialog box (that appears) to name the file and also specify which folder to save it to.

Figure 6-21

 Note that choosing File➪Exit closes all open documents in an application. Choose File➪Close to close only the currently active document and keep the application and any other open documents open.

 You don't have to close an application to open or switch to another. To switch between open applications, press Alt+Tab and use the arrow keys to move to the application (or document if multiple documents are open in an application) in which you want to work.

Setting Up Your Display

You chose your designer Day Planner, paper-clip holder, and solid maple inbox for your real-world desktop, right? Why shouldn't the Windows desktop give you the same flexibility to make things look the way you like? After all, this is the main work area of Windows, a space that you traverse many, many times in a typical day. Take it from somebody who spends many hours in front of a laptop: Customizing your desktop pays off in increased productivity as well as decreased eyestrain.

To customize your desktop, you can do the following:

➡ Set up Windows to display images and colors.

➡ Use screen-saver settings to switch from everyday work stuff to an attractive animation when you've stopped working for a time.

➡ Modify your *screen resolution* setting, which controls how sharp and detailed a picture your screen displays. (See Chapter 8 for more about settings that help those with visual challenges.)

Get ready to . . .

➠ Modify Windows transparency. Windows Aero Glass is an effect that makes the borders of your windows transparent so you can see other windows layered underneath the active window. You might love it, or hate it, but you should know how to turn the effect on or off.

Customize Windows' Appearance

When you take your laptop out of the box, Windows comes with certain preset, or default, settings that determine the appearance of the desktop and a color scheme for items you see on your screen. Here are some of the things you can change about the Windows environment and why you might want to change them:

➠ As you work with your laptop, you might find that changing the appearance of various elements on your screen not only makes it more pleasant to look at, but also helps you see the text and images more easily. You can change the graphic that's shown as the desktop background, even displaying your own picture there.

➠ You can adjust your screen resolution, which not only affects the crispness of images on your screen, but lower resolutions will display items larger on your screen, which could help you if you have visual challenges or a smaller laptop screen. (See Chapter 8 for more about Windows features that help people with visual, hearing, or dexterity challenges.)

➠ Windows has built-in *themes* that you can apply quickly. Themes save sets of elements that include menu appearance, background colors or patterns, screen savers, and even mouse cursors and system sounds. If you choose a theme and then modify the way your laptop looks in some way — for example, by changing the color scheme — that change overrides the setting in the theme you last applied.

➠ Screen savers are animations that appear after your laptop has remained inactive for a time. In the early days of personal computers, screen savers helped to keep your monitor from burning out from constant use. Today, people use screen savers to automatically conceal what they're doing from passersby or just to enjoy the pretty picture. Note, however, that if you are running your laptop off the battery, you might want to disable the screen saver so it doesn't use up your power.

Set Your Screen's Resolution

1. Changing screen resolution can make items onscreen easier to see. Choose Start⇨Control Panel⇨Appearance and Personalization and click the Adjust Screen Resolution link.

2. In the resulting Screen Resolution window, click the arrow to the right of the Resolution field.

3. Use the slider (as shown in **Figure 7-1**) to select a higher or lower resolution.

You can also change the orientation of your display by making a choice in the Orientation drop-down list.

4. Click OK to accept the new screen resolution and then click the Close button to close the window.

Higher resolutions, such as 1400 × 1250, produce smaller, crisper images. Lower resolutions (such as 800 × 600) produce larger, somewhat jagged images. The upside of higher resolution is that more stuff fits on your screen; the downside is that words and graphics can be hard to see because they're smaller.

The Advanced Settings link in the Screen Resolution window displays another dialog box where you can work with color management and monitor settings.

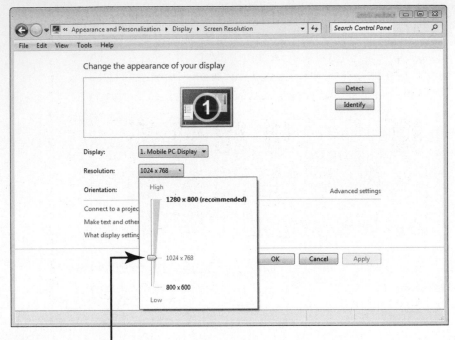

Click and drag the Resolution slider
Figure 7-1

 Remember that you can also use your View settings in most software programs to get a larger or smaller view of your documents without having to change your screen's resolution. Consult the program's Help feature for instructions on how to adjust the view.

Change the Desktop Background

1. You can display a picture or color that appeals to you on your desktop. Right-click the desktop and choose Personalize from the shortcut menu.

2. In the resulting Personalization window, click the Desktop Background link to display the Desktop Background window, as shown in **Figure 7-2**.

3. Select a category of desktop background options from the Picture Location drop-down menu (see **Figure 7-3**), and thumbnails of your choices display in the viewing area.

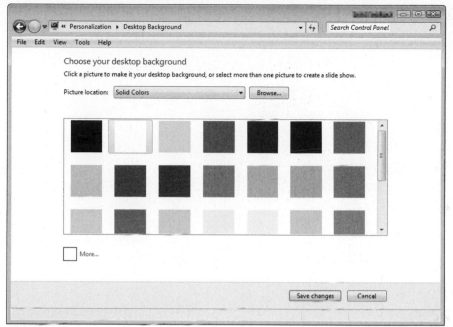

Figure 7-2

Select a location   Click a picture

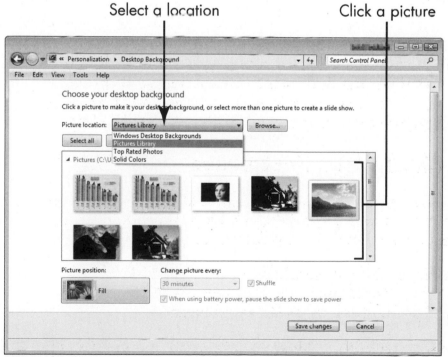

Figure 7-3

4. Click the image that you want to use. The background is previewed on your desktop.

5. Click Save Changes to apply the settings and close the window, and then close the Personalization window.

 If you apply a desktop theme (see the "Choose a Desktop Theme" task later in this chapter), you overwrite whatever desktop settings you've made in this task. If you apply a desktop theme and then go back and make desktop settings, you replace the theme's settings. However, making changes is easy and keeps your desktop interesting, so play around with themes and desktop backgrounds all you like!

Use Your Own Picture as a Background

1. You can display a picture or color that appeals to you on your desktop. Right-click the desktop and choose Personalize from the shortcut menu.

2. In the resulting Personalization window, click the Desktop Background link to display the Desktop Background window, as shown back in **Figure 7-2**.

3. Click the Browse button to display the Browse For Folder dialog box shown in **Figure 7-4**.

4. Click the folder where your picture is stored (for example, click Libraries and then Pictures to access your Pictures folder) and then click OK.

5. The pictures in that folder appear in the Choose Your Desktop Background window. Click a picture, and then click Save Changes to make that picture your background.

6. Click the Close button to close the Control Panel. Your new picture appears as your desktop background.

Figure 7-4

Choose a Desktop Theme

1. Themes apply several color and image settings at once. Right-click the desktop and choose Personalize. The Personalization window opens.

2. In the resulting Personalization window, as shown in **Figure 7-5**, select a theme. Your options include the following groups:

- **My Themes:** Uses whatever settings you have and saves them with that name.

- **AeroThemes:** Offers up themes related to nature, landscapes, light auras, and your country of residence.

- **Basic and High Contrast Themes:** Offers a variety of easy to read contrast settings in a variety of themes.

3. Click Close to close the dialog box.

 Themes affect sets of elements that include menu appearance, background colors or patterns, screen savers, and even cursors and sounds. If you modify any of these individually — for example, by changing

the screen saver to another one — that change overrides the setting in the theme you last applied.

 You can save custom themes. Simply apply a theme,
make any changes to it you like by using the various
Appearance and Personalization settings options, and
then — in the Personalization window — click Save
Theme. In the resulting dialog box, give your new
theme a name and click Save. It will now appear on
the Theme list.

Select a desktop theme

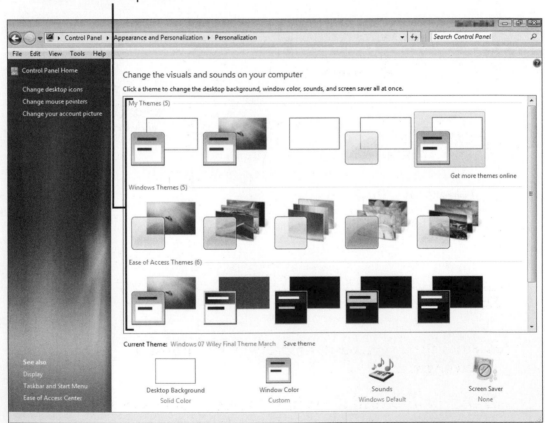

Figure 7-5

Set Up a Screen Saver

1. If you want an animated sequence to appear when your laptop is not in use for a period of time, set up a screen saver. Right-click the desktop and choose Personalize. In the resulting Personalization window, click the Screen Saver button in the bottom-right corner of the window to display the Screen Saver Settings dialog box, as shown in **Figure 7-6.**

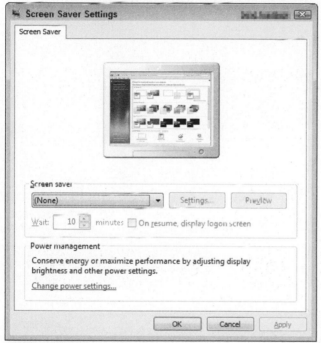

Figure 7-6

2. From the Screen Saver drop-down list, choose a screen saver.

3. Use the arrows in the Wait *xx* Minutes text box to set the number of inactivity minutes that Windows 7 waits before displaying the screen saver. If you choose a lower setting such as 5 minutes, you save battery power; but if you choose a higher setting, you avoid sometimes annoying screen blackouts causing you to have to log in again. You can always change this setting if you want to make a different choice in the future.

4. Click the Preview button to take a peek at your screen saver of choice. (See **Figure 7-7**.) When you're happy with your settings, click to stop the preview, and then click OK.

Figure 7-7

5. Click the Close button in the Personalization window to close it.

Some screen savers allow you to modify their settings: for example, how fast they display or how many lines they draw onscreen. To customize your screen saver, click the Settings button when you're in the Screen Saver Settings dialog box.

Change the Color and Appearance of Windows

1. You can modify the appearance of elements on your screen one by one. Right-click the desktop and choose Personalize.

2. In the resulting Personalization window, click the Window Color button to display the Window Color and Appearance dialog box.

3. Click the Advanced Appearance Settings link.

4. In the resulting Window Color and Appearance dialog box (see **Figure 7-8**), select items one by one from the Item drop-down list. Make any changes you wish by using the Size, Color, and Font settings.

5. Click OK to accept the settings, and then click Save Changes to return to the Personalization window.

6. Click the Close button to close the Personalization window.

 When customizing a color scheme, be aware that not all screen elements allow you to modify all settings. For example, setting an Application Background doesn't make the Font setting available — because it's just a background setting. Makes sense, huh?

Some colors are easier on the eyes than others. For example, green is more restful to look at than orange. Choose a color scheme that is pleasant to look at and easy on the eyes!

Figure 7-8

Modify Windows' Transparency

1. You can apply a Windows Aero theme to get a transparent effect on windows you display. Choose Start⇨ Control Panel⇨Appearance and Personalization. In the Appearance and Personalization window that appears (see **Figure 7-9**), click Personalization.

2. In the resulting Personalization window (see **Figure 7-10**) click a theme in the Aero Themes section.

3. Click the Close button to close the Personalization window and see the results.

Click the Personalization link

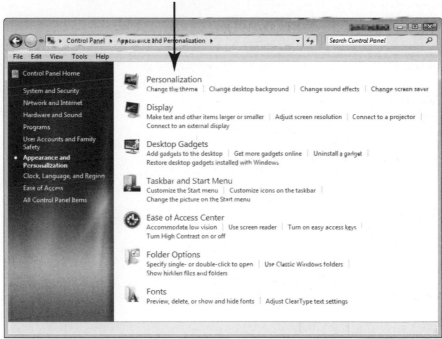

Figure 7-9

Select a theme from the Aero Themes section

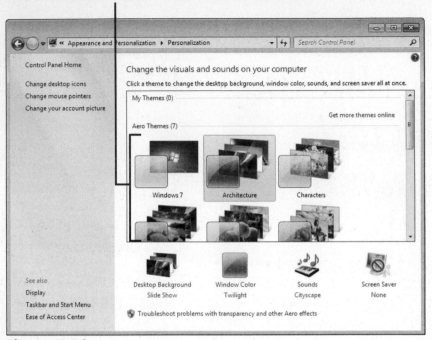

Figure 7-10

Getting Help with Vision, Hearing, and Dexterity Challenges

Though Windows knows how to do a lot of things right out of the box, when it comes to being more accessible to each person using it, it has to be taught how to behave. For example, if you have a vision challenge that requires special help, or prefer a certain cursor, or have difficulty using a keyboard, Windows depends on you to make settings that customize its behavior. This is good news for you because the ability to customize Windows gives you a lot of flexibility in how you interact with it.

Here's what you can do to customize Windows:

➡ Control features that help visually challenged users work with a laptop, such as setting a higher screen contrast, using the Narrator feature to read the onscreen text aloud, or increasing the size of text onscreen.

➡ Work with the Speech Recognition feature, which allows you to input data into a document using speech rather than a keyboard or mouse.

➡ Modify the touchpad functionality, change the mouse cursor to sport a certain look, or make your cursor easier to view as it moves around your screen.

➡ Work with keyboard settings that make input easier for those who are challenged by physical conditions such as carpal tunnel syndrome or arthritis.

Use Tools for the Visually Challenged

1. You can set up Windows to use higher screen contrast to make things easier to see, read descriptions to you rather than make you read text, and more. Choose Start⇨ Control Panel.

2. In the Control Panel window, click the Optimize Visual Display link under the Ease of Access tools.

3. In the resulting Make the Computer Easier to See dialog box (as shown in **Figure 8-1**), select the check boxes for features you want to use:

• **High Contrast:** Turn on the Higher Contrast When Alt+Left Shift+Print Screen Is Pressed setting. High contrast is a color scheme that increases the darkness of darker elements and the lightness of lighter elements so it's easier for your eyes to distinguish one from the other. You can also choose to have a warning message appear when you turn this setting on, or play a sound when it's turned off or on.

• **Hear Text and Descriptions Read Aloud:** You can turn on a Narrator feature that reads onscreen text or an Audio Description feature to describe what's happening in video programs.

• **Make Things on the Screen Larger:** If you click Turn on Magnifier, there will be two cursors displayed

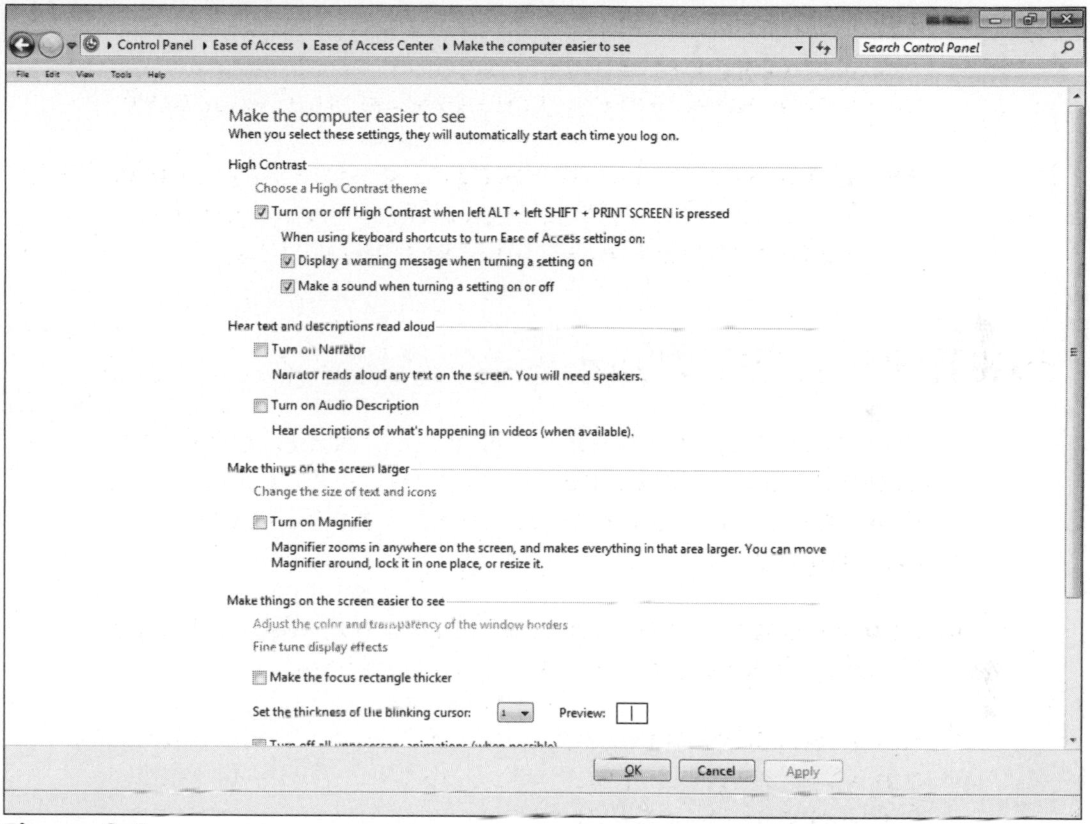

Figure 8-1

onscreen. One cursor appears in the Magnifier window, where everything is shown enlarged, and one appears in whatever is showing on your laptop (for example, your desktop or an open application). You can maneuver either cursor to work in your document. (They're both active, so it does take some getting used to.)

- **Make Things On the Screen Easier to See:** Here's where you make settings that adjust onscreen contrast to make things easier to see, enlarge the size of the blinking cursor (see **Figure 8-2**), and get rid of distracting animations and backgrounds.

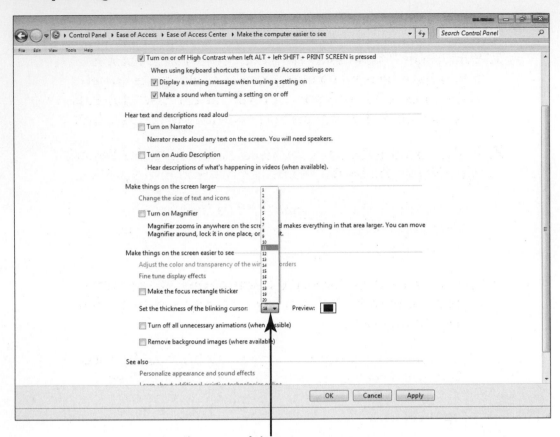

Set the size of the mouse cursor

Figure 8-2

4. When you finish making your settings, click OK to apply them and then click the Close button to close the dialog box.

 If you bought a laptop with a 12-inch screen and find things are hard to read, don't run out and buy a new laptop. It's possible to connect your laptop to a standalone monitor using a VGA port. If you mainly use your laptop at home, this may be a less expensive way to upgrade your screen to a larger size. Consult your laptop manual for instructions on how to hook up to a separate monitor.

Replace Sounds with Visual Cues

1. Sometimes Windows alerts you to events with sounds. If you have hearing challenges, you might prefer to get visual cues. Choose Start⇨Control Panel⇨Ease of Access and then click the Replace Sounds with Visual Cues link.

2. In the resulting Use Text or Visual Alternatives for Sounds window (see **Figure 8-3**), make any of the following settings:

- Select the Turn on Visual Notifications for Sound (Sound Sentry) option so that Windows gives you a visual alert when a sound plays.

- Chose a setting for visual notifications. These warnings essentially flash a portion of your screen to alert you to an event.

- To control text captions for any spoken words, select Turn on Text Captions for Spoken Dialog (When Available). *Note:* This isn't available with some applications.

3. To save the new settings, click OK, and then click the Close button to close the window.

Visual cues are useful if you're hard of hearing and don't always pick up system sounds that play to alert you to error messages or a device disconnect. After the setting is turned on, it is active until you go back to the Use Text or Visual Alternatives for Sounds window and turn it off.

This may seem obvious, but if you're hard of hearing, you may want to simply increase the volume of the sound coming out of your speakers. You can modify your system volume by choosing Hardware and Sound in the Control Panel and then clicking the Adjust System Volume link. Most laptop keyboards also offer special volume keys you can click to quickly adjust system sounds.

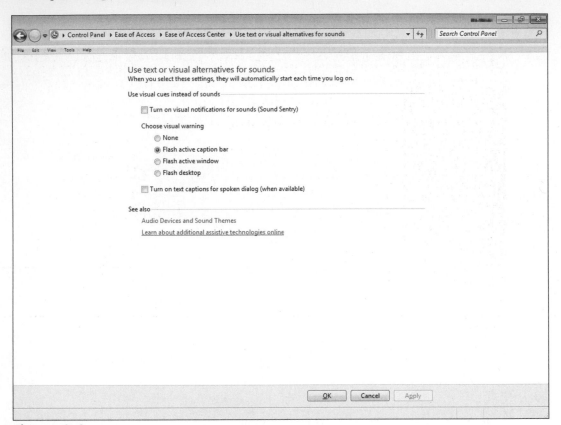

Figure 8-3

Make Text Larger or Smaller

1. Choose Start⇨Control Panel⇨Appearance and Personalization. In the resulting window, click Make Text and Other Items Larger or Smaller.

2. In the resulting Display window (see **Figure 8-4**), click the radio button for the size of text you prefer. Smaller is the default, but you can expand text size to 125 percent with the Medium setting and 150 percent with the Larger setting.

3. Click Apply and then click the Close button to close the window. You'll see the results (see **Figure 8-5,** which shows the Larger setting applied) next time you log on to Windows.

Make your text size selection

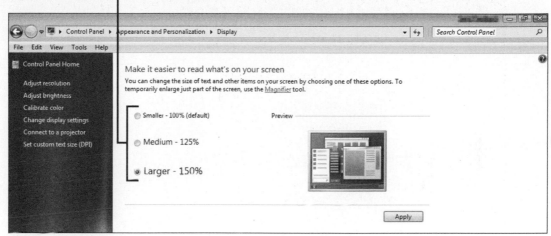

Figure 8-4

Figure 8-5

Set Up Speech Recognition

1. If you have dexterity challenges from a condition such as arthritis, you might prefer to speak commands using a technology called *speech recognition* rather than type them. If your laptop doesn't have a built-in microphone (most do), plug a headset with a microphone into your laptop headset ports.

2. Choose Start⇨Control Panel⇨Ease of Access⇨Start Speech Recognition.

3. The Welcome to Speech Recognition message appears; click Next to continue. (*Note:* If you've used Speech Recognition before, this message does not appear.)

4. In the resulting Set Up Speech Recognition dialog box (as shown in **Figure** 8-6), select the type of microphone that you're using and then click Next. The next screen tells you how to place and use the microphone for optimum results. Read the message and click Next.

5. In the dialog box that appears (see **Figure** 8-7), read the sample sentence aloud to help train Speech Recognition to your voice. When you're done, click Next. A dialog box appears, telling you that your microphone is now set up. Click Next.

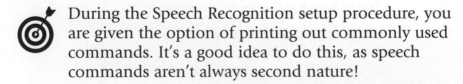 During the Speech Recognition setup procedure, you are given the option of printing out commonly used commands. It's a good idea to do this, as speech commands aren't always second nature!

6. In the resulting dialog box, choose whether to enable or disable *document review*, which allows Windows to review your documents and e-mail to help it recognize the way you typically phrase things. Click Next.

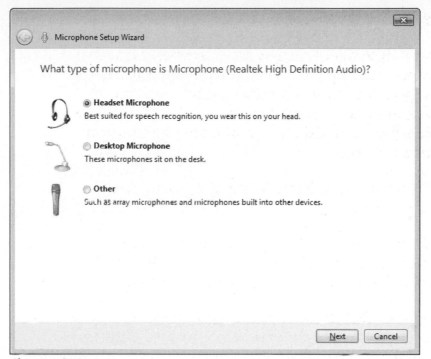

Figure 8-6

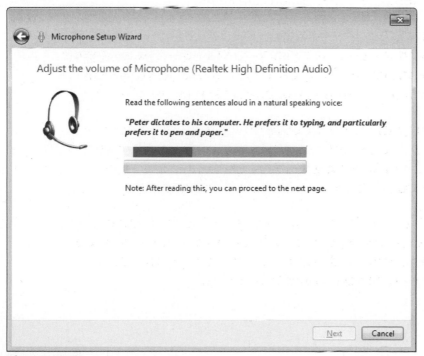

Figure 8-7

7. In the next dialog box, choose either Manual Activation mode, where you can use a mouse, pen, or keyboard to turn the feature on; or Voice Activation mode, which is useful if you have difficulty manipulating devices because of arthritis or a hand injury. Click Next.

8. In the resulting screen, if you wish to view and/or print a list of speech recognition commands, click the View Reference Sheet button and read about or print reference information, and then click the Close button to close that window. Click Next to proceed.

9. In the resulting dialog box, either click Run Speech Recognition at Startup to disable this feature or leave the default setting. Click Next.

10. The final dialog box informs you that you can now control the laptop by voice, and it offers you a Start Tutorial button to help you practice voice commands. Click that button, or click Skip Tutorial to skip the tutorial and leave the Speech Recognition setup.

11. The Speech Recognition control panel appears. (See **Figure 8-8.**) Say "Start listening" to activate the feature if you used voice activation in Step 6, or click the Start Speech Recognition link if you chose manual activation in Step 8. You can now begin using spoken commands to work with your laptop.

To stop Speech Recognition, click the Close button on the Control Panel. To start the Speech Recognition feature again, choose Start⇨Control Panel⇨Ease of Access and then click the Start Speech Recognition link. To learn more about Speech Recognition commands, click the Take Speech Tutorial link in the Speech Recognition Options window accessed from the Ease of Access window of the Control Panel.

The Speech Recognition control panel

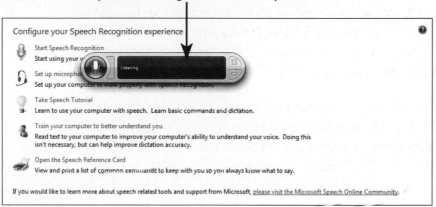

Figure 8-8

Modify How Your Keyboard Works

1. If your hands are a bit stiff with age or you have carpal tunnel problems, you might look into changing how your keyboard works. Choose Start⇨Control Panel⇨Ease of Access and then click the Change How Your Keyboard Works link.

2. In the resulting Make the Keyboard Easier to Use dialog box (see **Figure 8-9**), make any of these settings:

- **Turn on Mouse Keys:** Select this option to control your cursor by entering keyboard commands. If you turn on this setting, click the Set Up Mouse Keys link to specify settings for this feature.

- **Turn on Sticky Keys:** Select this option to enable keystroke combinations (such as Ctrl+Alt+Delete) to be pressed one at a time, rather than simultaneously.

- **Turn on Toggle Keys:** You can set up Windows to play a sound when you press Caps Lock, Num Lock, or Scroll Lock (which I do all the time by mistake!).

- **Turn on Filter Keys:** If you sometimes press a key very lightly or press it so hard that it activates twice, you can use this setting to adjust repeat rates to adjust for that. Use the Set Up Filter Keys link to fine-tune settings if you make this choice.

- **Make It Easier to Use Keyboard Shortcuts:** To have Windows underline keyboard shortcuts and access keys wherever these shortcuts appear, click this setting.

- **Make It Easier to Manage Windows:** If you want to avoid windows shifting automatically when you move them to the edge of your screen, use this setting.

3. To save the new settings, click OK, and then click the Close button to close the Ease of Access Center.

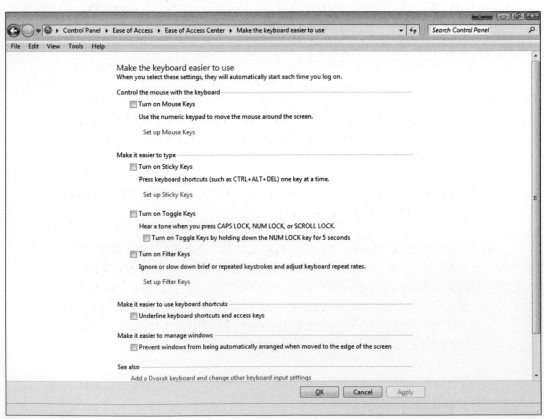

Figure 8-9

You can click the Learn about Additional Assistive Technologies Online link to go the Microsoft web site and discover add-on and third-party programs that might help you if you have a visual, hearing, or input-related challenge.

 Keyboards all have their own unique feel. When you buy a laptop, it's important to try different keyboards to see if one works better for you than another. See Chapter 2 for more about selecting the right laptop for you.

Use the Onscreen Keyboard Feature

1. Some people have problems pressing the keys on a regular keyboard. If you have a tablet style computer such as an iPad, there's a handy onscreen keyboard feature you can tap with your fingers. If you have another style of laptop, Windows offers its own onscreen keyboard you can use by clicking its (virtual) keys with your mouse. To use the onscreen keyboard, choose Start⇨Control Panel⇨Ease of Access category.

2. In the resulting window, click the Ease of Access Center link to open the Ease of Access Center window. (See **Figure 8-10.**)

3. Click Start On-Screen Keyboard. The onscreen keyboard appears. (See **Figure 8-11.**)

4. Open a document in any application where you can enter text, and then click the keys on the onscreen keyboard with your mouse to make entries. (If you have a tablet with a touchscreen and Windows 7 operating system so you can use the Windows keyboard feature, tap the keyboard with your finger.)

Click this link

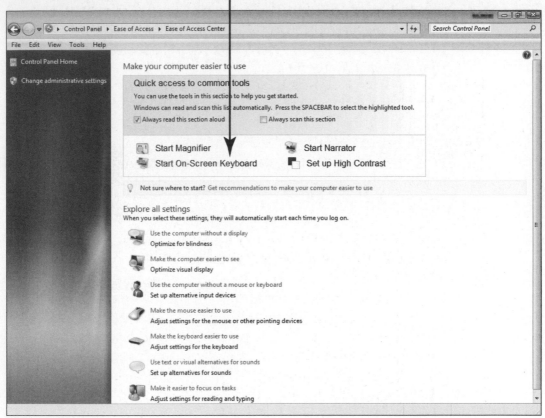

Figure 8-10

Figure 8-11

 To use keystroke combinations (such as Ctrl+Z), click the first key (in this case, Ctrl), and then click the second key (Z). You don't have to hold down the first key as you do with a regular keyboard.

5. To change settings, such as how you select keys (Typing Mode) or the font used to label keys (Font), click the Options key on the onscreen keyboard. Choose one of the four options shown in the Options dialog box and click OK.

6. Click the Close button on the onscreen keyboard to remove it from your screen.

 You can set up the Hover typing mode to activate a key after you hover your pointer over it for a predefined period of time (*x* number of seconds). If you have arthritis or some other condition that makes clicking difficult, this option can help you enter text. Click the Hover over Keys item in the Options dialog box and use the slider to set how long you have to hover before activating a key.

Set Up Keyboard Repeat Rates

1. Adjusting your keyboard settings might make it easier for you to type, and it can be helpful to people with dexterity challenges. To see your options, choose Start⇨Control Panel⇨All Control Panel Items. In the resulting window, click the Keyboard link.

2. In the Keyboard Properties dialog box that appears, click the Speed tab (see **Figure 8-12**) and drag the sliders to adjust the two Character Repeat settings, which do the following:

- **Repeat Delay:** Affects the amount of time it takes before a typed character is typed again when you hold down a key.

- **Repeat Rate:** Adjusts how quickly a character repeats when you hold down a key after the first repeat character appears.

If you want to see how the Character Repeat rate settings work in action, click in the text box below the two
settings and hold down a key to see a demonstration.

Figure 8-12

3. Drag the slider in the Cursor Blink Rate section. This affects
cursors, such as the insertion line that appears in text.

4. Click OK to save and apply changes and close the dialog box.
Click the Close button to close the Control Panel window.

 If you have trouble with motion (for example,
because of arthritis or carpal tunnel syndrome), you
might find that you can adjust these settings to make
it easier for you to get your work done. For example,
if you can't pick up your finger quickly from a key, a
slower repeat rate might save you from typing more
instances of a character than you'd intended. This is
especially helpful for laptops with smaller keyboards,
such as netbooks.

Customize Touchpad Behavior

1. To avoid having to click your touchpad too often, you can use your keyboard to move the cursor instead of moving your mouse with your hand, or you can activate a window by hovering your mouse over it rather than clicking. Choose Start➪Control Panel➪Ease of Access and then click the Change How Your Mouse Works link. The Make the Mouse Easier to Use dialog box opens (as shown in **Figure 8-13**).

2. To use the numeric keypad to move your cursor on your screen, choose the Turn on Mouse Keys setting. If you turn this feature on, click Set Up Mouse Keys to fine-tune its behavior.

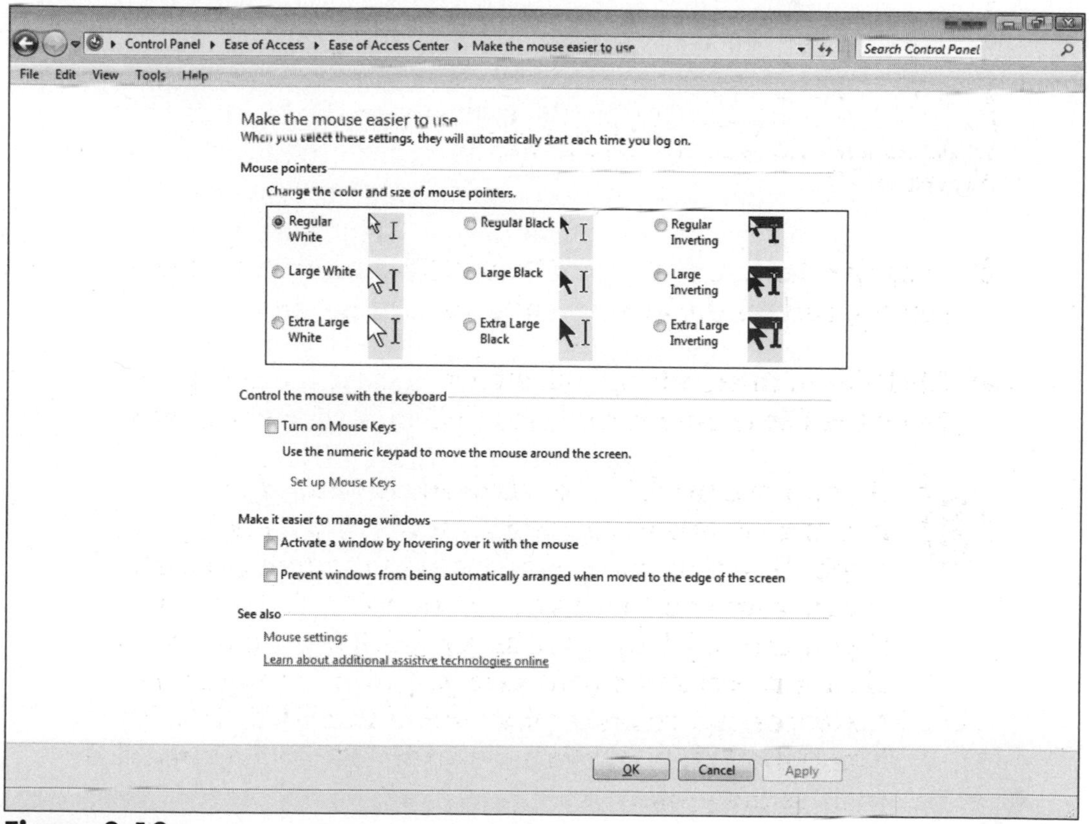

Figure 8-13

3. Select the Activate a Window by Hovering Over It with the Mouse check box to enable this (pretty self-explanatory!) feature.

4. Click OK to save the new settings and then click the Close button to close the Ease of Access Center.

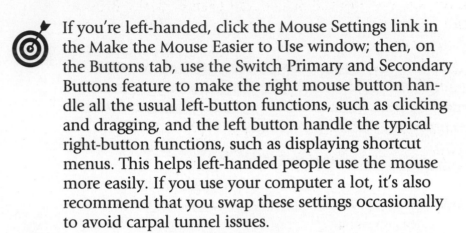 If you're left-handed, click the Mouse Settings link in the Make the Mouse Easier to Use window; then, on the Buttons tab, use the Switch Primary and Secondary Buttons feature to make the right mouse button handle all the usual left-button functions, such as clicking and dragging, and the left button handle the typical right-button functions, such as displaying shortcut menus. This helps left-handed people use the mouse more easily. If you use your computer a lot, it's also recommend that you swap these settings occasionally to avoid carpal tunnel issues.

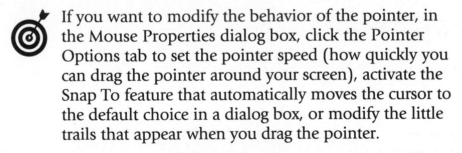 If you want to modify the behavior of the pointer, in the Mouse Properties dialog box, click the Pointer Options tab to set the pointer speed (how quickly you can drag the pointer around your screen), activate the Snap To feature that automatically moves the cursor to the default choice in a dialog box, or modify the little trails that appear when you drag the pointer.

Though some laptop keyboards have separate number pads, many have them embedded in the regular keyboard to save space. Using these embedded keys requires that you press the Fn key and then the letter key where the number you want is embedded. (The numbers are usually included on the key in a different color, such as red or blue.)

Change the Cursor

1. Having trouble finding the mouse cursor on your screen? You might want to enlarge it or change its shape. Choose

Start⇨Control Panel⇨Ease of Access⇨Change How Your Mouse Works. In the resulting Make the Mouse Easier to Use dialog box, click the Mouse Settings link.

2. In the resulting Mouse Properties dialog box, on the Pointers tab, as shown in **Figure 8-14,** click to select a pointer, such as Normal Select, and then click the Browse button. (*Note:* This dialog box may have slightly different tabs depending on your mouse model features.) In the Browse dialog box that appears, click an alternate cursor and then click Open.

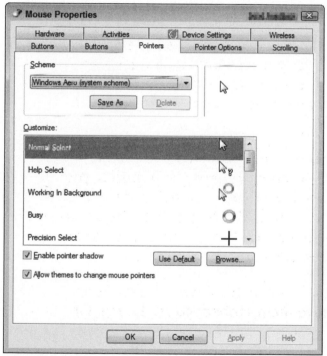

Figure 8-14

3. Click Apply to use the new pointer setting and then click the Close button to close the Mouse Properties dialog box.

 Be careful not to change the cursor to another standard cursor (for example, changing the Normal Select cursor to the Busy hourglass cursor). This could

prove slightly confusing for you and completely baf-
fling to anybody else who works on your laptop. If
you make a choice and decide it was a mistake, click
the Use Default button on the Pointers tab in the
Mouse Properties dialog box to return a selected
cursor to its default choice.

 You can also choose the color and size of mouse
pointers in the Make the Mouse Easier to Use dialog
box. A large white or extra large black cursor might
be more visible to you, depending on the color
scheme you've applied to Windows 7.

Setting Up Printers and Scanners

A laptop is a great place to store data, images, and other digital information. Sometimes you need ways to turn that data into printed documents or change printed text into electronic files you can work with on your laptop. Here are a few key ways to do just that:

➠ **Printers** allow you to create *hard copies* (a fancy term for printouts) of your files on paper, transparencies, or whatever stock your printer can accommodate. To use a printer, you have to install software — called a *printer driver* — and use certain settings to tell your laptop how to find the printer and what to print.

➠ You use a **scanner** to create electronic files from hard copies of newspaper clippings, your birth certificate, driver's license, pictures, or whatever will fit into/onto your scanner. You can then work with the electronic files, send them to others as e-mail attachments, or print them. Scanners also require that you install a driver that comes with your machine.

Install a Printer

Read the instructions that came with your printer. Some printers require that you manually install software before connecting them, but others install the needed software automatically and can be connected right away. After reading the instructions, turn on your laptop and then follow the option that fits your needs:

➡ If your printer is a Plug and Play device, connect it and power it on; Windows installs what it needs automatically.

➡ Insert the disc that came with the device and follow the onscreen instructions.

➡ If you have a wireless printer, choose Start➪Devices and Printers and click the Add a Printer link in the window that appears. Choose the Add a Network, Wireless, or Bluetooth Printer option and follow the instructions provided.

   Note: In the step that follows the one where you name the printer, you can indicate whether you want to share the printer on your network. You can select the Do Not Share This Printer option to prevent others from using the printer, or you can select the Share Name option and enter a printer name to share the printer on your network. This means that others can see and select this printer to print their documents.

If none of those options are suitable, follow these steps:

1. Choose Start➪Devices and Printers.

2. In the Devices and Printers window that appears, click the Add a Printer link near the top.

3. In the resulting Add Printer Wizard window (the first of a series of windows that will guide you through a task) shown in **Figure** 9-1), click the Add a Local Printer option and click Next.

Select this option and click Next

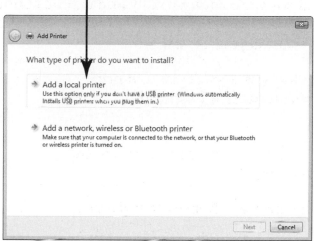

Figure 9-1

4. In the Choose a Printer Port dialog box shown in **Figure** 9-2, click the down arrow on the Use an Existing Port field and select a port, or just use the recommended port setting that Windows selects for you. Click Next.

Select a printer port

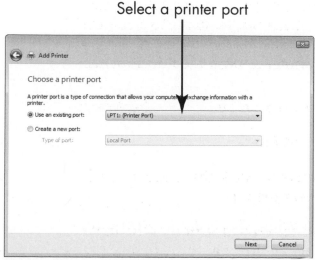

Figure 9-2

5. In the Install the Printer Driver dialog box, shown in
Figure 9-3, choose a manufacturer and then choose a
printer. You then have two options:

- If you have the manufacturer's disc, insert it in the
appropriate CD or DVD drive now and click the Have
Disk button. Click Next.

- If you don't have the manufacturer's disc, click the
Windows Update button to see a list of printer drivers
that you can download from the Microsoft web site.
Click Next.

Choose a manufacturer   Then choose a printer

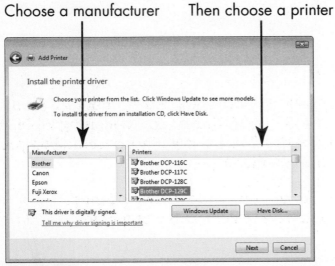

Figure 9-3

6. In the resulting Type a Printer Name dialog box (see
Figure 9-4), enter a printer name. Click Next.

7. In the resulting dialog box, click Finish to complete the
Add Printer Wizard.

If you need to print on the go, consider a portable
printer. These lightweight (5 pounds or less) units
don't offer the best print quality, but for quick, on-
the-fly printing, they can be useful. See Chapter 2
for more about buying laptop accessories.

Enter a name for your printer

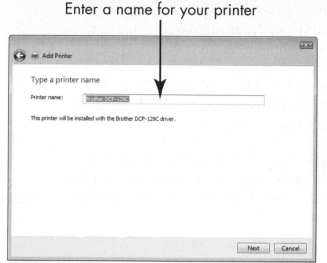

Figure 9-4

Set Up a Wireless Printer

A wireless printer connects to your laptop either through a technology called Bluetooth or, if you have a wireless network, using Wi-Fi. Here's a rundown of things you should be aware of when setting up your laptop to connect to a wireless printer:

➟ Bluetooth and Wi-Fi are short-range wireless connections (meaning you have to be near the printer to connect to it).

➟ To use a Bluetooth-based wireless printer, you may have to connect a Bluetooth transmitter to a USB port on your laptop. This transmitter is a small device about the size of a flash storage drive that transmits a signal to your printer. If you have a Wi-Fi–enabled laptop, you can skip this step.

➟ You should run through the procedure in the previous task to set up the printer in Windows Control Panel and install any required drivers. After you click Add a Printer in the Sound and Hardware window, choose Add a Network, Wireless, or Bluetooth Printer in the first dialog box that appears and follow the instructions. (You can also accomplish the setup for a Bluetooth connection by clicking the Add A Bluetooth Device choice instead of Add A Printer — and then letting Windows detect the device.)

➥ The Add a Printer wizard walks you through the process of pairing your laptop and printer; you may need a passcode (provided with your printer) for this.

➥ Once you've installed the printer, you should be able to print just as you would with any other kind of printer, but without the hassle of extra wires littering your desk.

If you run into a problem, check your wireless printer's instructions for help.

Set a Default Printer

1. You can set up a default printer that will be used every time you print so that you don't have to select a printer each time. Choose Start⇨Devices and Printers.

2. In the resulting Devices and Printers window, the current default printer is indicated by a check mark (as shown in **Figure 9-5**).

3. Right-click any printer that isn't set as the default and choose Set as Default Printer from the shortcut menu, as shown in **Figure 9-6**.

4. Click the Close button in the Devices and Printers window to save the new settings.

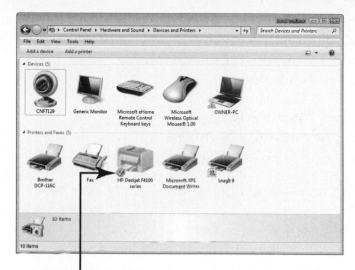

The default printer is checked

Figure 9-5

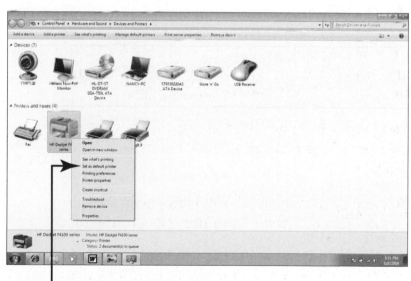

Choose Set As Default Printer

Figure 9-6

To modify printing properties that are available for your particular printer model (for example, whether the printer prints in draft or high-quality mode, or whether it uses color or only black and white), right-click a printer in the Devices and Printers window (refer to **Figure 9-6**) and choose Printing Preferences. This same dialog box is available from most common Windows-based software programs, such as Microsoft Word or Excel, by clicking the Properties button in the Print dialog box.

 If you right-click the printer that is already set as the default, you'll find that the Set as Default Printer command will not be available on the shortcut menu mentioned in Step 3.

Set Printer Preferences

1. Your printer might offer you a choice of capabilities — such as printing in color or black and white, printing in draft quality (which uses less ink), or high quality (which produces a darker, crisper image). To modify these settings for all documents you print, choose Start➪Devices and Printers (in the Hardware and Sound group).

2. In the resulting Devices and Printers window, any printers you have installed are listed. Right-click a printer and then choose Printing Preferences.

3. In the Printing Preferences dialog box that appears (as shown in **Figure 9-7**), click any of the tabs to display various settings, such as Color. (See **Figure 9-8**.) Note that different printers might display different choices and different tabs in this dialog box, but common settings include the following:

- **Color/Grayscale:** If you have a color printer, you have the option of printing in color or not. The grayscale option uses only black ink. When printing a draft of a color document, you can extend the life of your color ink cartridge (which is more expensive to replace or refill than the black one) by printing in grayscale.

- **Quality:** If you want, you can print in fast or draft quality (these settings might have different names depending on your manufacturer) to save ink, or you can print in a higher or best quality for your finished documents. Some printers offer a dpi setting for quality — the higher the dpi setting, the better the quality.

- **Paper Source:** If you have a printer with more than one paper tray, you can select which tray to use for printing. For example, you might have 8 ½ x 11 paper (letter sized) in one tray and 8 ½ x 14 (legal sized) in another.

- **Paper Size:** Choose the size of paper or envelope you're printing to. In many cases, this option displays a preview that shows you which way to insert the paper. A preview can be especially handy if you're printing to envelopes and need help figuring out how to insert them in your printer.

4. Click the OK button to close the dialog box and save settings and then click the Close button to close other open Control Panel windows.

 Also, the settings in the Printing Preferences dialog box might differ slightly depending on your printer model; color printers offer different options from black and white ones, for example.

Click a tab to see different settings

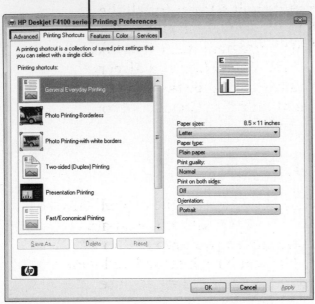

Figure 9-7

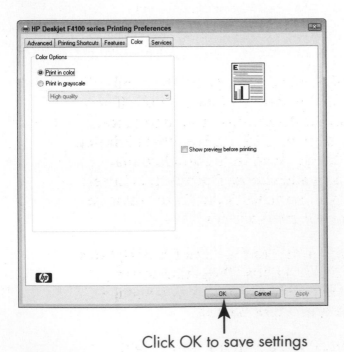

Click OK to save settings

Figure 9-8

The settings you make using the procedure in this task will become your default settings for all the printing you do. However, when you're printing a document from within a program, such as Works Word Processor, the Print dialog box you display gives you the opportunity to change the printer settings for that document only. See Chapter 14 for information about printing a document.

View Currently Installed Printers

1. Over time, you might install multiple printers; in which case, you might want to remind yourself of the capabilities of each or view the documents you have sent to be printed. To view the printers you have installed and view any documents currently in line for printing, choose Start⇨View Devices and Printers.

2. In the resulting Devices and Printers window (see **Figure** 9-9), a list of installed printers and fax machines appears.

If a printer has documents in its print queue, the number of documents is listed at the bottom of the window. If you want more detail about the documents or want to cancel a print job, select the printer and click the See What's Printing button at the top of the window. In the window that appears, click a document and choose Document⇨Cancel to stop the printing, if you want. Click the Close button to return to the Devices and Printers window.

3. You can right-click any printer to display a list of options (see **Figure** 9-10), and then choose Properties to see details about that printer such as which port it's plugged into or whether it can print color copies.

4. Click the Close button (the red X in the upper-right corner) to close the Devices and Printers window.

The number of documents in queue to print

Figure 9-9

Figure 9-10

Remove a Printer

1. Over time, you might upgrade to a new printer and toss the old one (recycling it appropriately, of course). When you do, you might want to also remove the older printer driver from your laptop so that your Printers window isn't cluttered with printers that you don't need anymore. To remove a printer, choose Start⇨Devices and Printers (in the Hardware and Sound group).

2. In the resulting Devices and Printers window, right-click a printer and choose Remove Device (as shown in **Figure 9-11**). (Or you can select the printer and click the Remove Device button at the top of the window.)

3. In the Printers dialog box that appears, click Yes; the Devices and Printers window closes, and your printer is removed from the printer list.

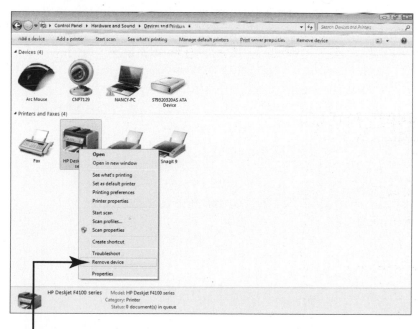

Click Remove Device

Figure 9-11

If you remove a printer, it's removed from the list of installed printers; if it was the default printer, Windows makes another printer you have installed the default printer. You can no longer print to it, unless you install it again. See the task, "Install a Printer," if you decide you want to print to that printer again.

Install a Scanner

1. Before you can scan documents into your laptop, you need to install the scanner driver so that your scanner and laptop can communicate. Start by connecting the scanner to your laptop's USB port. (See your scanner manual for information about how it connects to your laptop.)

2. Turn the scanner on. Some scanners use Plug and Play, a technology that Windows uses to recognize equipment, install it automatically, and set it up.

   If your scanner is Plug and Play–enabled, Windows 7 shows a Found New Hardware message on the taskbar notification area (in the lower-right corner). Most Plug and Play devices will then install automatically; then the message changes to indicate that the installation is complete, and that's all you have to do.

   If that doesn't happen, either you're not using a Plug and Play device or Windows doesn't have the driver for that device. So you should click the Found New Hardware message to proceed.

3. In the resulting Found New Hardware Wizard (this starts only if you don't permit Windows 7 to connect automatically to Windows Update), click Yes, This Time Only and then click Next.

4. If you have a CD for the scanner, insert it in your CD/DVD drive and click Next. Windows 7 searches for your scanner driver software and installs it.

5. Choose Start➪Control Panel. In the Search box, type **scanners.** Windows returns a set of links. Click the View Scanners and Cameras link. In the resulting Scanners and Cameras window, click the Add Device button.

6. In the resulting Scanners and Cameras Installation Wizard window, click Next. In the next screen of the wizard (see **Figure 9-12**), click your scanner's manufacturer in the list on the left and then click the model in the list on the right.

Select a manufacturer   Then select a model

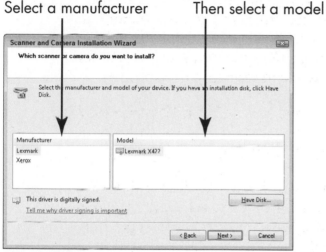

Figure 9-12

7. Follow the wizard directions for the model of scanner you chose in Step 6. Note whether you have a manufacturer's disc (a CD- or DVD-ROM) for your scanner; if you don't have a disc, Windows will help you download software from the Internet. When you reach the end of the wizard, click Finish to complete the installation.

Modify Scanner Settings

1. After you install a scanner, you might want to take a look at or change its default settings — for example, whether you usually want to print in color or grayscale. To do so,

choose Start⇨Control Panel. Type scanners in the
Control Panel search field and press Enter.

2. In the resulting Control Panel window, click View
Scanners and Cameras.

3. In the resulting Scanners and Cameras dialog box, a list
of installed scanners appears (see **Figure 9-13**). In the
Scanners and Cameras area, click the scanner for which
you'd like to modify the settings, and then click the Scan
Profiles button.

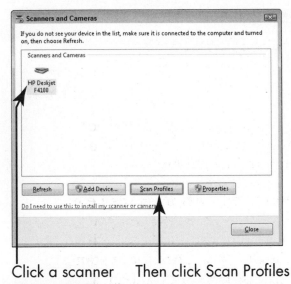

Click a scanner   Then click Scan Profiles

Figure 9-13

4. In the resulting Profiles dialog box, select a scanner and
click Edit. In the Edit Default Profile dialog box (see
Figure 9-14), review the settings, which might include
(depending on your scanner model) color management
for fine-tuning the way colors are scanned and resolution
settings that control how detailed a scan is performed. (The
higher the resolution, the crisper and cleaner your electronic
document, but the more time it might take to scan.)

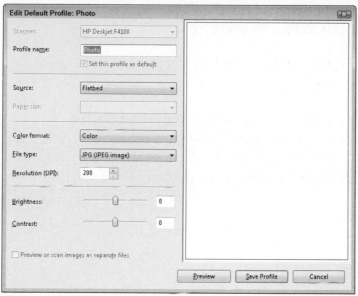

Figure 9-14

5. Click Save Profile to return to the Properties dialog box and then click the Close button twice to close the Scan Profiles and Scanners and Cameras windows.

 When you're ready to run a scan, you place the item to be scanned in your scanner. Depending on your model, the item may be placed on a flat "bed" with a hinged cover or fed through a tray. Check your scanner manual for the specific procedure to initiate a scan (for example, clicking a Scan or Start button). After you begin the scan, your laptop automatically detects it and displays a dialog box that shows you the scan progress and allows you to view and save the scanned item.

Getting Help

Chapter 10

*T*hough designed for ease of use, Windows is so feature-rich, you're bound to run into something that doesn't work the way you expected it to, or isn't easy to figure out. If you can't find your answer in this book, that's when you need to call on the resources that Microsoft provides to help you out.

Through the Help and Support Center, you can get assistance in various ways, including the following:

➡ **Access information that's stored in the Help system database.** Logically enough, a database contains data; in this case, it contains information about Windows 7, organized by topics such as Printers or Using Your Mouse. You can *drill down* (get more detail) by moving from a general topic to a detailed topic, or use a powerful search feature to search by keywords such as *printer*. There's even a troubleshooting feature that helps you pin down your problem.

➡ **Get help from your fellow Windows users.** Tap in to information exchanged by users in Windows communities (sort of like the bulletin board in your local community center) or by using a little feature called Remote Assistance, which allows you to let another user take over your laptop from a distance (via the Internet) and figure out your problem for you.

➠ **Open your wallet and pay for it.** Microsoft offers some help for free (for example, help for installing its software that you paid good money for), but some help comes at a price. When you can't find help anywhere else, you might want to consider forking over a few hard-earned bucks for this option.

Explore the Help Table of Contents

1. Your first stop in searching for help is likely to be the built-in help database. (It's also the only help feature that doesn't require an Internet connection.) One of the simplest ways to find what you need here is to use the Table of Contents, which is similar to a book's Table of Contents. Choose Start⇨Help and Support to open Windows Help and Support, as shown in **Figure 10-1**. *Note:* If your copy of Windows came built in to your laptop, some computer manufacturers (such as Hewlett-Packard) customize this center to add information that's specific to your laptop system.

Click this link

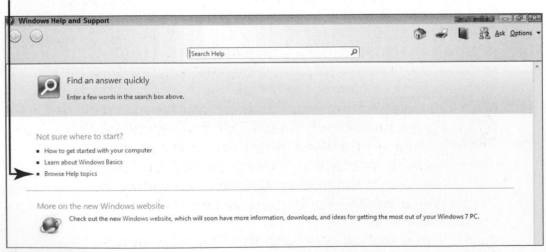

Figure 10-1

2. Click the Browse Help Topics link to display a list of topics. Click any of the topics to see a list of subtopics. Eventually, you get down to the deepest level of detailed subtopics, as shown in **Figure 10-2**.

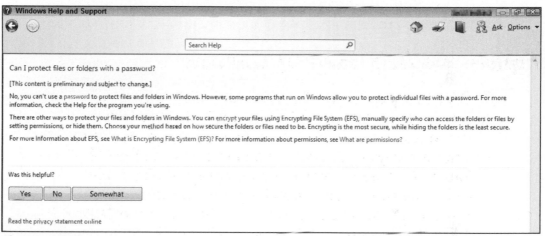

Figure 10-2

3. Click a *subtopic* (more detailed topic) to read its contents. Some subtopics contain blue links that lead to related topics or perform an action such as opening a dialog box. Green links display a definition or explanation of a term when clicked.

4. When you finish reading a help topic, click the Close button to close the Windows Help and Support window.

You can click the Print icon in the set of tools at the top-right corner of the Windows Help and Support window to print any displayed topic, if you have a printer connected to your laptop. You can also click the Minimize button in the title bar to minimize the window and keep it available while you work on your laptop.

Windows Help and Support will get the most up-to-date help information for you automatically if you're

connected to the Internet. See Chapter 19 for help
with connecting to the Internet.

Search for Help

1. If you don't find what you need by using the Table of
Contents (for instance, say you wanted help using your
mouse but didn't realize that's listed under the topic
Getting Started), you might want to use the Help search
feature to find what you need by entering keywords such
as *mouse* or *input*. Start by opening the Windows Help
and Support window.

2. Enter a search term in the Search Help box and then click
the Search Help button. Search results, such as those
shown in **Figure 10-3,** appear. Windows searches online
help by default, if you are connected to the Internet. If you
wish to use only offline help, click the Online Help link in
the bottom-right corner and choose Get Offline Help.

3. Explore topics by clicking various links in the search
results. These links offer a few different types of help:

- Procedures, such as "Make the mouse easier
  to use."

- Troubleshooting help items are phrased as statements,
  such as "I can't hear any text read aloud with
  Narrator." Clicking one of these opens a
  troubleshooter wizard.

- Some items provide general information rather than
  procedures, such as "Tips for searching the Internet."
  (See **Figure 10-4.**)

4. If you have no luck, enter a different search term in the
Search Help text box and start again.

Enter a search term here

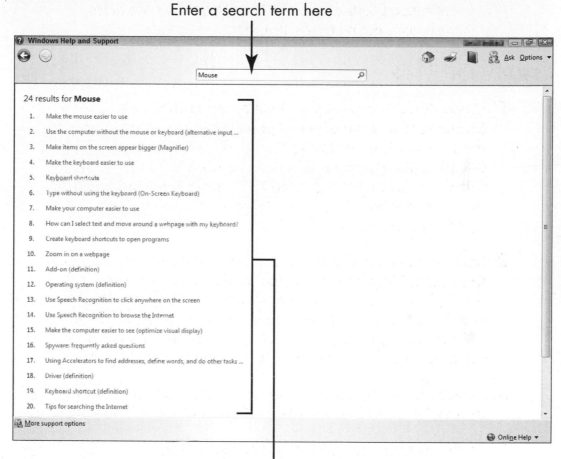

Figure 10-3

View the search results here

 If you don't find what you need with Search, consider clicking the Browse Help button in the top-right corner of the Windows Help and Support window (it sports a little blue icon in the shape of a book) to display a list of major topics. These topics may provide what you need, or give you some ideas for good search terms to continue your search.

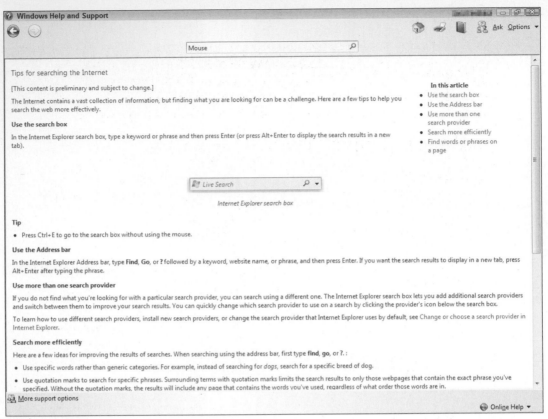

Figure 10-4

Post a Question in Windows Communities

1. If you want to see how other Windows users have solved a problem, you can visit Windows communities on the Internet, read posted messages, or even post one yourself and see if others can help you out. Open the Windows Help and Support window. Click the Ask button in the top-right corner.

2. Click the Windows web site link.

3. In the Windows page that opens in your browser, click the Help & How-To menu and then click Windows 7.

4. Click the Windows Community link and then, on the following page, click the Windows 7 Forums link. (See Figure 10-5.)

Click this link

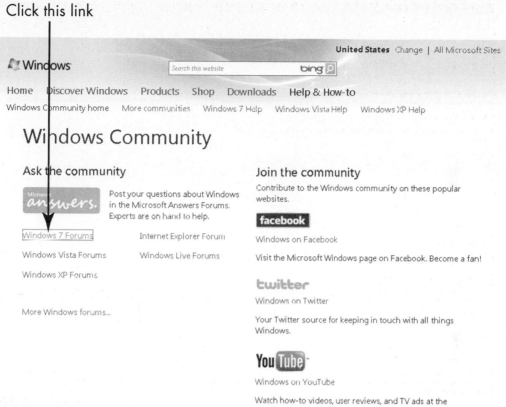

Figure 10-5

5. In the list of forums that is displayed (see **Figure 10-6**), click a forum, which displays a page with discussion summaries and the number of views and replies in each.

6. Click a thread title with a green check mark, which means a posted question has been answered, to open it. Scroll through the original posting and replies to it. If you'd like to add your own question or comment, follow these instructions:

- **Post a new message:** To post a message, you have to sign in to Microsoft TechNet using a Windows Live ID (which you can get for free by going to www. windowslive.com).

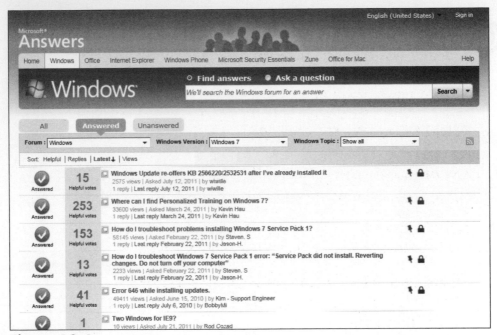

Figure 10-6

When you have your Windows Live ID, go back to the Forum and select the discussion group to participate in. Then click the Ask a Question button. If you have never participated in a discussion, you'll be asked to create a profile. Enter a display name and click the Accept button.

In the Ask Your Question form, enter the title and message body in their respective text boxes. Click Submit to post your question.

• **Reply to a message in a discussion:** With the list of postings and replies displayed, click the Reply button, fill in the message, and then click Post.

 You can also use the Search feature to search for keywords or phrases in discussions. Enter a word or phrase in the Search Answers with Bing text box and then click Go. Relevant messages are displayed; click one to read it.

If you have a question specific to the workings of your particular laptop model, consider visiting your manufacturer's site. They usually post helpful information by model, including an online version of your users' manual.

Access Windows Online Help

1. Enter **http://windows.microsoft.com/en-us/windows7/ help** in your browser address line and click the Go button.

2. On the Windows 7 Help & How-To page (see **Figure 10-7**), use the links in the following sections to get help:

   • **Getting Started:** Includes topics such as installing Windows or hardware and personalizing your PC. (See **Figure 10-8**.)

   • **Top Solutions:** Takes you to the most-viewed troubleshooting topics that help you work with Windows features and settings.

   • **More to Explore:** Offers information on upgrading to Windows 7, a link to community forums, and how-to videos.

3. Click the Close button to close the online help window in your browser, and then click the Close button to close Windows Help and Support.

 To set up Help and Support to always include Windows Online Help and Support when you search for help, with Help and Support open click the Options button and choose Settings. Be sure the check box labeled Improve My Search Results by Using Online Help (Recommended) is selected, and click OK to accept the change.

Use these sections to get help

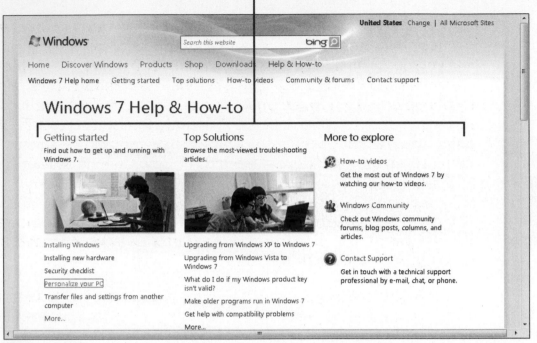

Figure 10-7

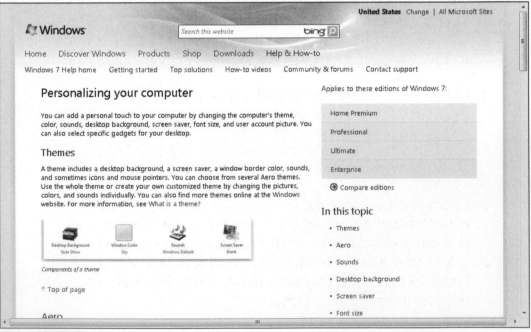

Figure 10-8

Connect to Remote Assistance

Remote Assistance can be a wonderful feature for new laptop users; if you're having laptop trouble and have asked for help, the people you've asked can view or take control of your laptop from their own computers, no matter where they are. You can contact such a person by phone or e-mail, for example, and ask for help. Then you send an invitation using Windows 7 Help. When that person accepts the invitation, you can give permission to access your system. Be aware that by doing so you give the person access to all your files, so be sure this is somebody you trust. When that person is connected, he or she can either advise you on your problem or actually make changes to your laptop to fix the problem for you. Of course you should be careful that the person you give access to is a trusted person or representative of a company you know and trust.

To use Remote Assistance, you and the other person first have to have Windows and an Internet connection. Then follow these instructions:

1. Enable Remote Assistance by choosing Start⇨Control Panel⇨System and Security⇨System⇨Allow Remote Access.

2. On the Remote tab of the System Properties dialog box that is displayed, select the Allow Remote Assistance Connections to This Computer check box, and then click OK.

3. Open the Windows Help and Support window by selecting Start⇨Help and Support.

4. Click the Ask button at the top of the page, and then click the Windows Remote Assistance link.

5. In the window that appears, as shown in **Figure 10-9**, click the Invite Someone You Trust to Help You link. If you have Windows Firewall or a third-party firewall active, you may have to disable that feature (Control Panel⇨System Security⇨Windows Firewall) to allow remote access to your laptop.

Click to invite a helper

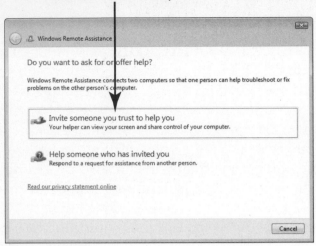

Figure 10-9

6. On the page that appears, you can choose to use your e-mail to invite somebody to help you. You have two options:

- Click the Save This Invitation as a File option and follow the instructions to save it as a file; then you can attach it to a message using your web-based e-mail program.

- Click the Use E-mail to Send an Invitation option to use a pre-configured e-mail program to send an e-mail. (See **Figure 10-10.**) Enter an address and additional message content, if you like, and send the e-mail.

7. In the Windows Remote Assistance window, as shown in **Figure 10-11,** note the provided password. When an incoming connection is made, use the tools there to adjust settings, chat, send a file, or pause, cancel, or stop sharing.

8. When you're finished, click the Close button to close the Windows Remote Assistance window.

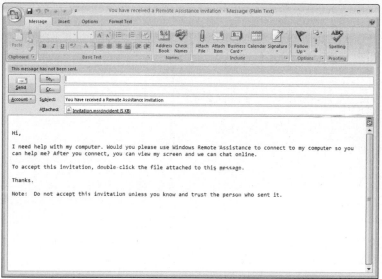

Figure 10-10

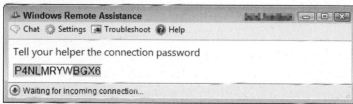

Figure 10-11

 Setting a time limit to not more than a few hours is a good idea. After all, you don't want somebody trying to log on to your laptop unexpectedly two weeks from now when you've already solved the problem some other way. You can make these timing settings in the Remote Assistance settings in the System Properties dialog box. (Choose Start➪Control Panel➪System and Security➪Allow Remote Access and click the Advanced button to bring up that dialog box.)

 Remember that it's up to you to let the recipient know the password — it isn't included in your e-mail unless you add it. It may be safer to call your friends with the password instead of including it in the invitation

e-mail in case it's intercepted by a cybercrook.
Although using a password used to be optional in
Windows XP, it's mandatory in Windows 7.

Change Windows Help and Support Display Options

1. If you're having trouble reading help topics, get some
help with modifying text size. Open the Windows Help
and Support window.

2. Choose Options⇨Text Size and then choose one of the
text size options: Largest, Larger, Medium (the default),
Smaller, or Smallest. (See **Figure 10-12**.)

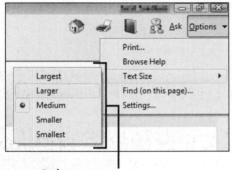

Select a text size option

Figure 10-12

3. Your new settings take effect immediately; click the Close
button or navigate to another area of the Windows Help
and Support window.

> If you don't like the colors in your Help and Support
> screen, you can change them by choosing a different
> color scheme in the Control Panel, Appearance and
> Personalization settings.

> Don't forget that you can reduce the size of the Help
> and Support window by clicking the Restore Down
> button in the upper-right corner of the window. This
> is especially useful with the Help window. You can

display it side by side with an application or Control Panel window where you're trying to troubleshoot the displayed help topic.

Contact Microsoft Customer Support

1. Enter this address in your browser and click Go: **support. microsoft.com.**

2. Click the View Our Solutions Centers button. On the page that appears, click the link for Windows 7.

3. In the page that appears, as shown in **Figure 10-13,** click any link along the left of the page to explore a topic of interest to you.

Click a link to explore a topic

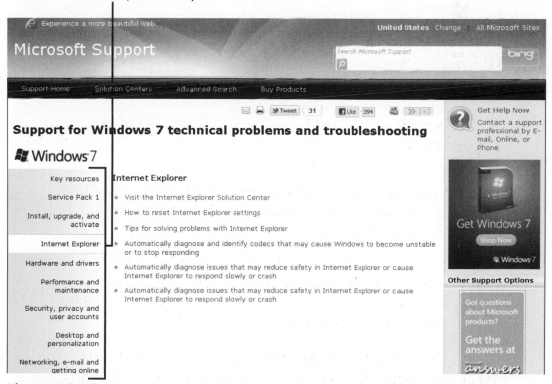

Figure 10-13

4. To get immediate help, click the Get Help Now link in the top-right corner of the page to get information about connecting with support through e-mail, in an online chat, or by phone.

5. When you're done, click the Close button to close the Internet Explorer browser.

Typically, you can contact Microsoft support for two free help sessions or unlimited installation support. You can submit a request via e-mail or call 1-800-936-3500. If Windows 7 came preinstalled on your laptop, you may be able to contact your manufacturer for support questions.

Note on the Windows support pages there are two icons, a small envelope and a printer. Use these to e-mail a link to the page to someone else or yourself or to print a topic.

Part III

Having Fun and Getting Things Done with Software

The 5th Wave   By Rich Tennant

"Can't I just give you riches or something?"

Working with Software Programs

Windows 7 is, first and foremost, an operating system — its main purpose is to enable you to run and manage *other* software programs. Using tools in Windows, you can run and work with programs that do anything from managing your finances to playing a great game of solitaire. By using the best methods for accessing and running programs with Windows 7, you save time; and setting up Windows 7 in the way that works best for you can make your life easier.

In this chapter, you explore several simple and very handy techniques for installing, launching, and moving information between applications. You go through step-by-step procedures ranging from setting program defaults to removing programs when you no longer need them. I even provide tips for accessing programs online, such as Google Docs or Office Live.

Install a Program

The typical laptop comes with Windows or another operating system installed, as well as several other programs. For example, Windows computers usually have Microsoft's Works suite of programs pre-installed, as well as several handy accessory programs such as Paint and the Internet Explorer browser.

These pre-installed programs get you started, but you're likely to want to install other programs such as games or a financial management program. Today you buy software programs in two ways: you can buy a packaged product which will include a CD or DVD disc or you can buy software online and download it directly to your computer. Here's how the installation process varies, depending on which option you choose:

➡ If you buy a boxed product, you simply take out the disc, insert it into the CD/DVD drive of your laptop, and then follow the onscreen instructions. If no instructions appear, you should open Windows Explorer (right-click the Start menu and choose Open Windows Explorer), locate your CD/DVD drive, and double-click the program name. This should launch the wizard that will walk you through the installation.

➡ If you purchase software online at a store such as Amazon.com or NewEgg.com, or from the software manufacturer's site, you simply click the appropriate button to buy the product, follow the directions to pay for it, and then download the product. Typically during this process you will see a dialog box that asks if you want to save or run the program. Running it should start the installation. If you save it, then you have to locate the downloaded software with Windows Explorer, and then double-click the application file (which usually ends with .exe).

Launch a Program

1. Once you've installed a program, it's time to use it. First, you have to open the program, referred to as *launching* it. Launch a program by using any of the following four methods:

  • Choose Start➪All Programs. Locate the program name on the All Programs list that appears and click it.

Clicking an item with a folder icon displays a list of programs within it; just click the program on that sublist to open it (as shown in **Figure 11-1**).

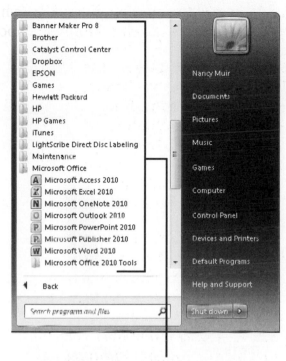

Click an item to launch it or click a folder to see its contents

Figure 11-1

- Double-click a program shortcut icon on the desktop. (See **Figure 11-2**.)

- Click an item on the taskbar. The taskbar should display by default; if it doesn't, press the Windows logo key (on your keyboard) to display it, and then click an icon on the taskbar (as shown in **Figure 11-2**), just to the right of the Start button. See Chapter 5 for more about working with the taskbar.

Double-click a program's shortcut icon to launch it...

Or click an icon on the taskbar

Figure 11-2

- If you used the program recently and saved a document, choose it from the list of recently used programs displayed when you first open the Start menu. Then click a document created in that program from the list that displays. (See Chapter 11 for information about displaying recently used files on the Start menu.)

2. When the application opens, if it's a game, play it; if it's a spreadsheet, enter numbers into it; if it's your e-mail program, start deleting junk mail. . . . You get the idea.

Not every program that's installed on your laptop appears as a desktop shortcut or taskbar icon. To add a program to the taskbar or add a desktop shortcut, see Chapter 6.

Move Information between Programs

1. What if you have a list of items in a letter created with a word processor and you want to copy it to a slide show created in another program? You can easily take text and objects such as pictures and move them to another program. Open documents in two programs. (See the next task for more about opening applications.) Right-click the taskbar on the Windows desktop and choose Show Windows Side by Side. (See **Figure 11-3**.)

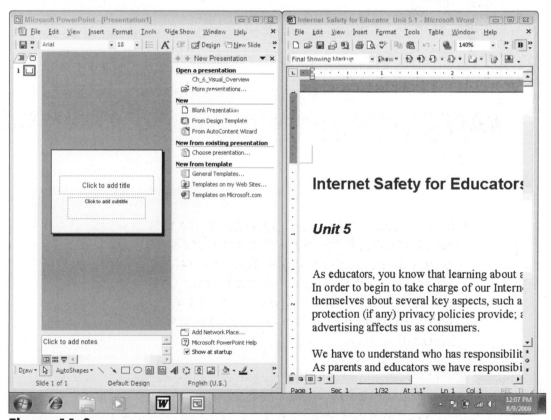

Figure 11-3

2. If you don't need one of the active programs displayed, click the Minimize button in that program so that just the programs you're working with appear.

3. Select the information that you want to move (for example text, numbers, or a graphical object in a document) and drag it to the other application document. (See **Figure 11-4**.)

4. Release your mouse, and the information is copied to the document in the destination window.

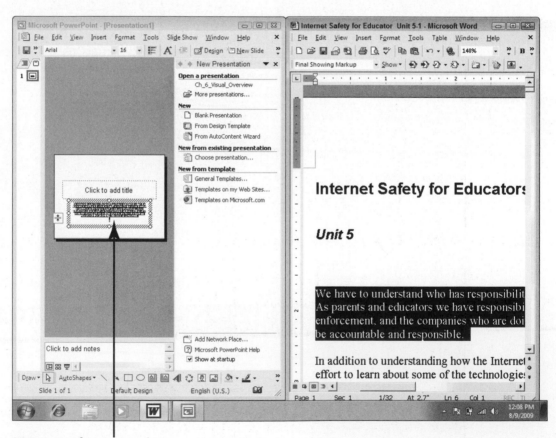

Moving information between programs

Figure 11-4

You can also use simple cut-and-paste or copy-and-paste operations to take information from one application and move it or place a copy of it into a document in another application. To do this, first click and drag over the information in a document, and then press Ctrl+X to cut or Ctrl+C to copy the item. Click in the destination document where you want to place the item and press Ctrl+V.

In addition, some applications have Export or Send To commands to send the contents of a document to another application. For example, Microsoft Word has a File⇨Save and Send set of commands to save a Word document quickly in PDF format.

 Remember, this won't work between every type of program. For example, you can't click and drag an open picture from Paint into the Windows Calendar. Moving content will work most dependably when you're dragging text or objects from one Office 2010 or other standard program — word-processing, presentation, database, or spreadsheet — to another.

Start a Program Automatically

1. If you use a program often, you might want to set it to start every time you start your laptop. Click Start⇨All Programs.

2. Right-click the Startup folder and click Open. (See **Figure 11-5**.)

3. Right-click Start and choose Open Windows Explorer. In the window that appears, locate and open the folder where the program you want to start when you start Windows is located. Click to select it.

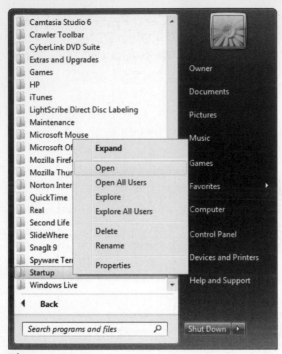

Figure 11-5

4. Drag the item to the Startup window that you opened in Step 2. The program appears in the Startup folder. (See **Figure 11-6.**)

5. When you finish moving programs into the Startup folder, click the Close button in the upper-right corner of both windows. The programs you moved will now open every time you start Windows 7.

 If you place too many programs in Startup, it might take a minute or two before you can get to work because you have to wait for programs to load. Don't overfill your Startup folder: Use it just for the programs you need most often.

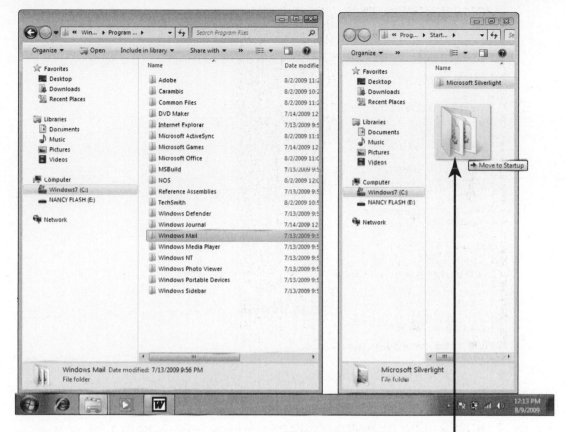

Moving the item to the Startup window

Figure 11-6

 You can remove an application from Startup folder by right-clicking the application in the Startup folder in Windows Explorer and choosing Delete.

Set Program Defaults

1. To make working with files easier, you may want to control which programs are used to open files of different types. Choose Start⇨Control Panel⇨Programs.

2. In the resulting Programs window, as shown in **Figure 11-7**, click the Set Your Default Programs link in the Default Programs section to see specifics about the programs that are set as defaults.

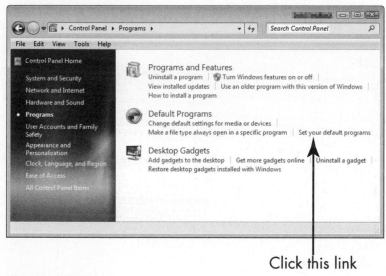

Click this link

Figure 11-7

3. In the resulting Set Default Programs window, click a program in the list on the left (see **Figure 11-8**) and then click the Set This Program as Default option. You can also click Choose Defaults for this Program and select specific file types (such as the .jpeg graphics file format or .docx Word 2007 and 2010 file format) to open in this program; click Save after you've made these selections.

4. Click OK to save your settings.

You can also choose which devices to use by default to play media such as movies or audio files. Click the Change Default Settings for Media or Devices link in the Programs window you opened in Step 1 to do so.

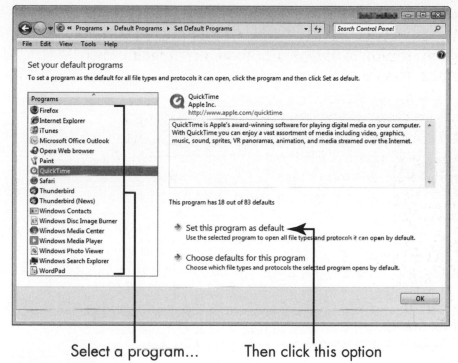

Select a program...   Then click this option

Figure 11-8

Access a Program Online

Today, many programs are being made available online so you never have to install them on your laptop hard drive to use them. This makes it easy to access them from any computer, and you can store your files online — which means you can work on your files from anywhere.

A couple of online software sources that are popular today are Google Docs (www.docs.google.com) and Office Live (www.officelive.com). Both allow you to upload and share documents, as well as edit the documents online. Both these services allow you to create word-processed documents, spreadsheets, and presentations. Google Docs also lets you create forms and drawings, while Office Live lets you also create One Note notebooks. One Note is a great tool for researching as you can cut and paste text into it, along with links that show the online source of the information.

Most online applications have a bit more limited functionality than their offline counterparts, if they have any. However, they work with documents created in most other programs easily and they're free!

Remove a Program

1. If you don't need a program, removing it might help your laptop's performance, which can get bogged down when your hard drive is too cluttered. Choose Start⇨Control Panel⇨Uninstall a Program (under the Programs and Features category).

2. In the resulting Uninstall or Change a Program window, as shown in **Figure 11-9,** click a program and then click the Uninstall (or sometimes this is labeled Uninstall/ Change) button that appears. Although some programs will display their own uninstall screen, in most cases, a confirmation dialog box appears. (See **Figure 11-10.**)

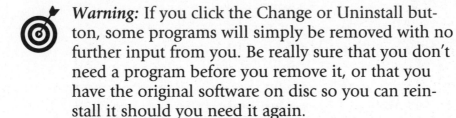 *Warning:* If you click the Change or Uninstall button, some programs will simply be removed with no further input from you. Be really sure that you don't need a program before you remove it, or that you have the original software on disc so you can reinstall it should you need it again.

3. If you're sure that you want to remove the program, click Yes in the confirmation dialog box. A dialog box shows the progress of the procedure; it disappears when the program has been removed.

4. Click the Close button to close the Uninstall or Change a Program window.

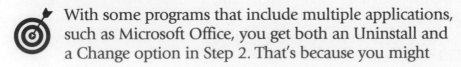 With some programs that include multiple applications, such as Microsoft Office, you get both an Uninstall and a Change option in Step 2. That's because you might

want to remove only one program, not the whole shooting match. For example, you might decide that you have no earthly use for Access but can't let a day go by without using Excel and Word — so why not free up some hard drive space and send Access packing? If you want to modify a program in this way, click the Change button in Step 2 of this task rather than the Uninstall button. The dialog box that appears allows you to select the programs that you want to install or uninstall, or it might open the original installation screen from your software program.

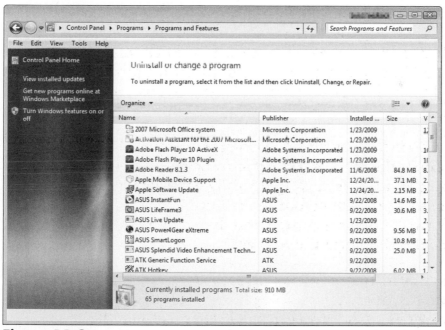

Figure 11-9

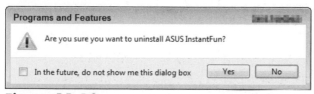

Figure 11-10

When you buy your laptop, you may be offered a service to clean out all the preinstalled programs your manufacturer added. This can help your laptop's performance. If you feel capable of uninstalling programs yourself, skip paying the fee for this service. If you can't, consider paying for it — though it's undeniably irritating to have to pay to remove things that you never asked for that make your laptop perform more slowly!

Working with Files and Folders

*I*f you worked in an office before computers came along, you remember the metal filing cabinets and manila file folders holding paper rather than the sleek computer workstations and boxes of DVDs we use today to store our documents.

With a computer, you still organize the work you do every day in files and folders, but today, the metal and cardboard have been dropped in favor of electronic bits and bytes. *Files* are the individual documents that you save from within applications, such as Word and Excel, and you use folders and subfolders to organize several files into groups or categories, such as by project or by year.

In this chapter, you find out how to organize and work with files and folders, including

➠ **Finding your way around files and folders:** This includes tasks such as locating and opening files and folders.

➠ **Manipulating files and folders:** These tasks cover moving, renaming, deleting, and printing a file.

➠ **Squeezing a file's contents:** This involves creating a compressed folder to reduce a large file to a more manageable creature.

Chapter 12

Get ready to . . .

➡ **Backing up files and folders:** To avoid losing valuable data, you should know how to make backup copies of your files and folders on a recordable CD/DVD or *flash drive* (a small, stick-shaped storage device that slots right into a USB port on your laptop).

Understand How Windows Organizes Data

When you work in a software program, such as a word processor, you save your document as a file. Files can be saved to your laptop hard drive, removable storage media such as USB flash drives (which are about the size of a package of gum), or to recordable CDs or DVDs (small, flat discs you insert into a disc drive on your laptop).

You can organize files by placing them in folders. The Windows operating system helps you to organize files and folders in the following ways:

➡ **Take advantage of predefined folders.** Windows sets up some folders for you. For example, the first time you start Windows 7, you find folders for Documents, Pictures, Videos, and Music already set up on your laptop. You can see them listed in Windows Explorer (right-click the Start menu button and choose Open Windows Explorer), as shown in **Figure 12-1.** (See Chapter 6 for a more detailed explanation of Explorer.)

The Documents folder is a good place to store letters, presentations for your community group, household budgets, and so on. The Pictures folder is where you store picture files, which you may transfer from a digital camera or scanner, receive in an e-mail message from a friend or family member, or download from the Internet. Similarly, the Videos folder is a good place to put files from your camcorder, and the Music folder is where you place tunes you download or transfer from a music player.

Predefined folders help organize files

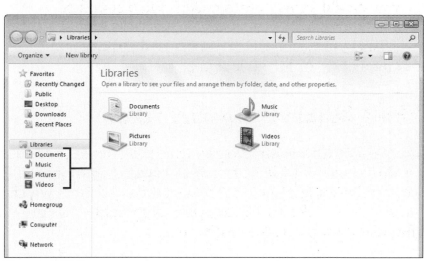

Figure 12-1

▬▶ **Create your own folders.** You can create any number of folders and give each one a name that identifies the types of files you'll store in it. For example, you might create a folder called *Digital Scrapbook* if you use your laptop to create scrapbooks, or a folder called *Taxes* where you save e-mailed receipts for purchases and electronic tax-filing information. The task "Create a Shortcut to a File or Folder" later in this chapter explains how to create a shortcut to a folder.

▬▶ **Place folders within folders to further organize files.** A folder you place within another folder is called a *subfolder*. For example, in your Documents folder, you might have a subfolder called *Holiday Card List* that contains your yearly holiday newsletter and address lists. In my Pictures folder, I organize the picture files by creating subfolders that begin with the year and then a description of the event or subject, such as *Home Garden Project, 2010 Christmas, 2009 San Francisco Trip, Family Reunion, Pet Photos,* and so on. In **Figure 12-2,** you can see subfolders and files stored within the Pictures folder.

Folder   Subfolders   Files in Pictures folder

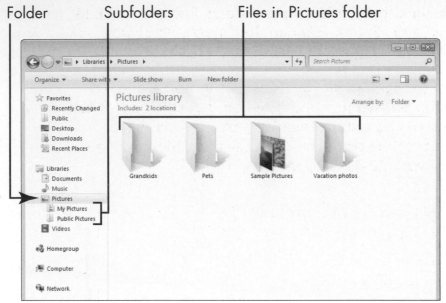

Figure 12-2

➟ **Move files and folders from one place to another.**
Being able to move files and folders helps you if you
decide it's time to reorganize information on your laptop. For example, when you start using your laptop,
you might save all your documents to your Documents
folder. That's okay for a while, but in time, you might
have dozens of documents saved in that one folder. To
make your files easier to locate, you can create subfolders by topic and move files into them.

Access Recently Used Files

1. If you worked on a file recently, Windows offers a shortcut to finding and opening it to work on again. Open the
Start menu and right-click any blank area. From the
resulting shortcut menu, choose Properties.

2. In the Taskbar and Start Menu Properties dialog box
that appears, click the Start Menu tab (if that tab isn't
already displayed).

3. Make sure that the Store and Display Recently Opened Items in the Start Menu and the Taskbar check box is selected (see **Figure 12-3**) and then click OK.

4. Open the Start menu and hover your mouse over any recently opened program listed on the left side that has an arrow and a submenu of recently opened items appears to the right. Choose a file from the submenu (see **Figure 12-4**) to open it.

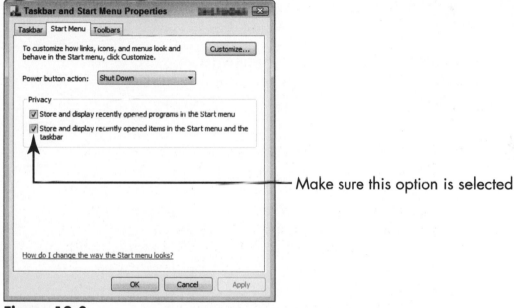

Make sure this option is selected

Figure 12-3

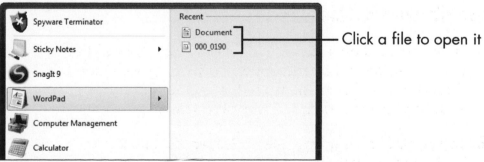

Click a file to open it

Figure 12-4

Recently opened programs should be displayed in the Start menu by default, but if they aren't, follow directions in Step 1 to open the Taskbar and Start Menu Properties dialog box and make sure that the Store and Display Recently Opened Programs in the Start Menu check box is selected.

Locate Files and Folders in Your Laptop

1. Can't remember what you named a folder or where on your laptop or storage media you saved it? You can open the Computer window to locate it. Choose Start➪Computer.

2. In the resulting Computer window (see **Figure 12-5**), double-click an item, such as a USB drive, a CD-ROM drive, or your laptop hard drive, to open it.

3. If the file or folder you want is stored within another folder (see **Figure 12-6** for an example of the resulting window), double-click the folder or a series of folders until you locate it.

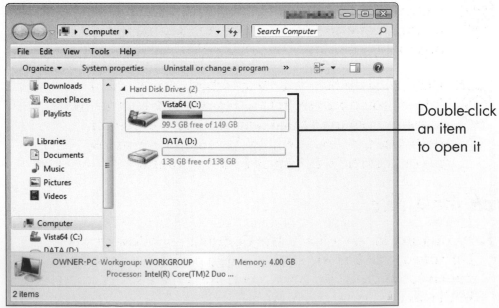

Double-click an item to open it

Figure 12-5

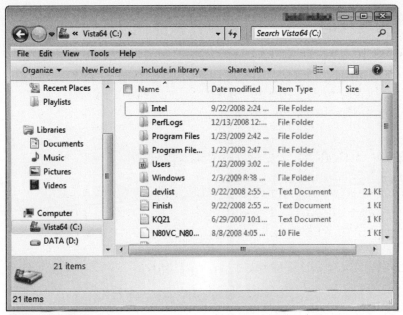

Figure 12-6

4. When you find the file you want, double-click it to open it in the application in which it was created.

> Note the buttons near the top of the window in **Figure 12-6.** Use the commands in this area to perform common file and folder tasks, such as organizing, sharing, or opening files.

> Depending on how you choose to display files and folders, you might see text listings (as in **Figure 12-6**), icons, or even thumbnail representations of file contents. Use the View menu in the Computer window to configure how to display files and folders.

Search for a File

1. If you can't locate a file in the Computer window or your Documents folder, you could simply perform a simple search for it. Open the Start menu and type a search term in the search box at the bottom.

2. A list of search results appears, divided into categories based on the locations of the results. (See **Figure 12-7**.)

Figure 12-7

3. Click the See More Results link.

4. In the window that appears (see **Figure 12-8**) click an item to view it.

5. When you locate the file you want, you can double-click it to open it.

 Search Folders was a new feature in Windows Vista that has carried over to Windows 7. To save the results of a search, you can click the Save Search button. In the Save As dialog box that appears, provide a filename and type, set the location to save it to, and then click Save. The search results are saved as a search folder on your laptop in your username folder.

 You can modify the Search feature's settings. When you're in the Search Results window shown in **Figure 12-8**, click the arrow on the Organize button and choose the Folder and Search Options command. Using the Search tab in the Folder Options dialog box that appears, indicate what locations to search, whether to find partial matches for search terms, and more.

Click an item to view it

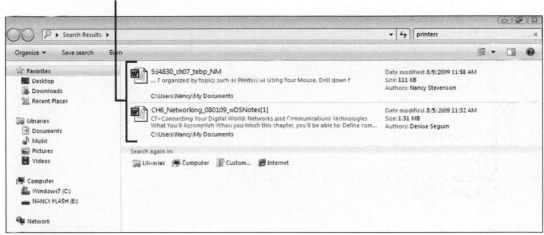

Figure 12-8

Move a File or Folder

1. Sometimes you save a file or folder in one place but, in reorganizing your work, decide you want to move the item to another location. To do so, right-click the Start menu button and choose Open Windows Explorer.

2. In Windows Explorer, double-click a folder or series of folders to locate the file that you want to move. (See **Figure 12-9**.)

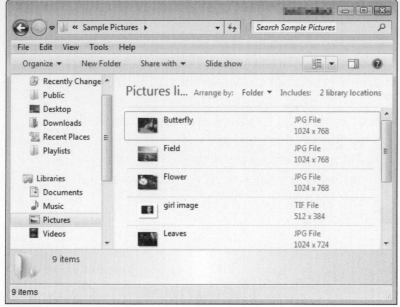

Figure 12-9

3. Take one of the following actions:

- Click and drag the file or folder to another folder in the Navigation pane on the left side of the window. If you right-click and drag, you are offered the options of moving, copying, or creating a shortcut to the item when you place it via the shortcut menu that appears.

- Right-click the file and choose Send To. Then choose from the options shown in the submenu that appears (as shown in **Figure 12-10**); these options may vary slightly depending on the type of file you choose and what software you have installed.

4. Click the Close button in the upper-right corner of Windows Explorer to close it.

> If you change your mind about moving an item using the right-click-and-drag method, you can click Cancel on the shortcut menu that appears.

Figure 12-10

 If you want to create a copy of a file or folder in another location on your laptop, right-click the item and choose Copy. Use Windows Explorer to navigate to the location where you want to place a copy, right-click, and choose Paste or press Ctrl+V.

Rename a File or Folder

1. You may want to change the name of a file or folder to update it or make it more easily identifiable from other files or folders. Locate the file that you want to rename by using Windows Explorer. (Right-click Start, choose Open Windows Explorer, and then browse to find the file you want to rename.)

2. Right-click the file and choose Rename. (See **Figure 12-11.**)

3. The filename is now available for editing. Type a new name, and then click anywhere outside the filename to save the file with its new name.

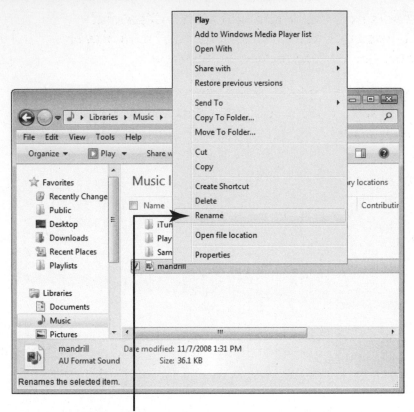

Select Rename

Figure 12-11

 You can't rename a file to have the same name as another file located in the same folder. To give a file the same name as another, cut it from its current location, paste it into another folder, and then follow the procedure in this task. Or open the file and save it to a new location with the same name, which creates a copy. Be careful, though: Two files with the same name can cause confusion when you search for files. If at all possible, use unique filenames.

Create a Shortcut to a File or Folder

1. You can place a shortcut to a file or folder you used recently on the desktop to make it quick and easy to open. Locate the file or folder by using Windows Explorer. (Right-click Start and choose Open Windows Explorer, and then browse to find the file you want to make a shortcut to.)

2. In Windows Explorer, right-click the file or folder that you want and choose Send To⇨Desktop (Create Shortcut) as shown in **Figure 12-12.**

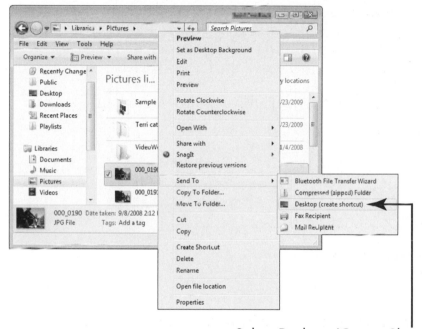

Select Desktop (Create Shortcut)

Figure 12-12

3. A shortcut appears on the desktop.

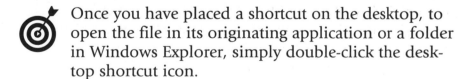

Once you have placed a shortcut on the desktop, to open the file in its originating application or a folder in Windows Explorer, simply double-click the desktop shortcut icon.

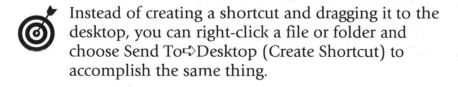

Instead of creating a shortcut and dragging it to the desktop, you can right-click a file or folder and choose Send To⇨Desktop (Create Shortcut) to accomplish the same thing.

Delete a File or Folder

1. If you don't need a file or folder anymore, you can clear up clutter on your laptop by deleting it. Locate the file or folder by using Windows Explorer. (Right-click Start, choose Open Windows Explorer, and then browse to locate the file you want to delete.)

2. In Windows Explorer, right-click the file or folder that you want to delete and then choose Delete from the shortcut menu, as shown in **Figure 12-13.** (Or you can simply click the file to select it and then press the Delete key.)

3. In the resulting Delete File dialog box (see **Figure 12-14**), click Yes to delete the file.

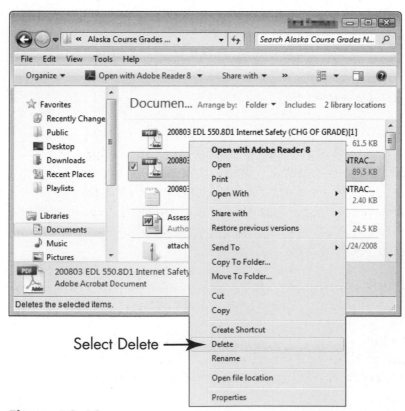

Figure 12-13

Figure 12-14

 When you delete a file or folder in Windows, it's not really gone. It's removed to the Recycle Bin. Windows periodically purges older files from this folder, but you might still be able to retrieve recently deleted files and folders from it. To try to restore a deleted file or folder, double-click the Recycle Bin icon on the desktop. Right-click the file or folder and choose Restore. Windows restores the file to wherever it was when you deleted it.

Compress a File or Folder

1. To shrink the storage size of a file, or of all the files in a folder, you can compress the file(s). This is often helpful when you're sending an item as an attachment to an e-mail message. Locate the files or folders that you want to compress by using Windows Explorer. (Right-click Start, choose Open Windows Explorer, and then browse to locate the file(s) or folder(s).)

2. (Optional) In Windows Explorer, you can do the following (as shown in **Figure 12-15**) to select multiple items:

- **Select a series of files or folders.** Click a file or folder, press and hold Shift to select a series of items listed consecutively in the folder, and click the final item.

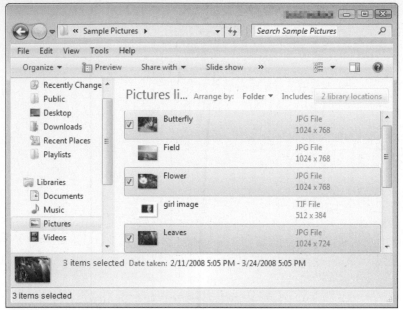

Figure 12-15

- **Select nonconsecutive items.** Press the Ctrl key and click the items.

3. Right-click the selected item(s). In the resulting shortcut menu (see **Figure 12-16**), choose Send To⇨Compressed (Zipped) Folder. A new compressed folder appears below the last selected file in the Windows Explorer list. The folder icon is named after the last file you selected in the series, but it's open for editing. Type a new name or click outside the item to accept the default name.

 You might want to subsequently rename a compressed folder with a name other than the one that Windows automatically assigns to it. See the task "Rename a File or Folder," earlier in this chapter, to find out just how to do that.

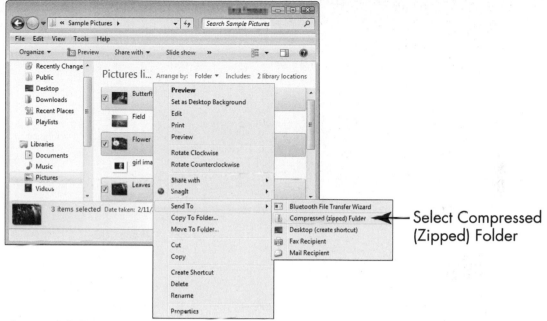

Figure 12-16

Add a File to Your Favorites List

1. The Favorites list in the Start menu offers another quick way to access frequently used items. Locate the files or folders that you want to add to the Favorites list by using Windows Explorer. (Right-click Start and choose Open Windows Explorer.)

2. In Windows Explorer, click a file or folder and drag it to any of the Favorites folders in the Navigation pane on the left. (See **Figure 12-17.**)

3. To see a list of your Favorites, choose Start⇨Favorites.

4. In the resulting submenu (see **Figure 12-18**), click an item to open it.

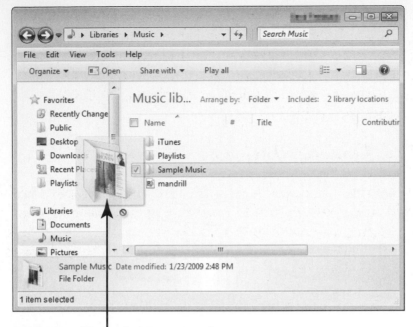

Adding a file to the Favorites list
Figure 12-17

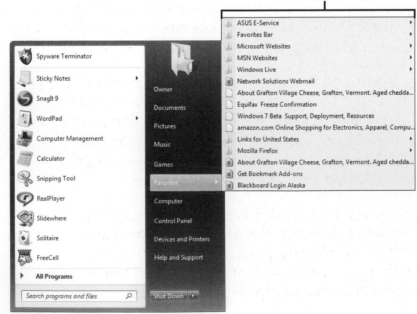

Figure 12-18

If the Favorites item doesn't display on your Start menu, right-click the Start menu and choose Properties. On the Start Menu tab in the Taskbar and Start Menu Properties dialog box, click the Customize button. Make sure that Favorites Menu is selected, and then click OK twice to save the setting.

Understand File Storage Options

You may want to save copies of your files somewhere other than your laptop's hard drive. You might, for example, want to keep a copy of your work just in case you lose your laptop or the hard drive fails. Or, you may want to copy a file onto a DVD so you can hand it on to a friend to read or work on.

You have four main options for storing your files:

➡ **Utilize a USB stick:** You can purchase a USB stick (also called a *flash drive*) to store your files on. These are about the dimensions of a stick of gum (though designs vary — some are very tiny). You insert the stick into a USB port on your laptop (most laptops have three or four of these). Then you can use Windows Explorer (or the Finder on a Mac) to copy files onto the drive.

➡ **Use a CD or DVD to store files, if your laptop has a CD/DVD slot:** Some laptops, especially smaller ones like netbooks, don't have a CD/DVD drive, but most do. Slip a disc into your laptop just as you would a music CD or DVD you were going to play, and copy files to it (see the next task for detailed steps).

➡ **Attach an external hard drive to your laptop:** You can buy what amounts to a second hard drive and attach it to your laptop to store and retrieve files. This will run you around $50–$100, depending on the model and storage capacity.

➠ **Store files online:** Today you can use an online service such as Windows SkyDrive (www.skydrive.com), Google Docs (docs.google.com), or Dropbox (www.dropbox.com) to store your files online, usually for free. The handy thing about this option is that you can then easily access your files from anywhere without carrying a storage device. It's also a great way to share files (for example, photos or a set of meeting minutes) with others.

Back Up Files to a Read/Writable CD or DVD

1. If your laptop is damaged or loses data, you'll want to have a copy safely tucked away. Storing data on a CD or DVD disk is a popular choice. If your laptop doesn't have a CD/DVD drive built in, you'll have to purchase an external CD/DVD drive and connect it to your laptop to perform these steps. Place a blank writable CD-R/RW (read/writable) or DVD-R/RW in your CD-RW or DVD-RW drive and then choose Start⇨Documents.

2. In the resulting Documents window, select all the files that you want to copy to disc.

3. Right-click the files that you want and then choose Copy to Folder (see **Figure 12-19**).

4. In the Copy Items dialog box that appears, click the CD-R/RW or DVD-RW drive and click Copy.

5. Click the Close button to close the Document window.

If you want to back up the entire contents of a folder, such as the Document folder, you can just click the Documents folder itself in Step 2 and follow the rest of the steps.

Figure 12-19

 You can also back up to a network or another drive by using the Back Up Your Computer link in the Control Panel. Using Windows Backup, you can make settings to regularly back up to a local disk or CD-R/RW/DVD drive, or to a network. Backing up to a CD/DVD is a little different from burning a disc: After you back up your files, then later changes are saved only each subsequent time a backup is run.

Using the Desktop Gadget Gallery and Gadgets

Windows 7 has a feature called the *Desktop Gadget gallery.* The gallery contains little applications, called *gadgets,* that you can display as icons on the desktop. Using gadgets, you can quickly access various handy features to check the time, organize your schedule with a calendar, feed online data direct to your desktop, and more. Here are some of the things you can do with the Windows gadgets that we cover in this chapter:

→ **Work with images.** Slide Show displays a continuous slide show of the photos in your Pictures folder.

→ **Organize your time.** The Calendar gadget displayed on your desktop helps you keep track of the days, weeks, and months. The Clock gadget displays the time using an old-style wall clock and allows you to make changes to your time zone.

→ **Play with a puzzle.** A neat little Picture Puzzle allows you to play a game that's so tiny, even your boss or spouse won't notice you're not actually working.

➠ **Work with online data.** The Feed Headlines gadget allows you to grab data from online RSS feeds (a format used for syndication of news and other content), such as the latest headlines or other useful information. Stocks and Currency conversion gadgets provide up-to-the-minute data on stocks and currency values.

➠ **Keep an eye on your system's performance.** The CPU Meter provides up-to-date information about your laptop's processor speed and available memory.

Open the Gadget Gallery and Add Gadgets to the Desktop

1. Right-click the desktop and choose Gadgets to open the Gadget Gallery window, as shown in **Figure 13-1**.

2. Click any gadget and drag it to the desktop. (See **Figure 13-2**.)

3. Click the Close button to close the Gadget Gallery.

Figure 13-1

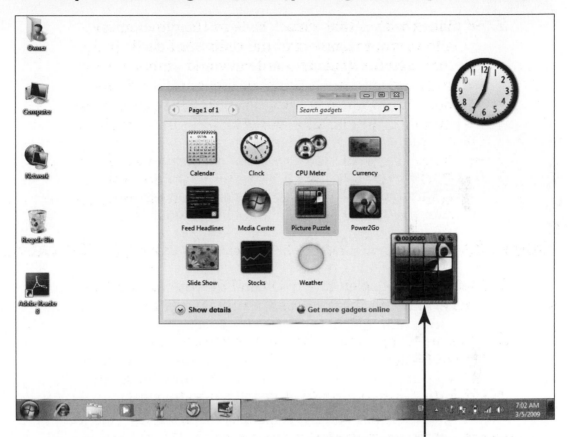

Dragging a gadget to the desktop

Figure 13-2

 If you want to remove a gadget from your desktop, just place your pointer over it and then click the Close button (marked with an X) that appears next to it. The gadget closes. Just follow the steps above to display it on the desktop again at any time.

Check the Time

1. To display a clock on your desktop, right-click the desktop and choose Gadgets.

2. In the Gadget Gallery that appears, click the clock and drag it to the desktop.

3. To make changes to the clock style or change the time zone, place your mouse over the Clock and click the Settings button. (It sports a little wrench symbol.)

4. In the resulting Clock dialog box (see **Figure 13-3**), click the Next or Previous buttons to move through the various available clock styles.

5. If you wish, you can enter a name for the clock in the Clock Name field. To change the time zone, click the arrow in the Time Zone field and choose your local time.

6. Click OK to save the clock settings.

> You can display a second hand on your clock by clicking the Show the Second Hand check box in the Clock dialog box.

> If you are on the road with your laptop and want to keep track of the local time and the time back home, you can display more than one clock by simply dragging the clock gadget to the desktop from the Gadget gallery again. Make changes to the time zone settings and even use two different styles of clock to tell them apart at a glance.

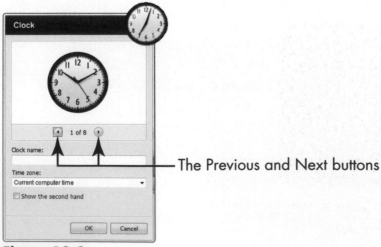

The Previous and Next buttons

Figure 13-3

Display a Continuous Slide Show

1. You can display a continuous show of the pictures in your Pictures folder to keep you entertained as you work or play on your laptop. Add the Slide Show gadget to the desktop. (See the earlier task, "Open the Gadget Gallery and Add Gadgets to the Desktop.")

2. Move your mouse over the Slide Show gadget and use the tools along the bottom of the slide show (see **Figure 13-4**) to do the following:

- Click the View button to display the current slide in Windows Photo Viewer.

- Click Pause to stop the slide show at the current slide.

- Click Previous to go to the previous slide.

- Click Next to go to the next slide.

3. The Slide Show uses the Sample Pictures folder contents by default, but you can display pictures in any folder. Click the Settings button (it looks like a wrench). In the resulting Slide Show dialog box (see **Figure 13-5**), change the picture folder to include in the slide show.

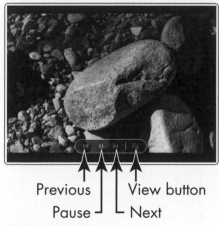

Previous | View button

Pause ┘ └ Next

Figure 13-4

Figure 13-5

In this dialog box, you can also modify the number of seconds to display each slide or specify a transition effect to use between slides. Click the arrow to display and select your options.

4. Click OK to close the dialog box.

> When you click the View button to display the current slide in Windows Photo Viewer, you can use tools to modify the image, print it, e-mail it, or even create a movie. See Chapter 15 for more about using Windows Photo Viewer.

> Note that continuously playing features like the slide show, or continuously updating features such as the stock ticker, may put a drain on your laptop's battery. If you're running on battery power, you might hide the Gadget gallery to save juice.

Use the Windows Calendar

1. The Calendar gadget isn't an organizer; it just helps you remember the date with a Calendar display you can place on your desktop. Add the Calendar gadget (see **Figure 13-6**) to the desktop. (See the earlier task, "Open the Gadget Gallery and Add Gadgets to the Desktop.")

Figure 13-6

2. Move your pointer over the Calendar and click the Size tool to move between the larger size, which displays both the monthly and daily sections (as shown in **Figure 13-7**), and the smaller size, which shows only the daily display by default.

←—The Size tool

Figure 13-7

3. With the larger calendar displayed, click the Next or Previous arrows to move to another month; double-click a date to display it in the lower part of the calendar; and click the red tab in the lower-left corner to return to today's date in the lower area.

If you prefer to use the smaller size calendar but have it display the monthly calendar rather than daily, just double-click the small display and it toggles between month and day.

With the monthly display shown in the smaller size, you can jump to the daily display for a specific date by double-clicking that date in the monthly view.

Play with Puzzles

1. Add the Picture Puzzle gadget to the Desktop. (See the earlier task, "Open the Gadget Gallery and Add Gadgets to the Desktop.")

2. Click any of the tools along the top of the puzzle (see **Figure 13-8**) to do the following:

- **Pause timer:** Stops the automatic count of seconds of play.

- **Show Picture:** Displays the completed picture; release it, and you go back to where you were in the game.

- **Solve:** Ends the game and displays the completed picture.

3. To play the game, click any piece adjacent to a blank square. It moves into the blank space. Keep clicking and moving pieces until you get the picture pieces arranged to form a picture.

4. Click the Settings button to the right of the puzzle to display the Settings dialog box. (See **Figure 13-9.**)

5. Click the Previous or Next button to scroll through available pictures for the puzzle.

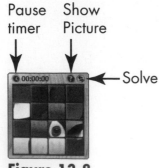

Pause   Show
timer   Picture

Solve

Figure 13-8

Figure 13-9

6. When you find the picture you want, click OK to close the dialog box.

Convert Currency

1. Are you shopping in a market in Paris with your laptop under your arm and need to change dollars to euros? If you have an Internet connection, you can get up-to-the-minute currency values. Start by adding the Currency Conversion gadget to the desktop. (See the earlier task, "Open the Gadget Gallery and Add Gadgets to the Desktop.")

2. Connect to the Internet to access the latest currency rates (as shown in **Figure 13-10**) and do any of the following.

- Enter the number of dollars; the number of equivalent euros is displayed.

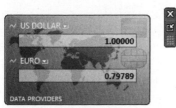

Figure 13-10

- Click one of the currency names, and a list of available currencies appears. (See **Figure 13-11**.) Click another currency in this list to change which currencies to convert from and to.

Figure 13-11

 To view the online source for the latest currency conversion rates, with the larger size Currency gadget displayed, click the Data Providers link. The MSN Money page opens. Click the Investing tab and then click the Markets tab on the page that appears, and finally click the Currencies tab on that page to view current rates.

 If you want to, you can display several Currency Conversion gadgets to compare multiple currencies at the same time. You can also click the plus symbol (+) opposite Data Providers to add another country to a gadget. Get rid of a country by clicking the X next to it.

Use the Feed Headlines Gadget

1. If you like to read the latest headlines (this requires an Internet connection) add a news feed to your desktop. First, add the Feed Headlines gadget to the desktop. (See the earlier task, "Open the Gadget Gallery and Add Gadgets to the Desktop.")

2. Click the Feed Viewer window to connect to the default RSS feed. (**Figure 13-12** shows what the feed might look like.)

3. At the web site that appears, you can view blog entries, submit an entry, or subscribe to additional feeds.

Figure 13-12

4. Click the Settings button. In the resulting Feed Viewer dialog box (see **Figure 13-13**), select the default feed.

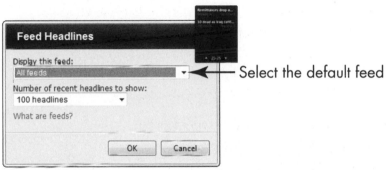

Select the default feed

Figure 13-13

5. Click OK to close the dialog box.

 Use the Show Next Set of Feeds and Show Previous Set of Feeds arrows that appear at the bottom of the Feed Headlines gadget when you move your pointer over it to scroll through available feeds.

Monitor Your CPU

1. Is your laptop acting sluggish? Check its performance by using the CPU Meter (see **Figure 13-14**). Add the CPU Meter gadget to the desktop. (See the earlier task, "Open the Gadget Gallery and Add Gadgets to the Desktop.")

Figure 13-14

2. Use the readouts to monitor the following:

- **CPU** (on the left) monitors how hard your CPU is working to process various programs and processes running on your laptop.

- **Memory** (on the right) monitors the percent of your laptop memory that is being used.

That's about all there is to CPU Meter! You can click the Size button to toggle between a larger and smaller version, but you can't make any settings for it. It's just a little reminder that helps you keep track of your laptop's performance. If memory is almost at 100%, consider freeing some space. If the CPU usage is at a higher percentage, odds are you've got lots of programs running — which could be slowing down your laptop's performance; consider shutting some down!

If you want more detail about your laptop memory, use the Start menu to display the Control Panel and choose System and Security. The System links allow you to view the processor speed and the amount of RAM available.

Check the Weather

1. It's always handy to know what today's weather will be, and, luckily, there's a gadget for that. Add the Weather gadget to the desktop. (See the earlier task, "Open the Gadget Gallery and Add Gadgets to the Desktop.")

2. Click the Options button to see settings for the Weather gadget (see **Figure 13-15**). Choose one of two options:

- Enter a name in the Select Current Location textbox.

- Check the Find Location Automatically option.

Figure 13-15

3. Click to select either Fahrenheit or Celsius for your temperature setting.

4. Click OK to save the settings.

 To enlarge the Weather gadget and see more detail about the weather, click the Enlarge button along its right side.

Find More Gadgets Online

1. Right-click the desktop and choose Gadgets.

2. In the Gadgets window, click the Get More Gadgets Online link.

3. In the page that opens in your browser (see **Figure 13-16**) scroll down to view featured gadgets. When you find one that interests you, click on it to get more information and read user reviews.

4. Click the Download button if you want to get the gadget.

5. In the confirmation dialog box that appears, click Install to download the gadget.

6. In the dialog box that appears, click Open, and then in the Security Warning dialog box that appears, click Install (unless you've changed your mind, in which case, click Don't Install). The gadget appears on your desktop.

 Note that some gadgets work better on one version of Windows than on another. Read the information about a gadget to make sure it will run smoothly on a Windows 7 computer.

Figure 13-16

Using Microsoft Works

The two kinds of software programs that people use most often are word processors (for working with words) and spreadsheets (for working with numbers and organizing data). In this chapter, you get to see the basic tools of the word processor and spreadsheet programs built in to Microsoft Works 9.

Microsoft Works is a *suite* (a bundle that includes multiple programs). Works, or a trial version of the product, comes installed on many Windows-based laptops. If it's not installed on yours, the program is relatively inexpensive (anywhere from $30 to $40, depending on where you shop), so it's a good entry-level program you might want to have on your laptop. Note that if you don't have Works and want an entirely free word-processing program to try, many of these tasks will work similarly with Google Docs (www.docs.google.com), which you can use for free online, or OpenOffice.org (www.openoffice.org), which you can download for free. You can also access online versions of Microsoft Office applications at

```
http://office.microsoft.com/en-us/
office_live/?pid=CL101750181033
```

See Chapter 18 for more about working with applications online.

With a word processor, you can create anything from simple letters to posters or brochures. You can use both text and graphics to add style to your documents. You can even use a word processor to print envelopes or labels, so you can send those holiday newsletters or fundraising letters for the local food bank on their way.

Microsoft Works 9 also includes a spreadsheet program that provides some pretty sophisticated tools for working with numbers and charts.

A spreadsheet program allows you to organize data and automate both simple and complex calculations. You enter numbers and then perform actions on them such as calculating an average or generating a sum for a range of numbers. You can format the data in a spreadsheet and also generate charts based on the numbers you enter.

In this chapter, you explore the following features of Works Word Processor and Spreadsheet:

➡ Enter text in the Works Word Processor and format it by applying different fonts, colors, and effects.

➡ Prepare your document for printing by using spelling- and grammar-checking tools, modifying the page setup, and finally, printing it!

➡ Enter data into a spreadsheet and format it.

➡ Perform simple calculations on data.

Open a New Document and Enter and Edit Text

1. Your first step in creating any document is to open your word processor and enter and edit text. Choose Start➪All Programs➪Microsoft Works and then select Microsoft Works Word Processor. The program opens, and a blank document is displayed. (See **Figure 14-1.**)

Begin typing in a blank document

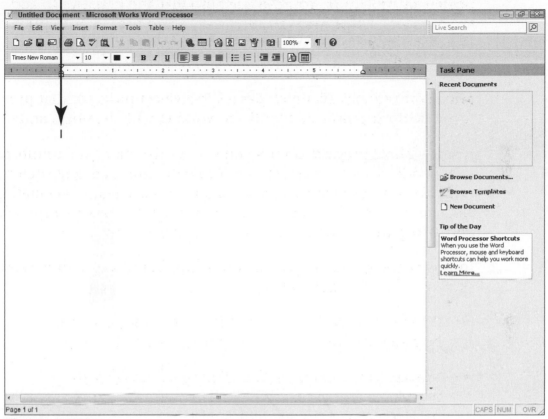

Figure 14-1

2. Begin typing your text. Word Processor (like all word processing programs) *wraps* the text, which means it moves automatically to the next line within a paragraph as you type. Press Enter twice on your keyboard only when you want to start a new paragraph.

3. To edit text you have entered, perform any of the following actions:

- Click anywhere within the text and press Backspace on the keyboard to delete text to the *left* of the cursor.

- Click anywhere within the text and press the Delete key to delete text to the *right* of the cursor.

- Click and drag your cursor over text to select it and press Delete or Backspace to delete the selected text.

- Click anywhere within the text and type additional text.

Save a Document

1. If you want to keep your document to use it again later or keep a copy for your records, you have to save it. To save a document for the first time, choose File⇨Save.

2. In the resulting Save As dialog box (see **Figure 14-2**), click the arrow on the right of the Save In field and click a different folder.

3. Type a name for the document in the File Name text box.

Type a name for your document

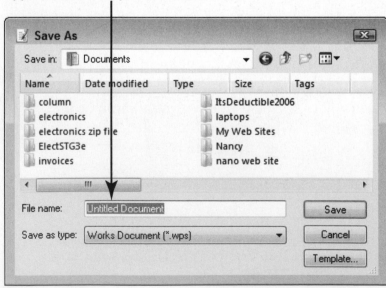

Figure 14-2

If you want to save the document in another format (for example, you can save a Works document as plain text so that any word processor can open it), click the arrow on the Save as Type field in the Save As dialog box and choose a different format before you click the Save button.

4. Click Save.

Open an Existing Document

1. After you create a file and save it, you can open it to add to or edit the contents, or print it. To open a file after you save it, with the Works word processor open, choose File➪Open.

2. In the Open dialog box that appears (see **Figure 14-3**), locate the file on your laptop, storage device, or disc by clicking the arrow on the Look In field and clicking the drive or folder where your file is located.

3. After you locate the file and click it, click the Open button. The file opens, ready for you to edit or print it.

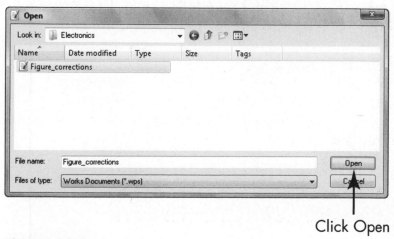

Figure 14-3

223

Cut, Copy, and Paste Text

1. You can cut and paste or copy and paste selected text to move or duplicate it in another location in your document. With a document open in Works word processor, click and drag over text to select it; the text is highlighted. (See **Figure 14-4**.)

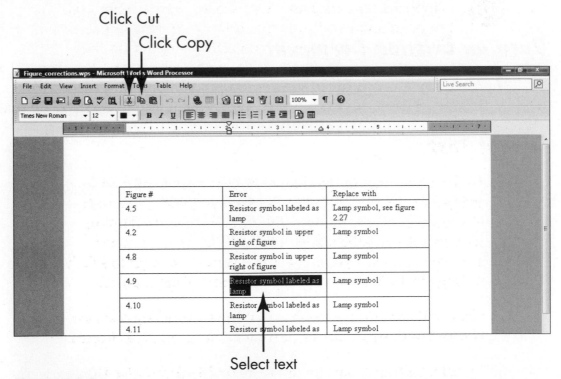

Click Cut

Click Copy

Select text

Figure 14-4

2. Perform either of the following two steps, depending on whether you want to *cut* the text (remove it) or *copy* it (leave the existing text and make a copy of it):

- Click the Cut button on the toolbar to cut the text.

- Click the Copy button on the toolbar to make a copy of the text.

3. Windows places the cut or copied text on its *Clipboard*, a temporary holding place for cut or copied text or objects. To paste the cut or copied text to another location within the document, click your mouse with the pointer sitting where you want the text to appear — and then click the Paste button on the toolbar. The text appears in the new location.

 After you place text or an object on the Windows Clipboard, you can paste it anywhere. For example, you can open another document and paste it there or paste it in an e-mail message. However, it won't stay on the Clipboard forever. If you cut or copy other text or objects, your earlier item will soon be removed from the Clipboard, which holds only a few items at a time.

Format Text

1. To *format* text means to change its size, apply effects such as bold or italic to it, or change the font (that is, a family of typeface style with a certain look and feel to it). You start by selecting the text you want to format. Click and drag your mouse over the text you want to format to select it. (**Figure 14-5** shows how selected text is highlighted.)

2. Choose Format⇨Font. In the resulting Font dialog box (see **Figure 14-6**), make any of the following formatting choices:

- Select a font from the list of available fonts. Use the arrows or scroll bar in this list to see more choices and click the one you want to select. The font is previewed in the large box near the bottom of the dialog box.

- Select a font style such as Bold or Italic from the Font Style list. Font styles are useful for emphasis.

- Choose a different text size by selecting a point-size setting from the Size list. The higher the point-size number, the larger the text.

Click and drag to select text

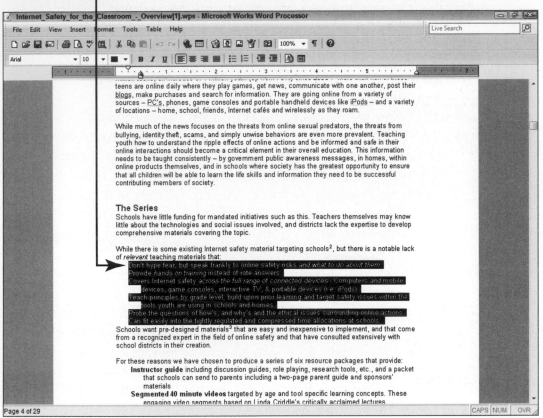

Figure 14-5

- If you want to underline the selected text, choose a style from the Underline drop-down list.

- Click the arrow on the Color drop-down list and select a different color for the text.

- Click any of the Effects check boxes to apply effects to the text.

3. Click OK to apply the formatting options you've selected.

Click the arrow to see options

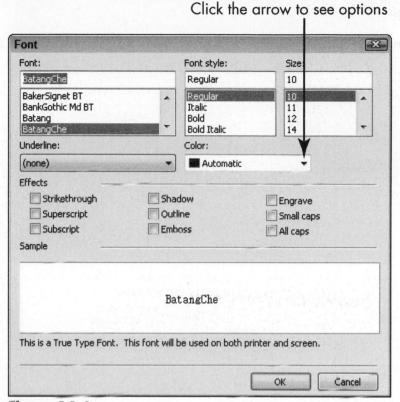

Figure 14-6

 You can also use the Formatting toolbar to apply individual formatting settings to selected text. For example, you can click the Bold button or choose a different font from the Font drop-down list. If you don't see the Formatting toolbar, choose View➪Toolbars➪Formatting.

 Try not to use too many formatting bells and whistles in a single document, as the formatting might become distracting or make the document difficult to read. A good guideline is to use only two fonts on a single page and use effects such as bold or shadowed text for emphasis only.

Check Spelling

1. Especially if you go on the road with your laptop and leave your hefty dictionary behind, you'll be glad to hear that Works has a tool that helps you check and correct your spelling. Although the tool won't catch every error (if you typed *sore* instead of *soar*, for example, the tool won't catch it), it can catch many spelling mistakes. With the document you want to check open, choose Tools⇨Spelling and Grammar. If you didn't make any discernable errors, a message appears that the spelling check is complete, but if you did, a dialog box appears.

2. In the resulting Spelling and Grammar dialog box (see **Figure 14-7**), take any of the following actions:

- Click a suggested spelling and then click Change to change just this instance of the word.

- Click a suggested spelling and click Change All to change all instances of the word in the document.

- Click Ignore Once to ignore the current instance of the word not found in the dictionary.

- Click Ignore All to ignore all instances of this word.

- Click Add to add the word to the dictionary so that it is no longer questioned in a Spelling and Grammar check.

3. The spell checker moves to the next suspect word, if any, and you can use any of the options in the preceding list to fix mistakes. This continues until the spell checker tells you that the spell check is complete.

4. Click Close to close the dialog box.

Click to select an alternate spelling

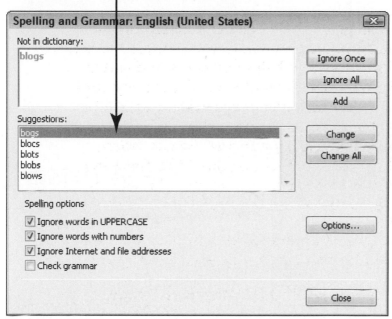

Figure 14-7

 If you would also like to have Works check your grammar, you can select the Check Grammar check box in the Spelling and Grammar dialog box. The next time you run the Spelling and Grammar check, Works displays sentences with possible grammatical errors and suggests how to fix them.

 It's a good idea to use the Add feature to put unusual words or acronyms you use often in the dictionary. For example, you might add unrecognized names of people or companies, scientific terms, or acronyms such as IBM or AARP. By adding such words to the dictionary, you save yourself the time it takes to tell Works over and over again that those words are correct.

Change Page Setup

1. Word processors have default page setup settings that determine, among other things, how wide or tall the margins are and which way the page is oriented. If you want to change those settings, you can do that when you first create the document, or you may wait until you're ready to print the document on paper. With the document whose setup you want to change displayed, choose File⇨Page Setup.

2. In the Page Setup dialog box that appears (see **Figure 14-8**), click the Margins tab. Use the up and down arrows (called *spinner arrows*) to increase or decrease margin settings, or type a new measurement in any of the Margins boxes.

3. Click the Source, Size & Orientation tab. (See **Figure 14-9**.) Select a radio button for either Portrait orientation (with the longer edges of the paper on the sides) or Landscape (with the shorter edges of the paper on the sides).

4. Also on the Source, Size & Orientation tab, you can use the Paper settings to specify the size of paper you want to print to — and, if your printer has multiple paper trays, select a tray to be the source for the paper.

Click arrows to change margin settings

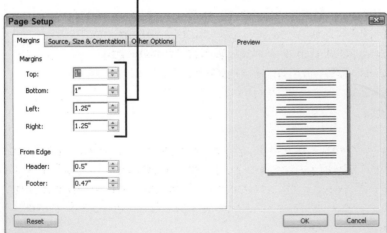

Figure 14-8

Choose an orientation

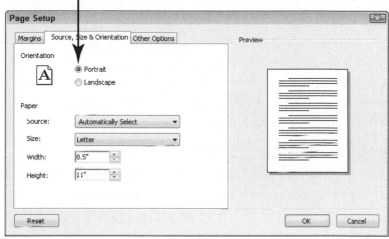

Figure 14-9

5. Click OK to save the new settings.

If you're inserting a header or footer (for example, a page number or the name of the document that you want to appear on every page on either the top or bottom), you should adjust some settings in the Page Setup dialog box. On the Margins tab, you can specify how far from the edge of the paper the header or footer should appear. On the Other Options tab, you can control what page number you start with and whether the header or footer should appear on the first page of the document. (To insert headers or footers into your document, use the Header and Footer command on the View menu.)

Print a Document

All Windows software uses a similar procedure to print files, and Works is only slightly different. You simply choose File⇨Print — or in Office 2007 and later programs, click the Office button and choose Print — and use the settings shown in **Figure 14-10** to determine these variables:

- **Number of Copies:** Be sure there's enough paper in your printer to handle them all!

- **Collate:** *Collating* assembles sets of documents in the correct page order rather than printing, say, five page 1s, then five page 2s, and so on. This can save you effort when you're assembling multiple copies of a document yourself.

- **Page Range:** The Print dialog box you see in Windows software allows you to print the current page, text you select before choosing the Print command, the entire document, or a specified page or range of pages.

- **Find Printer:** Click this button to open a dialog box where you can choose which printer to print to and indicate your preferences for that printer. You can determine preferences such as the print quality and whether to print in color or grayscale.

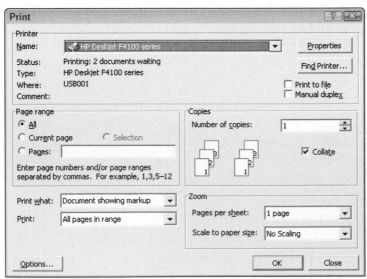

Figure 14-10

Always remember that — before you print — you should proofread your document and run a spell check to make sure it's letter-perfect.

Explore the Structure of a Spreadsheet

Spreadsheet software, such as Microsoft Works Spreadsheet and Microsoft Excel, uses a grid-like structure for entering data. The individual cells of the grid are formed by the intersection of a row with a column, so a cell is identified by a column letter followed by a row number. For example, B3 identifies the cell located at the intersection of the second column over and third row down.

Here are some additional facts you should know about spreadsheets:

⟶ You can enter text or numbers in spreadsheets.

⟶ When you click in a cell, the Formula bar becomes active. You can enter contents and edit those contents in the Formula bar. (See **Figure 14-11**.)

⟶ Use the two scrollbars, the one to the right and the one at the bottom, to move vertically or horizontally through a large spreadsheet.

Enter data in the Formula bar

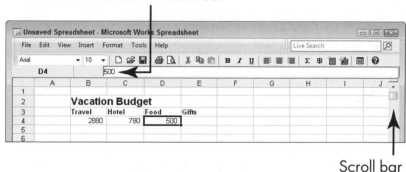

Scroll bar

Figure 14-11

➠ You can perform calculations on numbers that you've entered in a spreadsheet, such as adding up numbers or calculating an average of several numbers. See the "Perform Simple Calculations" task later in the chapter for instructions.

➠ You can format the contents of cells or use an AutoFormat feature to apply predesigned styles to selected cells. Note that in some predesigned formats, the grid lines are neither displayed nor printed. See the "Apply AutoFormats to Cells" task for more details.

➠ After you've entered some data into your spreadsheet, you can easily generate a chart to represent that data graphically.

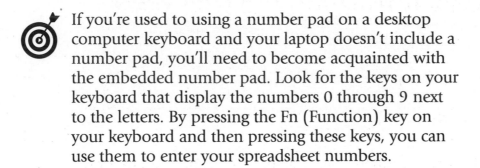 If you're used to using a number pad on a desktop computer keyboard and your laptop doesn't include a number pad, you'll need to become acquainted with the embedded number pad. Look for the keys on your keyboard that display the numbers 0 through 9 next to the letters. By pressing the Fn (Function) key on your keyboard and then pressing these keys, you can use them to enter your spreadsheet numbers.

Open Works Spreadsheet and Enter Data

1. To start a new spreadsheet and begin filling it with information, first choose Start⇨All Programs⇨ Microsoft Works⇨Microsoft Works Spreadsheet.

2. In the blank spreadsheet that appears, click in a cell to make it active. (See **Figure 14-12.**)

3. Begin typing; notice that what you type appears in both the cell and the Formula bar.

4. Press Tab to complete the entry and move to the next cell. Note that you can also click the Enter button in Works

Spreadsheet (see **Figure 14-13**), which looks like a check mark, to complete your entry and keep the current cell active.

Click a cell to make it active

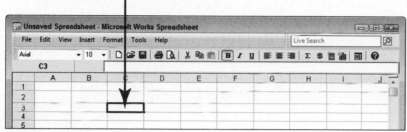

Figure 14-12

The Enter button

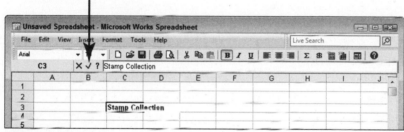

Figure 14-13

You can open a new, blank spreadsheet at any time by choosing File⇨New. To open an existing, saved file, choose File⇨Open to locate and open it.

Remember to save your work often to avoid losing anything. I like to back up all my work to a USB stick, which I can easily move between my desktop computer and laptop.

Format Numbers

1. You can format text in the cells of a spreadsheet, applying effects or changing the text font or color, just as you do for text in a word processor. However, formatting numbers in a spreadsheet is a bit different. In this procedure, you format the number to fit a category, such as currency, or include a certain number of decimal points. To begin formatting numbers, first click the cell containing the numbers you want to format. To select multiple cells, click a cell and drag up, down, right, or left to select a range of cells.

2. Choose Format⇨Number.

3. In the Format Cells dialog box that appears with the Number tab displayed (see **Figure 14-14**), click an option in the Select Format Type list, such as Currency or Percent.

Click a number format

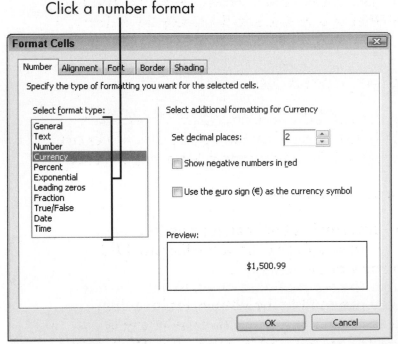

Figure 14-14

After you select a format, you'll usually see, on the right side of the dialog box, additional options for indicating how you want the data to display. For example, if you choose the Currency format, you can click the up or down arrow on the Set Decimal Places field to specify how many decimal places the number should have — for example, 22.10 (two decimals), 22.1 (one decimal), or 22 (no decimals). Your settings appear in the Preview box.

4. Click OK to apply your formatting selections and close the dialog box.

 Currency and General are common options for formatting numbers in lists or budgets, but they aren't the only ones. You can even format numbers to display as dates, times, or fractions. If you want a zero to appear as False (in other words, no value) and any number (that is, any value at all) to appear as True, choose the True/False format type.

Apply AutoFormats to Cells

1. You can also format sets of cells by using AutoFormats, which are predesigned sets of formatting choices such as cell shading or borders. Click and drag to select a range of cells.

2. Choose Format⇨AutoFormat.

3. In the AutoFormat dialog box that appears (see **Figure 14-15**), select a format from the list provided. You see a preview of the design.

4. If you like, you can modify the settings for including column and row headings and totals by selecting or deselecting any of the four check boxes on the right side of the dialog box.

5. Click OK to apply the selected formatting to the cell range.

Click a format

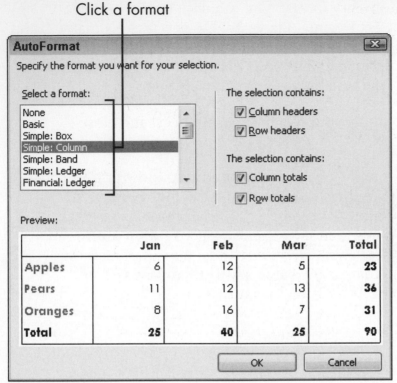

Figure 14-15

Perform Simple Calculations

1. A spreadsheet program is way more than just a place to list numbers and text. After you've entered some numbers in your spreadsheet, you can use powerful spreadsheet tools to perform simple or complex calculations, from averaging a set of numbers to complex statistical analysis. Click in a cell where you would like calculation results to appear.

2. Choose Tools⇨Easy Calc or press the Easy Calc button on the toolbar.

3. In the Easy Calc dialog box that appears (see **Figure 14-16**), click a function in the Common Functions list box and then click Next.

Click a function

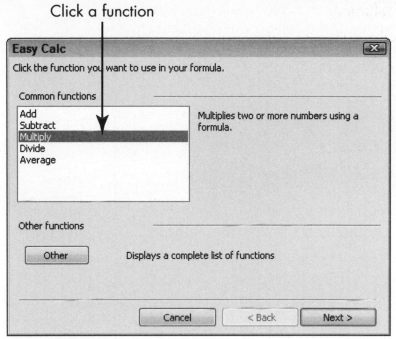

Figure 14-16

4. In the next Easy Calc dialog box (see **Figure 14-17**), enter a range of cells (such as **A1:C4**) in the Range field. Or click the button on the right of the Range field; the dialog box is hidden, allowing you to click and drag on your spreadsheet to select the cells you want to calculate. After you make the selection, the dialog box appears again.

5. Click Next. In the Final Result dialog box, you can enter a different cell location, such as G5, in the Result At text box, and the result will be saved in the cell you indicate. Click Finish to complete the calculation. The result of the calculation now appears in the designated cell.

 To add numbers quickly, you can simply click in the cell where you want to place the results and then click the AutoSum button on the toolbar (which looks kind of like a capital *M* turned sideways).

Spreadsheet suggests cells you might want to include in the calculation, but you can click and drag to select more or different cells. Click or press Enter to complete the sum.

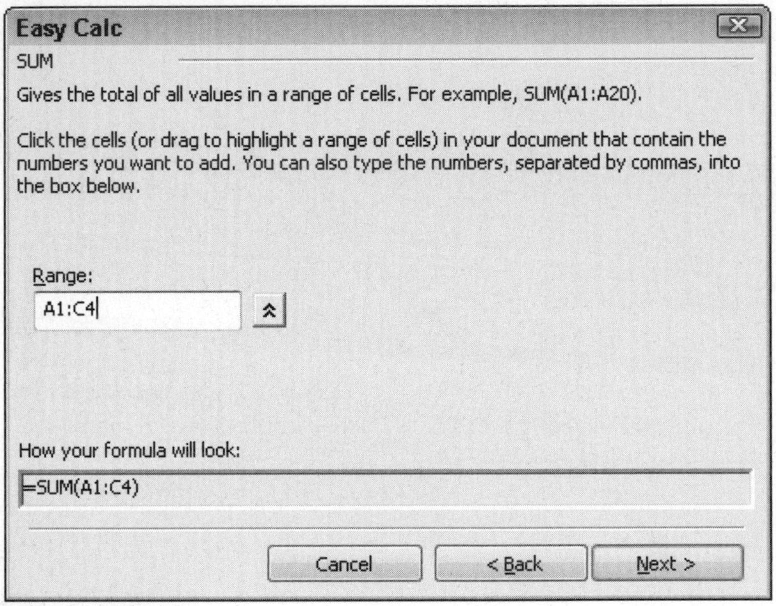

Figure 14-17

Getting the Most from Movies and Digital Photos

Most people today have access to a digital camera or video camera (even if only on their cellphones) and have started manipulating and swapping photos and videos, both online and off. Windows allows you to view, share, and organize photos and play movies with ease.

In this chapter you discover how to

→ Play movies with Windows Media Player.

→ Upload photos from your digital camera.

→ View your photos and add tags and ratings to help you organize and search through photos.

→ E-mail a photo to others.

→ Burn photos to a CD or DVD to pass around to your friends.

→ View movies online

Work with Media Software

Your laptop is a doorway into a media-rich world full of music, digital photos, and movies. Your laptop provides you with all kinds of possibilities for working with media. Windows 7 has two useful media programs built right into it: Windows Media Player and Windows Photo Viewer. In combination, they give you the ability to play music and set up libraries of music tracks; view, organize, and edit photos; and edit and play your own homemade movies.

Here's what you can do with each of these programs:

➡ **Windows Media Player** (see **Figure 15-1**) is just what its name suggests: a program you can use to play music, watch movies, or view photos. It also offers handy tools to create *playlists* (customized lists of music you can build and play) and set up libraries of media to keep things organized. You can even burn media to a DVD so that you can play it on your DVD player or another computer.

➡ **Windows Photo Viewer** (see **Figure 15-2**) enables you to work with digital photos; it opens automatically when you double-click a photo file. You can also *burn* (save) media to a disc or order prints from within Photo Viewer.

➡ Using photo properties in the **Pictures library** (see **Figure 15-3**), you can organize your photos by adding tags that help you search for just the photo you need. You can also run slide shows using the Pictures library.

Figure 15-1

Figure 15-2

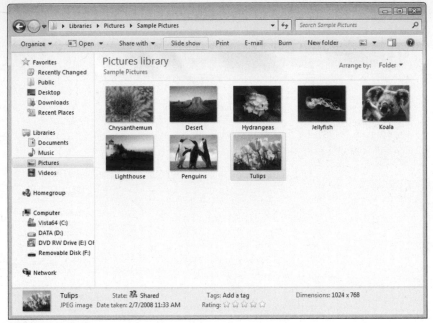

Figure 15-3

Play Movies with Windows Media Player

1. To open Windows Media Player and begin working with music and movie files, click the icon with an orange circle containing a right-facing arrow on the taskbar, or choose Start➪All Programs➪Windows Media Player. If this is your first time using the player, you may be prompted to make some basic settings.

2. Click the Maximize button in the resulting Media Player window. (Maximize is the square icon in the upper-right corner of the window, next to the X-shaped Close button.)

3. Click Videos in the navigation pane to the left.

4. In the window listing video files, click the Library folder that contains the movie you want to play (as shown in **Figure 15-4**).

Click the folder that contains the movie you want to play

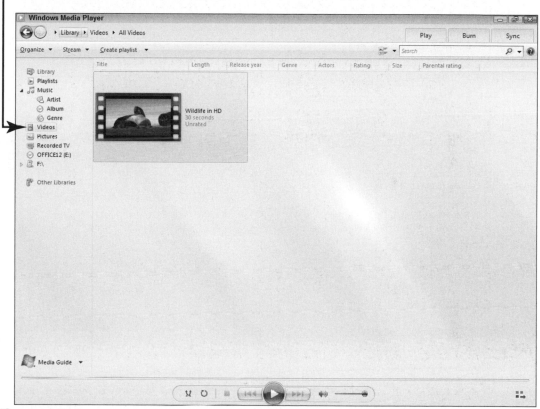

Figure 15-4

5. Double-click a file to begin the playback. (See **Figure 15-5.**)
Use tools at the bottom of the screen to do the following.
(If they disappear during playback, just hover your pointer
over that area to display them again.)

- Adjust the volume of any sound track by clicking and
  dragging the slider left (to make it softer) or right (to
  make it louder). Click the megaphone-shaped volume
  icon to mute the sound (and click it again to turn the
  sound back on).

- Pause the playback by clicking the round Pause button in the center of the toolbar. (Click it again to
  resume playback.)

- Stop the playback by clicking the square-shaped Stop button toward the left.

- Skip to the next or previous movie by clicking the Next (rewind) and Previous (fast forward) arrow buttons to the left and right of the Pause button.

Playing 'Wildlife in HD': 6134 K bits/second

00:04

Figure 15-5

6. Click the Close button to close Media Player when you're done viewing the movie.

 To stop the movie before it finishes, click the Stop button. Note that the Previous and Next buttons aren't available for single movie clips — they jump you from one track to another when playing sound files.

If you own a smaller laptop or netbook, you may not have a built-in DVD player. Consider buying an external DVD drive that you attach through a USB port. There are many small models that are highly portable.

Upload Photos from Your Digital Camera

Uploading photos from a camera to your laptop is a very simple process, but this task helps you understand what's involved. (Uploading photos is similar to the process you can use to upload movies from a camcorder — in both cases, check your manual for details.) Here are some highlights:

➡ **Installing software:** Digital cameras also typically come with software that makes uploading photos to your laptop easy. Install the software and then follow the easy-to-use interface to upload photos. If you're missing such software, you can simply connect your camera to your laptop and use Windows Explorer to locate the camera device on your laptop and copy and paste photo files into a folder on your hard drive. (Chapter 5 tells you how to use Windows Explorer.)

➡ **Making the connection:** Uploading photos from a digital camera to a laptop requires that you connect the camera to a USB port on your laptop using a USB cable that typically comes with the camera. Power on the camera or change its setting to a playback mode as instructed by your user's manual.

➡ **Printing straight from the camera:** Cameras save photos onto a memory card, and many printers include a slot where you can insert the memory card from the camera and print directly from it without having to first upload pictures. Some cameras also connect directly to printers. However, if you want to keep a copy of the photo and clear up space on your camera's memory card, you should upload even if you *can* print without uploading.

View a Digital Image in the Windows Photo Viewer

1. To peruse your photos and open them in Windows Photo Viewer, choose Start⇨Pictures.

2. In the resulting window, if there are folders in this library, double-click to display the files within it. Double-click any photo in any Pictures library folder. In Windows Photo Viewer, as shown in **Figure 15-6**, you can use the tools at the bottom (see **Figure 15-7**) to do any of the following:

Figure 15-6

• The **Display Size** icon in the shape of a magnifying glass displays a slider you can click and drag to change the size of the image thumbnails.

• The **Next** and **Previous** icons move to a previous or following image in the same folder.

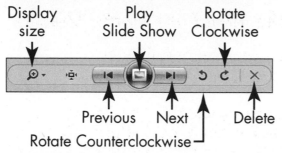

Figure 15-7

- The center **Play Slide Show** button with a slide image on it displays the images in your Picture folder in a continuous slide show.

- The **Rotate Clockwise** and **Rotate Counterclockwise** icons spin the image 90 degrees at a time.

- The **Delete** button deletes the selected image.

> If you want to quickly open a photo in another application, click the Open button at the top of the Windows Photo Viewer window and chose a program such as Paint or Microsoft Office Picture Manager.

Add a Tag to a Photo

1. Tags help to categorize photos so you can search for them easily. To create a new tag, choose Start⇨Pictures. Locate the photo you want, right-click it, and choose Properties.

2. In the Properties dialog box that appears, click the Details tab. (See **Figure 15-8**.)

3. Click the Tags item and a field appears. Enter a tag(s) in the field (see **Figure 15-9**) and click OK to save the tag.

4. If you display your Pictures library in Windows Explorer in Details view, you'll see the tag listed next to the photo. Tags are also used when you view photos in Windows Media Center.

Click the Details tab

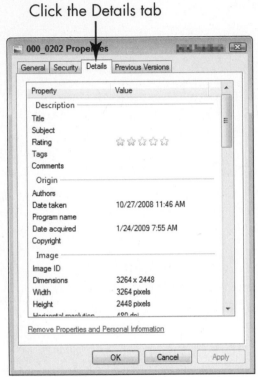

Figure 15-8

 To delete a tag, just display the photo Properties dialog box again, click to the right of the tag, and press Backspace.

 To see a list of all photos in the Photo gallery organized by tags, click the arrow on the Arrange By item and choose Tag.

Enter a tag here

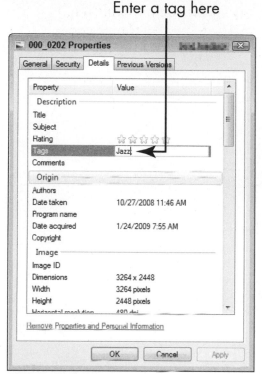

Figure 15-9

E-Mail a Photo

1. Choose Start⇨Pictures. In the Pictures library, shown in **Figure 15-10** in Details view, click the check box to the left of the thumbnail to select the photo; a check mark appears in the check box to indicate that it's selected. To choose multiple photos, click the check boxes next to additional thumbnails.

2. Choose File⇨Send To⇨Mail Recipient. In the Attach Files dialog box that appears (see **Figure 15-11**), change the photo size by clicking the Picture Size drop-down arrow and choosing another size from the list if you wish.

Selected photos

Figure 15-10

Choose smaller photos to attach to an e-mail because graphic files can be rather big. You might encounter problems sending larger files, or others might have trouble receiving them. Using a smaller size is especially important if you are sending multiple images.

Click to change the photo size

Figure 15-11

3. Click Attach. An e-mail form from your default e-mail appears with your photo attached.

4. Fill out the e-mail form with an addressee, subject, and message (if you wish), and then click Send.

Note that although you can send a video file as an e-mail attachment, you can't resize it; video files make photo files look tiny by comparison, so it's probably better to send one at a time, if at all. Consider using a video-sharing web site to post videos online to share with others.

Sometimes you'll send or receive a file with several photos or other documents compressed together (called a zip file). When you download the attachment to your computer it will appear as a little file with a zipper on it. Double-click the file to open it, and Windows offers a command to Extract All Files. Click that, and Windows creates a new folder with all the files unzipped so you can work with them.

Burn a Photo to a CD or DVD

1. You can burn (save) a copy of your photos to a writable disc to share them or back up your original copies. Insert a writable disc into your disc drive. (You can save photo files to CDs or DVDs.)

2. With the Pictures library open in Windows Explorer, display a photo by locating it with the Navigation pane and double-clicking the thumbnail to display it in Windows Photo Viewer.

3. Click the Burn button and then choose Data Disc.

4. A balloon message appears on the taskbar indicating that you have files waiting to be burned to disc. Click the balloon, and a list of files waiting to be burned appears, as shown in **Figure 15-12.**

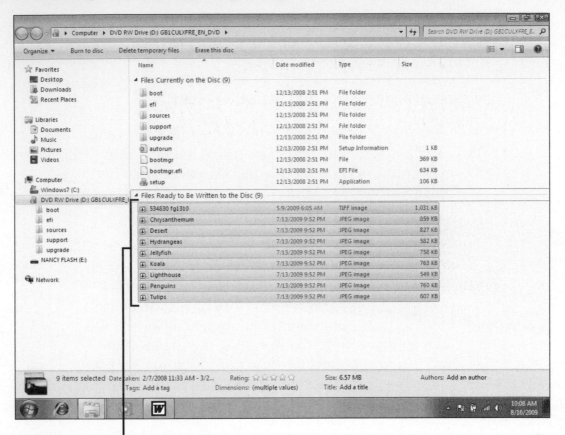

Files waiting to be burned

Figure 15-12

5. Click the Burn to Disc button. In the Burn to Disc dialog box that appears, enter a name in the Disc Title field (the default name is today's date). Click Next when you're ready to burn the disc.

6. A progress window appears. (See **Figure 15-13**.)

7. When the files have been burned to the disc, a confirmation dialog box appears, and your disc drawer opens. Click Finish to complete the process and close the dialog box.

If you want to check the photos you've added before you burn the DVD, click the Preview button in the Ready to Burn DVD window.

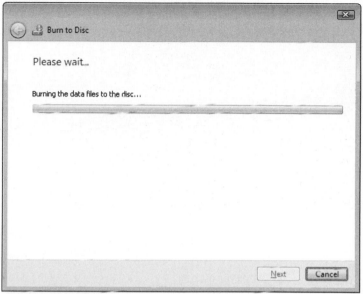

Figure 15-13

Create and Play a Slide Show

1. You can use the photos in your Pictures Library to run your own slide show. Choose Start⇨Pictures. Double-click the Pictures library to display all pictures within it.

2. Click an image to select it. Holding down the Ctrl key, click additional images to select all the photos you want to appear in the slide show. (See **Figure 15-14.**)

3. Click the Slide Show button. The first image appears in a separate full-screen display. The slides move forward automatically, cycling among the photos repeatedly. (See **Figure 15-15.**)

Photos selected for slide show

Figure 15-14

4. Press Escape to stop the slide show.

 If you want a more sophisticated slide show feature, check out Windows Media Center. Here you can create and save any number of custom slide shows, reorganize slides, and edit slide shows to add or delete photos. You might also consider a commercial slide-show program such as Microsoft PowerPoint if you want to create more complex slide shows.

Figure 15-15

Watch Movies Online

If you have an Internet connection, you can watch movies on your laptop using an online video sharing service such as YouTube or any of several free or paid movie sites such as Netflix and Hulu.

When you watch movies online, you're using a technology called *streaming*. The movie isn't downloaded to your laptop; rather, bits of the video are streamed to your computer over your Internet connection.

The plus side of video streaming is that you can watch videos — many of which are free — without overloading your laptop's memory. The negative side is that, depending on your Internet connection, streaming can be less than smooth. If you've tried watching a video online and gotten a message that the video is *buffering* (assembling content to show you), you know what I mean.

Try out YouTube (www.youtube.com) and Hulu (www.hulu.com) as a starting point. YouTube is made up of people who want to share their shorter video clips, from the guy next door to movie studios and news stations. Hulu offers many movies and TV shows for free, or you can get a paid subscription to access more content. Either service will give you a taste of how well your connection will deliver video to your laptop. Just go to their web sites, use the search feature to find a video, and then double-click a video to play it.

 Amazon.com recently added a lot of free instant video content to its Amazon Prime membership. If you pay the yearly fee for Amazon Prime ($79 as of this writing) — which gives you unlimited second-day free shipping on anything you buy on the site, you also get the free video content. If you buy much at all each year from the online retailer, this works out to be a great deal.

Playing Music in Windows 7

Music is the universal language, and your laptop opens up many opportunities for appreciating it at home or on the road. For example, on your laptop you can listen to your favorite music, download music from the Internet, play audio CDs and DVDs, and organize your music by creating playlists. You can also save (or *burn*, in computer lingo) music tracks to a CD/DVD or portable music device such as the hugely popular iPod.

With a sound card installed and your laptop's built-in speakers, you can use Windows media programs to do the following:

➡ Getting your laptop ready for listening by setting up your speakers and adjusting the volume

➡ Playing music using Windows Media Player

➡ Managing your music by creating playlists of tracks you download

➡ Burning tracks to CD/DVD or syncing with portable music devices

➡ Making settings to copy music from CD/DVDs to your laptop (called *ripping*)

Set Up Speakers

1. Your laptop probably has built-in speakers. If you prefer, you can attach external speakers to your laptop by plugging them into the appropriate connection (often labeled with a little megaphone or speaker symbol). You can set up your speakers with settings such as volume and the balance between the left and right speakers.

2. Choose Start⇨Control Panel⇨Hardware and Sound; then click the Manage Audio Devices link (under the Sound category).

3. In the resulting Sound dialog box (see **Figure 16-1**), click the Speakers item and then click the Properties button.

Figure 16-1

4. In the resulting Speakers Property dialog box, click the Levels tab and then use the Speakers slider, as shown in **Figure 16-2**, to adjust the speaker volume. *Note:* If there is a small red x on the speaker button, click it to activate the speakers.

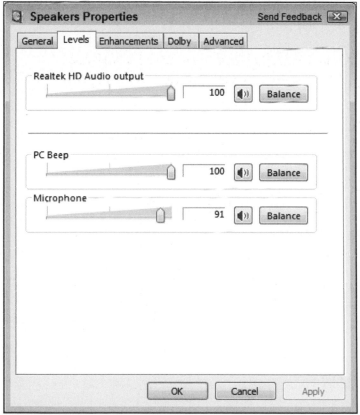

Figure 16-2

5. Click the Balance button. In the resulting Balance dialog box, use the L(eft) and R(ight) sliders to adjust the balance of sounds between the two speakers.

6. Click OK three times to close all the open dialog boxes and save the new settings.

Adjust System Volume

1. You can set the master system volume for your laptop to be louder or softer. Choose Start⇨Control Panel⇨ Hardware and Sound.

2. Click the Adjust System Volume link under Sound to display the Volume Mixer dialog box (as shown in **Figure 16-3**).

Figure 16-3

3. Make any of the following settings:

- Move the Device slider to adjust the system's speaker volume up and down.

- For sounds played by Windows (called *system sounds*), adjust the volume by moving the Applications slider.

- To mute either main or application volume, click the speaker icon beneath either slider so that a red circle appears.

4. Click the Close button on each of the dialog boxes.

 Here's a handy shortcut for quickly adjusting the volume of your default sound device. Click the Volume button (which looks like a little gray speaker) in the notifications area of the taskbar. To adjust the volume, use the slider on the Volume pop-up that appears, or select the Mute Speakers button to turn off sounds temporarily.

 Today, most laptop keyboards include volume controls and a mute button to control sounds; sometimes these are included in the function keys along the top of the keyboard. Some even include separate buttons to play, pause, and stop audio playback. Having these buttons and other controls at your fingertips can be worth a little extra in the price of your laptop.

Create a Playlist

1. A *playlist* is a saved set of music tracks you can create yourself — like building a personal music album. Choose Start⇨All Programs⇨Windows Media Player.

2. Click the Library button and then click the Create Playlist button. A playlist appears in the Navigation pane on the left, open for editing. Type a name for the playlist and then click anywhere outside the playlist to save the name.

3. Double-click a category (for example, Music) to display libraries, and then double-click a library in the left pane; the library contents appear. (See **Figure 16-4.**) Click an item and then drag it to the new playlist in the Navigation pane. Repeat this step to locate additional titles to add to the playlist.

Click an item in the Library contents

Then drag the item to the new playlist

Figure 16-4

4. To play a playlist, click it in the Library pane and then click the Play button.

5. You can organize playlists by clicking the Organize button (see **Figure 16-5**) and then choosing Sort By. In the submenu that appears, sort by features such as title, artist, or release date.

 You can also right-click a playlist in the Library pane and choose Play to play it or choose Delete to delete the list, though the original tracks that make up the list still exist.

Click the Organize button

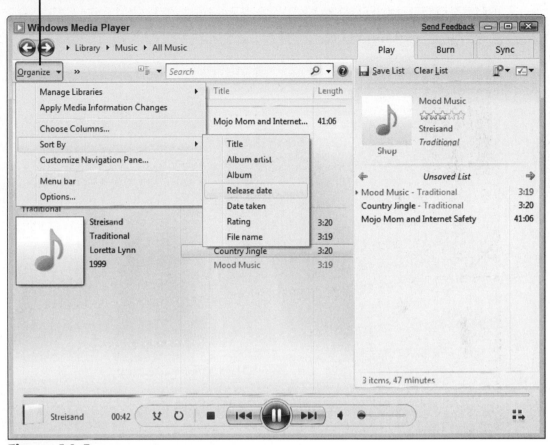

Figure 16-5

Burn Music to a CD/DVD

1. Saving music files to a storage medium such as a CD or DVD is referred to as *burning* (because the process uses a tiny internal laser). You might burn music to a disc so you can take it to a party or another location. Insert a blank CD or DVD suitable for storing audio files in your laptop CD/DVD-RW drive.

2. Open Windows Media Player, click the Burn tab, and then click one or more songs, albums, or playlists and drag them to the Burn pane. (See **Figure 16-6.**)

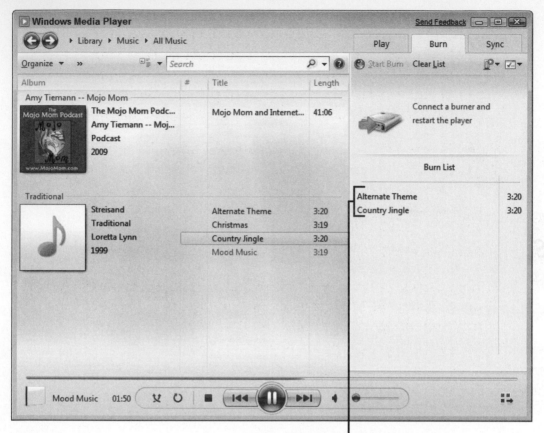

Songs placed in the Burn pane

Figure 16-6

3. Click Start Burn. Windows Media Player begins to burn the items to the disc. The Status column for the first song title reads `Writing to Disc` and changes to `Complete` when the track is copied.

4. When the burn is complete, your disc is ejected. (However, you can change this option by clicking the Burn Options button and choosing Eject Disc After Burning to deselect it.)

 If you swap music online through various music-sharing services and then copy them to CD/DVD and pass them around to your friends, always perform a virus check on the files before handing them off. Also, be sure you have the legal right to download and swap that music with others.

Note that optical discs come in different types, including CD-R (readable), CD-RW(read/writable), DVD+, DVD- and DVD+/-. You must be sure your optical drive is compatible with the disc type you are using; otherwise you can't burn the disc successfully. Check the packaging for the format before you buy!

 If you own a netbook, you should know by now that it doesn't include an optical drive. Your recourse is to buy an external drive that you can connect to your netbook using a USB port.

Sync with a Music Device

1. If you have a portable music player, such as an iPod or another type of MP3 player, you can sync it to your laptop to transfer music files. Connect the device to your laptop and open Windows Media Player.

2. Click the Sync tab; a Device Setup dialog box appears. (See Figure 16-7.)

Figure 16-7

3. Name the device and click Finish. The device is now synced
with Windows Media Player and will be automatically
updated whenever you connect it to your laptop.

 To add items to be synced to a device, with the Sync
tab displayed simply drag items to the right pane. If
you are connected (or the next time you do connect),
the items are copied onto the device automatically.

 If you want to be sure that the sync is progressing,
click the Sync Options button (it's on the far-right side
at the top of the Sync tab and looks like a little box
with a check mark in it) and choose View Sync Status.

Play Music

1. It's time to listen to some music. Choose Start⇨All
Programs⇨Windows Media Player.

2. Click the Library button and then double-click Music
or Playlists to display a library like the one shown in
Figure 16-8. Double-click an album or playlist to open
it; the titles of the songs are displayed in the right pane.

3. Use the buttons on the bottom of the Player window
(as shown in **Figure 16-9**) to do the following:

- Click a track, and then click the **Play** button to play it.
  When a song is playing, this button changes to the
  Pause button.

- Click the **Stop** button to stop playback.

- Click the **Next** or **Previous** buttons to move to the
  next or previous track in an album or playlist.

- Use the **Mute** and **Volume** controls to pump the
  sound up or down without having to modify the
  Windows volume settings.

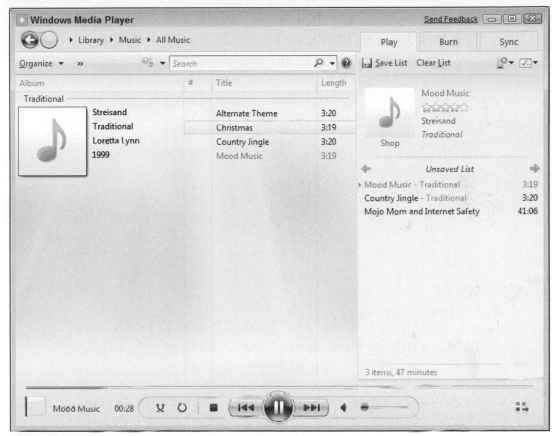

Figure 16-8

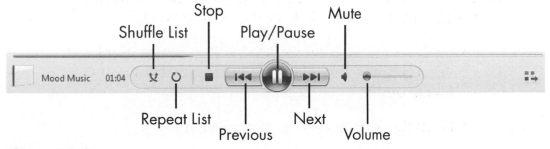

Figure 16-9

 Tired of the order in which your tracks play? You can use the List Options button on the Play Pane and chose Shuffle List to have Windows Media Player play the tracks on your album randomly. Click this button again to turn the shuffle feature off.

To jump to another track, rather than using the Next and Previous buttons you can double-click a track in the track list in the Media Player window. This can be much quicker if you want to jump several tracks ahead of (or behind) the track that's currently playing.

Make Settings for Ripping Music

1. If you place a CD or DVD in your disc drive, Windows Media Player will ask if you want to *rip* the music from the disc to your laptop. Doing so copies all the tracks to a storage space on your laptop. To control how ripping works, open Windows Media Player, click the Organize button, and choose Options.

2. Click the Rip Music tab to display it.

3. In the resulting Options window (see **Figure 16-10**) you can make the following settings:

- Click the **Change** button to change the location where ripped music is stored; the default location is your Music folder.

- Click the **File Name** button to choose the information to include in the filenames for music that is ripped to your laptop. The File Name Options dialog box appears, as shown in **Figure 16-11**. Click the check boxes for the items you want to include in your music's filenames; click OK when you're done.

- Choose the audio format to use by clicking the **Format** drop-down list.

- Many audio files are copyright-protected. If you have permission to copy and distribute the music, you might not want to choose the **Copy Protect Music** check box; however, if you are downloading music you paid for — and, therefore, should not give away

copies of — you should ethically choose to Copy
Protect music so that Windows prompts you to download media rights or purchase another copy of the
music when you copy it to another location.

- If you don't want to be prompted to rip music from
  CD/DVDs you insert in your drive, but instead want
  all music ripped automatically, click the **Rip CD
  Automatically** check box.

- If you want the CD/DVD to eject automatically after
  ripping is complete, select the **Eject CD after Ripping**
  check box.

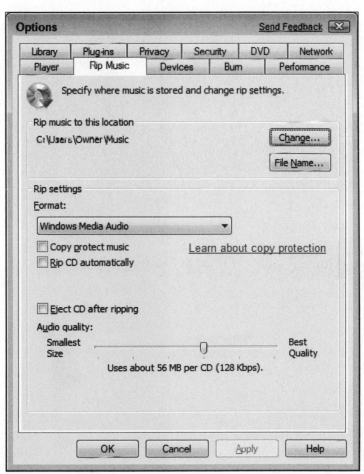

Figure 16-10

- Use the **Audio Quality slider** to adjust the quality of the
  ripped music. The Smallest Size will save space on your
  laptop by compressing the file, but this causes a loss of
  audio quality. The Best Quality will provide optimum
  sound, but these files can be rather large. The choice is
  yours — based on your tastes and your laptop's capacity!

Figure 16-11

4. When you finish making settings, click the OK button to
save them and close the Options dialog box.

Playing Games in Windows 7

As a senior, you may have earned your way to retirement and need fun activities to fill up your days. If so, you'll be happy to hear that Microsoft has built plenty of games into Windows 7 to keep you amused. If not, you need games to relieve the stress of your job!

Many computer games are essentially virtual versions of games that you already know, such as solitaire and chess. But Windows has added some interesting treats to the mix — several that depend to a great extent on some neat onscreen animation.

Altogether, you can access 14 games provided by Microsoft in Windows (although your computer manufacturer may have added more), and this chapter gives you a sampling of the best of them. Here's what you can expect:

➡ Traditional card games, such as Solitaire and Hearts

➡ Games of dexterity, such as Minesweeper, where the goal is to be the fastest, smartest clicker in the West

Get ready to . . .

➠ An online version of chess called Chess Titans that
helps you hone your chess strategy against another
player or your computer

➠ An Internet version of the popular game Checkers.

No matter what your comfort level with computers, these games are pretty darn
fun and easy to play, so why not give them a try?

Play Solitaire

1. Choose Start⇨Games. If this is the first time you're playing games, Windows displays a Set Up Game dialog box.
If it does, make choices (such as whether to check automatically for game updates) and click OK. In the resulting
Games window, (see **Figure 17-1**), double-click Solitaire.

Figure 17-1

2. In the resulting Solitaire window, if you need help with game rules, read the How to Play message that appears. When you're ready to play, click a card (see **Figure 17-2**) and then click a card in another deck that you want to move it on top of. The first card you click moves.

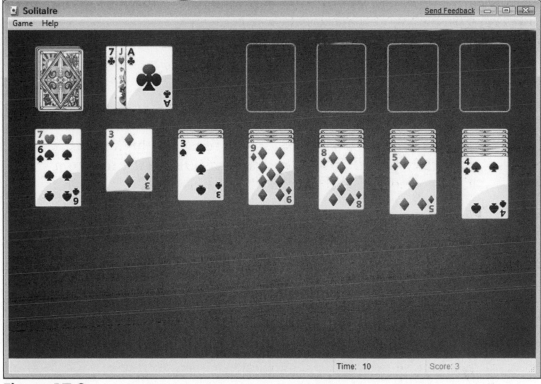

Figure 17-2

3. When playing the game, you have the following options:

- If no moves are available, click the stack of cards in the upper-left corner to deal another round of cards.

- If you move the last card from one of the six laid-out stacks, leaving only face-down cards, click the face-down cards to flip one up. You can also move a King onto any empty stack.

- When you reach the end of the stack of cards in the upper-left corner, click them again to redeal the cards that you didn't use the first time.

- You can play a card in one of two places: either building a stack from King to Ace on the bottom row, alternating suits; or starting from Ace in any of the top four slots, placing cards from Ace to King in a single suit.

- When you complete a set of cards (Ace to King), click the top card and then click one of the four blank deck spots at the top-right area of the window. If you complete all four sets, you win.

4. To deal a new game, choose Game⇨New Game (or press F2). Unlike life, it's easy to start over with Solitaire! When prompted, choose Quit and Start a New Game.

5. To close Solitaire, click the Close button.

 To change settings for the game, choose Game⇨ Options. The two main settings you'll probably deal with here are Draw (which gives you an option of turning over one card or a stack of three cards on each deal) and Scoring (which offers the option of not using scoring at all, or using Standard or Vegas-style scoring). Standard scoring starts you off with nothing in the bank and pays you $5 or $10 for every card you place, depending on whether you place it on the lower stacks or in the area where you place Aces. Vegas-style is a bit more complex, starting you off with a $52 debit ($1 per card in the deck), and crediting you $5 per card you place in the Aces area, with the object being to come out in the black (moneywise, that is) at the end. You can also choose to time your game.

Don't like a move you just made? Undo it by choosing Game⇨Undo. This works for the last move only, however. You can also get unstuck if you're on a losing streak by choosing Game⇨Hint.

 If you're using your laptop on battery power, keep an eye on the battery level as you play games. Because they use a bit more power to display graphics (and sometimes animations), you may find your battery drains quickly — and which can be an unwanted surprise if you've gotten absorbed in your game.

Play FreeCell

1. FreeCell is a variation on solitaire. Choose Start⇨Games; in the Games window, double-click FreeCell.

2. In the resulting FreeCell window, as shown in **Figure 17-3**, a game is ready to play. If you want a fresh game, you can always choose Game⇨New Game; a new game is dealt and ready to play.

 The goal is to move all the cards, grouped by the four suits, to the home cells (the four cells in the upper-right corner) stacked in order from Ace at the bottom to King at the top. The trick here is that you get four free cells (the four cells in the upper-left corner) where you can manually move a card out of the way to free up a move. You can also use those four slots to allow you to move up to four cards in a stack at once. (For example, you might want to move a Jack, 10, 9, and 8 all together onto a Queen.) You can move only as many cards as there are free cells available plus one. Free spaces in the rows of card stacks also act as free cells. You win when you have four stacks of cards for each of the four suits placed on the home cells.

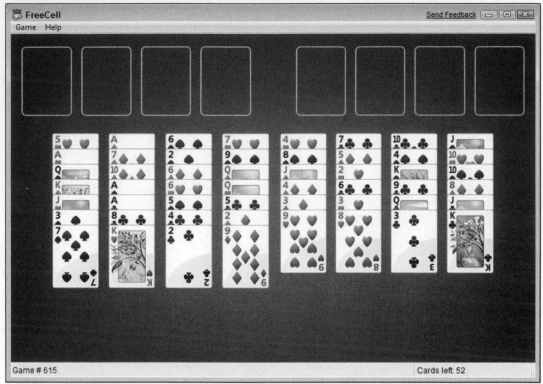

Figure 17-3

3. Click a card; to move it, click a free cell or another card at
the bottom of a column. **Figure 17-4** shows a game where
two free cells are already occupied.

> If you move a card to a free cell, you can move it back
> to the bottom of a column, but only on a card one
> higher in an alternate color. You could move a 3 of
> hearts to a 4 of spades, for example. You stack the cards
> in the columns in alternating colors, but the cards in
> the home cells end up in order and all in one suit.

> If you get hooked on this game, try going to www.
> freecell.org, a web site devoted to FreeCell. Here
> you can engage in live games with other players, read
> more about the rules and strategies, and even buy
> FreeCell merchandise. (Don't say I didn't warn you
> about the possibility of addiction.)

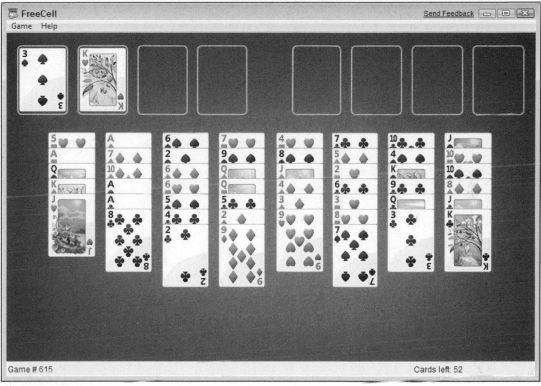

Figure 17-4

Play Spider Solitaire

1. Choose Start➪Games; in the Games window, double-click Spider Solitaire. If you've never played the game before, the Select Difficulty window appears. Click your comfort level: Beginner, Intermediate, or Advanced.

2. In the resulting game window, click a card and then click another card or drag it to the bottom of another stack or to an empty stack so that you match the same suit in each stack, moving in descending order from King to Ace. (See **Figure 17-5**.)

3. Move a card to turn over a new card automatically in the stack.

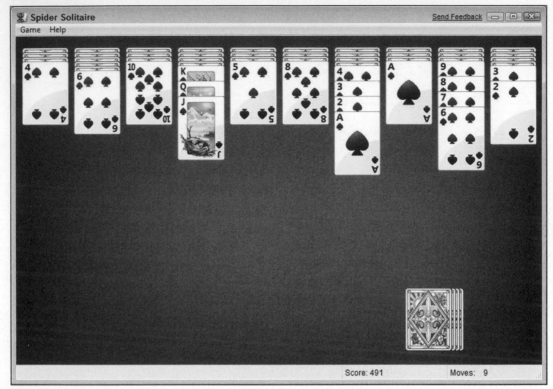

Figure 17-5

4. After you complete a set of cards in a suit, those cards are moved off the game area. The goal is to remove all the cards in the fewest moves. You can

- **Deal a new set of cards.** Choose Game⇨New Game or click the stack of cards in the bottom-right corner to deal a new set of cards. (*Note:* You are prompted to quit, restart, or keep playing; choose Keep Playing.)

- **Save your game.** Choose Game⇨Exit and then click Save in the Exit Game dialog box to save your game.

- **Change the options.** Choose Game⇨Options (see **Figure 17-6**) and select a new difficulty level. Other options mainly affect how (or whether) you save games and open them to continue, and whether the variously annoying or angelic sounds play when you click a card, deal a card, or fold a stack (assuming your laptop system is set up with a sound card and speakers).

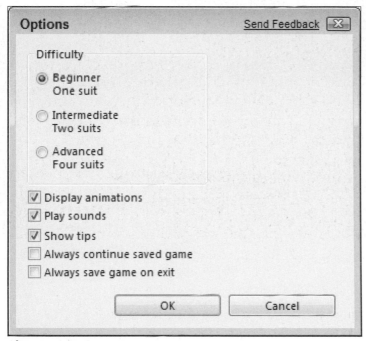

Figure 17-6

5. When you finish playing, click the Close button and either click Save or Don't Save in the Exit Game dialog box.

 Stuck for a move? Try choosing Game⇨Hint. Various combinations of cards are highlighted in sequence to suggest a likely next step in the game. If you're not stuck but just bored with the appearance of the game, choose Game⇨Change Appearance and select another desk and background style.

Play Minesweeper

1. Choose Start⇨Games; in the Games window, double-click Minesweeper. If you've never played the game, a Select Difficulty dialog box appears. Click your selection.

2. The Minesweeper game board opens. (See **Figure 17-7**.) Click a square on the board, and a timer starts counting the seconds of your game.

- If you click a square and numbers appear in various squares, the number tells you how many mines are within the up to eight squares surrounding that square; if it remains blank, there are no mines within the eight squares surrounding it.

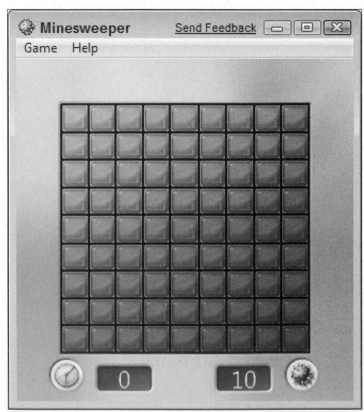

Figure 17-7

• If you click a square and a bomb appears, all the hidden bombs are exposed (see **Figure 17-8**), and the game is over.

• Right-click a square once to place a flag on it marking it as a mine. Right-click a square twice to place a question mark on it if you think it might contain a bomb to warn yourself to stay away for now.

3. To begin a new game, choose Game⇒New Game. In the New Game dialog box, click Quit and Start a New Game. If you want to play a game with the same settings as the previous one, click Restart This Game.

Figure 17-8

4. You can set several game options through the Game menu:

   • To change the expertise required, choose Game⇨ Options and then choose Beginner, Intermediate, or Advanced.

   • To change the color of the playing board, choose Game⇨Change Appearance.

   • If you want to see how many games you've won, your longest winning or losing streak, and other such figures, choose Game⇨Statistics.

5. To end the game, click the Close button and, when prompted to save the game, click Save or Don't Save.

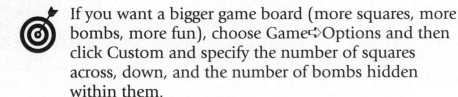 If you want a bigger game board (more squares, more bombs, more fun), choose Game⇨Options and then click Custom and specify the number of squares across, down, and the number of bombs hidden within them.

Play Hearts

1. Choose Start⇨Games and double-click Hearts.

2. In the resulting Hearts window, as shown in **Figure 17-9**, your hand is displayed while others are hidden. Begin play by clicking three cards to pass to your opponent, and then click the Pass Left button. (It's the big arrow above the bottom row of cards.)

3. Each player moving clockwise around the window plays a card of the same suit by clicking it. The one who plays the highest card of the suit in play wins the trick. (A *trick* is the cards you collect when you play the highest card of the suit.)

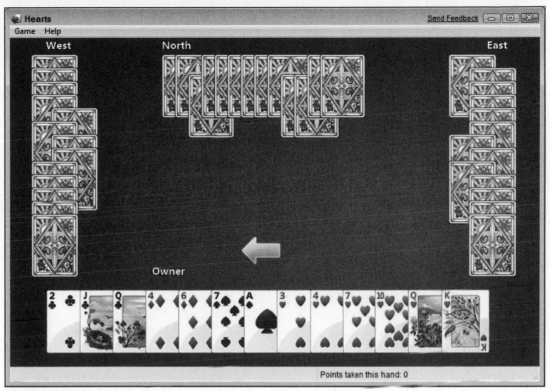

Figure 17-9

4. Choose Game⇨Options to change the settings shown in **Figure 17-10.** You can rename the other three players, play sounds, show tips, or specify how to save a game.

5. To end the game, choose Game⇨Exit or click the Close button. When prompted, either Save or Don't Save the game.

Check out the menus in the Games window for organizing and customizing the various games that Windows 7 makes available and to set Parental Controls.

Figure 17-10

Play Chess Titans

1. Chess is an ancient game of strategy. If you're a chess buff, you'll enjoy playing a computer opponent in the Windows version, Chess Titans. To begin playing chess, choose Start⇨Games; in the Games window, double-click Chess Titans. The first time you play the game, the Select Difficulty window appears. Click a skill level to start a game.

2. In the resulting Chess Titans window, a new game is ready to play. By default, a new game will be played against the computer, but you can choose to play another person when you start a new game. If you want to start a new game at any time, you can always choose Game⇨ New Game Against Computer or New Game Against Human; a new game is ready to play.

3. Click a piece; all possible moves are highlighted. To move the piece, click the space to which you want to move it. Once you make a play, your opponent (either the computer or another human) moves a piece. **Figure 17-11** shows a game in progress, with possible moves highlighted.

Possible moves are highlighted

Figure 17-11

 You can change the game options so that possible moves are not highlighted. Choose Game⇨Options. In the resulting Options window, deselect the Show Valid Moves check box and then click OK. The Options dialog box also lets you control a variety of other settings, including whether you're playing as black or white, whether to show tips or play sounds, and the quality of graphics. If you're new to the game, which is rather complex, try visiting www. chess.com for beginner instructions and strategies.

Don't like the look of your chessboard? You can modify it to look like a different material, such as wood.
Choose Game➪Change Appearance. In the Change
Appearance window, click a style of chess piece and a
style of chessboard. Click OK to save your settings.

Play Checkers Online

1. Just about everybody has played checkers. The Microsoft
version is an online game where you're matched with
another player. Click the Start menu and choose Games.
In the Games window, double-click Internet Checkers.

2. The game is displayed (see **Figure 17-12**) and indicates
which color you are (Red or White) and whose turn it is.
When it's your turn, click on a checker and drag it where
you want to go (moving kittycorner, one space to the
right or left of your current position).

Figure 17-12

3. When you're in a position to "jump" an opponent, drag your checker diagonally to the space on the other side of his piece. If you have two jumps, move the piece once and release the mouse, then move it again and release the mouse. Remember: Your goal is to get your checkers to the row on the opposite side of the board to get them kinged. Once kinged, a piece can move in any diagonal direction.

4. If you wish to chat during the game, click the arrow on the Select a Message to Send and choose a phrase. Your back-and-forth chat is displayed in the bottom window of the game, as shown in **Figure 17-13**.

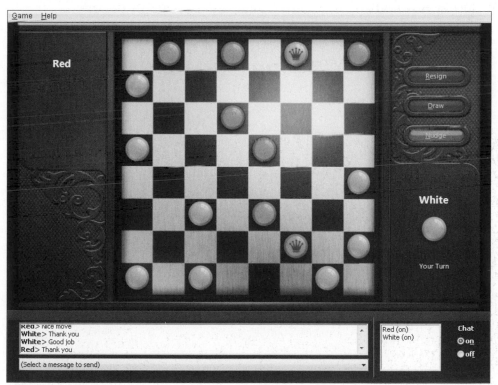

Figure 17-13

5. To end the game, play till somebody wins — or click the Resign button. If you have to leave before the game is over, it's polite to send a message such as "Sorry, I have to go now" through chat.

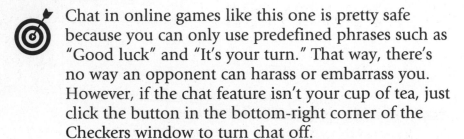 Chat in online games like this one is pretty safe because you can only use predefined phrases such as "Good luck" and "It's your turn." That way, there's no way an opponent can harass or embarrass you. However, if the chat feature isn't your cup of tea, just click the button in the bottom-right corner of the Checkers window to turn chat off.

If you aren't comfortable making the moves required when playing games with your laptop's touchpad or other style of built-in mouse, it might be worth investing in a wireless mouse. Many highly portable models exist, and they're easy to connect, use, and carry with you on the road.

Dabbling with Online Programs

*T*oday you can access a world of functional-ity from the Internet. You can create and share documents, share photos, and play online games, all without ever installing a piece of software on your laptop.

In this chapter, I give you a sampling of a few popular sites and tools you can use to really experience all the Internet offers you, but there are many more sites out there that you can explore on your own.

Understand the Cloud

You may have heard the term "cloud comput-ing" in recent years. The term "cloud" comes from networking: IT people would talk about anything that wasn't their network's own hardware as "being in the cloud" — in effect, "somewhere out there." Today, *cloud computing* refers to activities that once were bound to your computer but are now hosted on the Internet.

Yesterday you installed software on your com-puter to use it. Today, there are many software programs that are hosted online, such as Google Docs. Using these you can work on documents on the Internet without ever installing the software on your computer. In the past you stored documents and photos on your computer or on a disc. Today, you can store all kinds of content online and use tools and sites to edit that content and share it with others.

One of the major advantages of doing things in the cloud is the ability to access tools and content from anywhere. If you store files on your laptop but happen to be at your son's house without it, you can still show him those photos of your fishing trip from his family's computer using a photo sharing site such as Flickr. If you want to edit a spreadsheet but don't have Excel or Numbers installed on your laptop, you can find an online version of an Office program to get your work done.

Use Google Docs

1. Google Docs is a free, cloud-based set of tools for creating and sharing documents. You have to have a Gmail account to use Google Docs, so go to www.gmail.com and create an account if you don't already have one.

2. Next, go to www.docs.google.com. The sign-in page shown in **Figure 18-1** appears.

3. Enter your Google Username and Password and click the Sign In button. In the screen shown in **Figure 18-2**, click the Upload button to upload existing documents and share them, or click Create New to create a new document.

Figure 18-1

The Create New and Upload buttons

Figure 18-2

Note that, using the Create New menu, you can create a word-processed document, presentation, spreadsheet, form, or drawing. You can even create a document from a set of templates, as shown in **Figure 18-3.** Once you create a new document of any type, you'll encounter a software environment that you should find familiar if you've worked in any type of productivity software such as Works, iWorks, or Microsoft Office. When you finish working on a document, you can save it or share it with others.

Figure 18-3

 If you want to use Google Docs more after dabbling with it here, consider getting *Google Business Solutions All-In-One For Dummies* by Bud E. Smith and Ryan C. Williams (John Wiley & Sons, Inc.).

Exchange Files Using SkyDrive

There are several sites you can use to exchange documents. Google Docs allows you not only to create and work on documents, but also to share them with others. Another site called SkyDrive from Microsoft is also focused on sharing files with others.

To use SkyDrive, you have to have a Windows Live ID. To do that, go to www.live.com and create an account (this is an e-mail account but also allows you access many Microsoft online services, including SkyDrive).

Once you have a Windows Live account, go to www.skydrive.com sign in using your ID, and then follow these steps to upload a file:

1. Click the Add Files link shown in **Figure 18-4.**

Click this link

Figure 18-4

2. In the Select a Folder screen, click a folder to upload the file to.

If you have not yet created any folders, click New Folder and enter a name for the folder in the following screen and then click Next.

3. In the window shown in **Figure 18-5,** you have two options to choose what file(s) to upload:

- Open a new window in Windows Explorer and drag files to the empty box.

- Click to select a folder and locate documents from your computer and choose files from the Open dialog box and click the Open button.

Figure 18-5

4. Click the Continue button and your file is uploaded.

Now, from the SkyDrive home page (get there by moving your mouse pointer over the Windows Live logo in the upper-left corner and choosing SkyDrive from the drop-down menu), you can click any folder and add more files, share files with others, sort the files in the folder, or even create new documents and work on them with Office Web Apps online. When you share a file, a link to the file is e-mailed to the person you want to be able to access it.

Open E-mail Attachments in Office Online

If you get an e-mail with an attachment, certain e-mail programs such as Google's Gmail and Windows Live Hotmail allow you to open and even edit them using their productivity programs. Gmail uses Google Docs, and Windows Live Hotmail uses Office Web Apps.

To open an attachment from a Windows Live Hotmail e-mail account, follow these steps:

1. Click an e-mail message that includes an attachment in Windows Live Hotmail.

2. Click the View Online button (see **Figure 18-6**). The Word Web App opens, displaying the document.

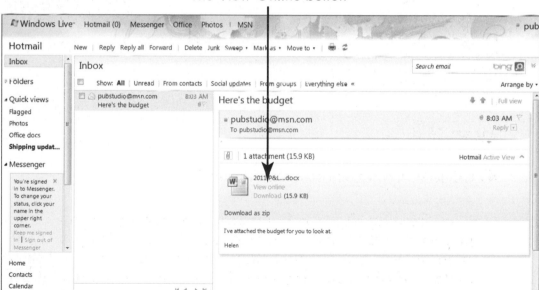

The View Online button

Figure 18-6

3. Click the Edit in Browser button, and the document opens for editing in the Word Web App shown in **Figure** 18-7.

This program offers a simplified version of tools contained in the full Microsoft Word program.

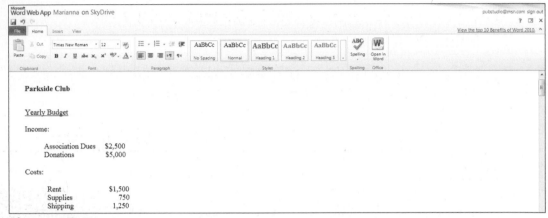

Figure 18-7

4. Use the buttons and menus in Word Web to work on the document, or click the Open in Word button to work on the document from the software installed on your computer.

5. When you've finished making changes, use the commands on the File menu to save, print, or share your changes with others.

 When you open and save a document in an Office Web app, it is saved to SkyDrive. See the previous task for information about accessing your SkyDrive account.

Share Photos and Videos Online

The ability to share photos and videos online gives you a chance to share memories with family and friends who are distant. Many image-sharing sites offer this service for free, including Snapfish, Shutterfly, and Flickr.

Many social networking sites such as Facebook also allow you to share photos and videos with those who have permission to view your page.

Flickr.com is owned by Yahoo!. Here's how to open an account on Flickr and share photos or videos:

1. Go to www.flickr.com and click the Sign Up Now button shown in **Figure 18-8**.

Note that if you already have a Yahoo! or Facebook account, you can use those to sign in to Flickr.

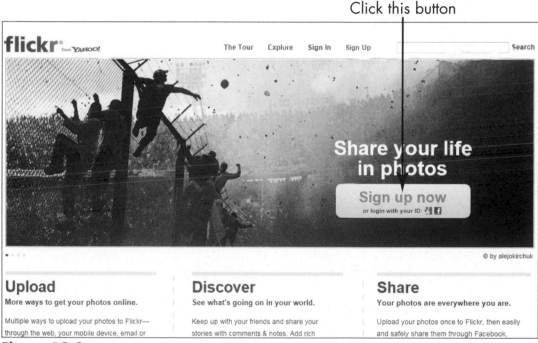

Figure 18-8

2. Click Create New Account.

3. In the form that appears, shown in **Figure 18-9**, enter the required information about you, your ID and password, and password questions.

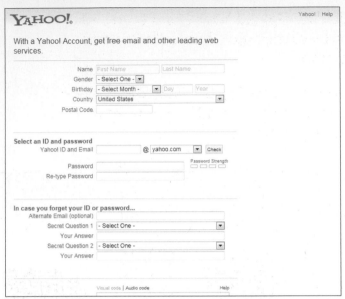

Figure 18-9

4. Enter the code that's displayed, and then click the Create My Account button. The screen shown in **Figure 18-10** appears, telling you how to get started using Flickr.

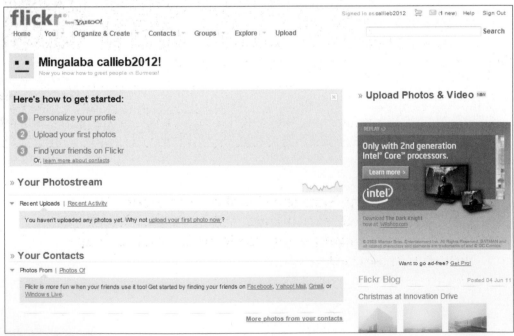

Figure 18-10

5. To upload files, click the Upload Your First Photos link. On the following screen, click the Choose Photos and Videos link that appears.

6. In the Select Files to Upload dialog box that appears (see **Figure 18-11**), locate the photo or video you want to upload and click the Open button.

Figure 18-11

7. Click to select a privacy level, as shown in **Figure 18-12**: Private — to make your images visible only to friends (or to friends and family) — or Public, which makes them viewable by anybody.

Select a privacy level

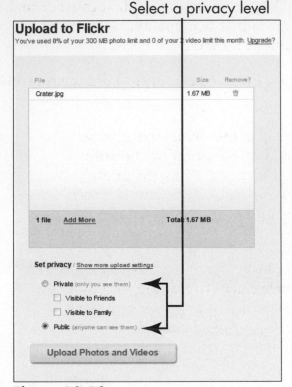

Figure 18-12

8. Click the Upload Photos and Videos button. A bar is displayed to show your upload in progress. At this point, you can add a description to the file if you like by clicking the Add a Description link.

 To see the photos you have uploaded to Flickr (called your Photostream), Click the You tab at the top of the screen. Once you've uploaded images you can tag them or identify which people appear in them so you can search them easily, set them up in Galleries, or designate Favorites.

Play Online Games

There are thousands of gaming sites online that let you interact with other players from around the world. Search in your browser using keywords such as *card games* or *chess* to find them. Some are simple games like poker or chess. Others are part of sophisticated virtual worlds where you take on an online personality, called an *avatar*, and can even acquire virtual money and goods.

Here are some tips for getting involved in online gaming and some advice for staying safe:

➡ Safety first! You're playing games with strangers, so avoid giving out personal information or choosing a revealing username. If somebody is inappropriately emotional or abusive while playing the game, leave the game immediately and report the player to the site owner.

➡ In some cases, you can play a computer; in others, you're playing against other people that the game site matches you up with. You can usually request a level of play, so if you're a beginner, you can feel comfortable that you'll be matched with other beginners.

➡ To play some games, you might need additional software, such as Adobe Shockwave Player or software to enable your laptop to play animations. If you see such a message on a game site, be sure you're downloading software from a reputable source that has a good privacy policy for users — and credentials like a Better Business Bureau seal so you don't download a virus or spyware.

➡ Many games are free, though some require that you enter information about yourself to become a member. Read the fine print carefully when signing up.

➡ Many game sites offer tutorials or practice games to help you learn and improve. **Figure 18-13** shows the Tutorial page for Legends of Norrath, a multiplayer online role-playing game.

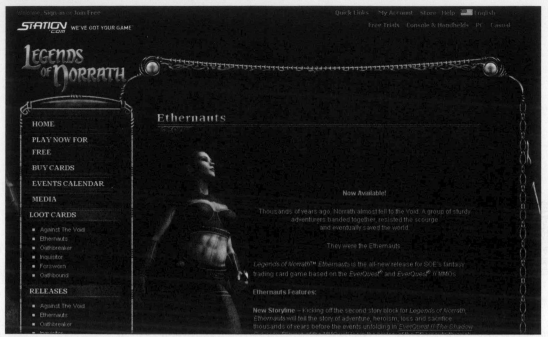

Figure 18-13

➡ Some games allow several players to participate at once, so you might have to be on your toes! In addition to manipulating pieces or characters, you might also be able to communicate with other players using instant messaging or even voice messages. Chapter 23 explains how instant messaging works.

➡ Online gaming can be addictive, so be as moderate in your playing online as you are offline. Remember that these games are just for fun.

 If you aren't comfortable making the moves required when playing games with your laptop's touchpad or other style of built-in mouse, it might be worth investing in a wireless mouse. Many highly portable models exist; they are easy to connect, use, and carry with you on the road.

Part IV
Exploring the Internet

The 5th Wave   By Rich Tennant

"He saw your laptop and wants to know if he can check his email."

Understanding Internet Basics

Many people buy a laptop mainly to tap in to the wonderful opportunities the Internet offers. You can use the Internet to check stock quotes, play interactive games with others, and file your taxes, for example. For seniors especially, the Internet can provide wonderful ways to keep in touch with family and friends located around the country or on the other side of the world via e-mail, video phone calls, or instant messaging. You can share photos of your grandchildren or connect with others who share your hobbies or interests.

But before you begin all those wonderful activities, it helps to understand some basics about the Internet and how it works.

This chapter helps you to understand what the Internet and World Wide Web are, as well as some basics about connecting to the Internet and navigating it.

Understand What the Internet Is

The Internet, links, the web . . . people and the media bounce around many online-related terms these days, and folks sometimes use them incorrectly. Your first step in getting familiar with the Internet is to understand what some of these terms mean.

Here's a list of common Internet-related terms:

➠ The *Internet* is a large network of computers that contain information and technology tools that can be accessed by anybody with an Internet connection. (See the next task for information about Internet connections.)

➠ Residing on that network of computers is a huge set of documents, which form the *World Wide Web*, usually referred to as just the *web*.

➠ The web includes *web sites*, which are made up of collections of *web pages* just as a book is made up of chapters that contain individual pages. Web sites can be informational and/or host communication tools such as *chats* or *discussion boards* that allow people to "talk" via text messages. They may also allow you to share files with others or use software applications without having to install them on your computer.

➠ You can buy, bid for, or sell a wide variety of items in an entire online marketplace referred to as the world of *e-commerce*.

➠ To get around online, you use a software program called a *browser*. There are many browsers available, and they're free. Internet Explorer is Microsoft's browser; others include Mozilla Firefox, Google Chrome, and Opera. Browsers offer tools to help you navigate from web site to web site and from one web page to another.

➠ When you open a web site, you might see colored text or graphics that represent *hyperlinks*, also referred to as *links*. You can click links to move from place to place within a web page, on a web site, or between web documents. **Figure 19-1** shows some hyperlinks indicated by highlighted text (such as Don't Miss Out) or graphics (such as the Free Download button).

Click a text hyperlink   Click a graphical hyperlink

Figure 19-1

 A link can be a graphic (such as a company logo) or text. A text link is identifiable by colored text, and it's usually underlined. After you click a link, it usually changes color to show that you've followed the link.

Explore Different Types of Internet Connections

Before you can connect to the Internet for the first time, you have to have certain hardware in place and choose your *Internet service provider* (also referred to as *ISP* or simply a *provider*). An ISP is a company that owns dedicated computers (called *servers*) that you use to access the Internet. ISPs charge a monthly fee for this service.

In the past, you could sign up with an ISP such as Microsoft's MSN to get dial-up access (that is, access via your regular phone line) to the Internet. Today, many people pay to access the Internet through their telephone or cable-television provider, whose connections are much faster than a dial-up connection.

You can choose a type of connection to go online. Depending on the type of connection you want, you'll go to a different company for the service. For example, a DSL connection might come through your phone company, whereas a cable connection is available through your cable-TV company. Wireless connections provide a convenient and sometimes free way to go online when you travel with your laptop. You can use them for free at Wi-Fi hotspots, or you can subscribe to a wireless network so that you can pick up Wi-Fi signals as you roam.

 Some laptops and tablet devices can pick up a connection from a 3G-enabled cellphone if they are out of range of a network, though this usually involves paying an additional fee to your cellphone company.

Not every type of connection is necessarily available in every area, so check with phone, cable, and small Internet providers in your town to find out your options and costs. (Some offer discounts to AARP members, for example.)

Here are the most common types of connections:

➡ **Dial-up connections:** With a dial-up connection, you plug your laptop into a phone line at home or at a hotel room or friend's house to connect to the Internet, entering a phone number that's provided by your ISP. This is the slowest connection method, but it's relatively inexpensive. Your dial-up Internet provider will give you *local access numbers*, which you use to go online. Using these local access numbers, you won't incur long distance charges for your connection. However, with this type of connection, you can't use a phone line for phone calls while you're connected to the Internet, so it's no longer a very popular way to connect.

➡ **Digital Subscriber Line:** DSL also uses a phone line, but your phone is available to you to make calls even when you're connected to the Internet. DSL is a form of broadband communication, which may use phone lines and fiber-optic cables for transmission.

You have to subscribe to a broadband service (check with your phone company) and pay a monthly fee for access.

➡ **Cable:** You can go through your local cable company to get your Internet service via the cable that brings your TV programming rather than your phone line. This is another type of broadband service, and it's also faster than a dial-up connection. Check with your cable company for monthly fees.

➡ **Satellite:** Especially in rural areas, satellite Internet providers may be your only option. This requires that you install a satellite dish. BlueDish and Comcast are two providers of satellite connections to check into.

➡ **Wireless hotspots:** If you take a wireless-enabled laptop computer with you on a trip, you can piggy-back on a connection somebody else has made. You will find wireless hotspots in many public places, such as airports, cafes, and hotels. If you're in range of such a hotspot, your laptop usually finds the connection automatically, making Internet service available to you for free or for a fee.

Internet connections have different speeds that depend partially on your laptop's capabilities and partially on the connection you get from your provider. Before you choose a provider, it's important to understand how faster connection speeds can benefit you:

➡ Faster speeds allow you to send data faster. In addition, web pages and images display faster.

➡ Dial-up connection speeds run at the low end, about 56 kilobits per second, or Kbps. Most broadband connections today are around 500 to 600 Kbps. If you have a slower connection, a file might take minutes to upload (for example, a file you're attaching to an e-mail). This same operation might take only seconds at a higher speed.

Depending on your type of connection, you'll need different hardware:

→ A broadband connection uses an Ethernet cable and a modem, which your provider should make available, as well as a connection to your phone or cable line.

→ Some laptops come with a built-in modem for dial-up connections (though these are being left out more and more as people move to wireless connections) or are enabled for wireless service. If you choose a broadband connection, your phone or cable company will provide you with an external modem and wireless router (usually for a price). Remember, though, that you can't use this connection when you travel with your laptop.

→ If you have a laptop that doesn't have a built-in wireless modem, you can add this hardware by buying a wireless CardBus adapter PC card at any office supply or computer store. This card enables a laptop to pick up wireless signals.

Many providers offer free or low-cost setup when you open a new account. If you're not technical by nature, consider taking advantage of this when you sign up.

If you fly with your laptop, you may not be able to connect to the Internet during the flight. Also, it's important to remember that during takeoff and landing, you'll be asked to turn off electronics so that they don't interfere with air traffic communications. Be alert to the announcement if you intend to use your laptop on the plane. Some tablet computers come with an Airport setting that disables any disruptive communications while in flight.

Set Up an Internet Connection

1. The first step in going online is to set up a connection in Windows so that you can access the Internet. Choose Start⇨Control Panel⇨Network and Internet.

2. In the resulting window, click Network and Sharing Center.

3. In the resulting Network and Sharing Center window (see **Figure** 19-2), click the Set Up a New Connection or Network link.

Click this link

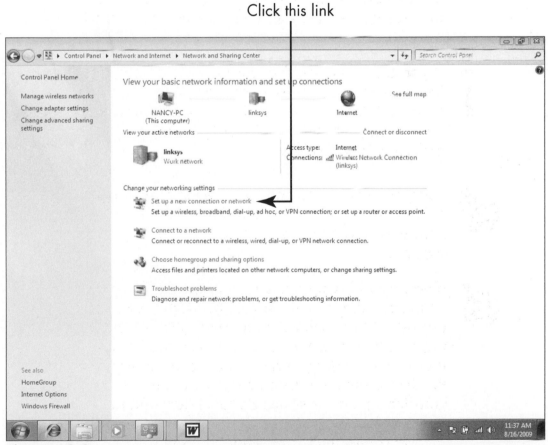

Figure 19-2

4. In the Choose A Connection Option window, click Next to accept the default option of creating a new Internet connection. If you are already connected to the Internet, a window appears; click Set Up A New Connection Anyway.

5. In the resulting dialog box, click your connection. (These steps follow the selection of Broadband.)

6. In the resulting dialog box, as shown in **Figure 19-3**, enter your username, password, and connection name (if you want to assign one) and then click Connect. Windows detects the connection automatically, and the Network and Sharing Center appears with your connection listed.

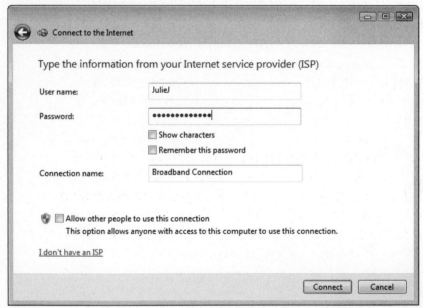

Figure 19-3

 In many cases, if you have a disc from your ISP, you don't need to follow the preceding steps. Just pop that DVD into your DVD-ROM drive, and in no time, a window appears that gives you the steps to follow to get set up.

Compare Popular Browsers

A *browser* is a program that you use to navigate around the Internet. Popular browsers include Internet Explorer from Microsoft, Firefox from Mozilla, Opera from Opera Software, Chrome from Google, and Safari from Apple.

Most browsers have similar features and all are free. Internet Explorer is pre-installed on Windows-based laptops, but you can download any browser by going to its associated web site. You can install and use multiple browsers if you like. Here are some features to consider when choosing a browser:

➡ **Safety features:** Browsing the web can be dangerous; certain sites will attempt to download dangerous programs such as viruses to your computer. Even if you have an antivirus program installed on your computer, choose a browser with robust security and privacy features. An advisor feature that ranks sites based on their safety record when they appear in search results is a good feature to have.

➡ **Favorites and Bookmarking:** The ability to save links to sites you like to visit often is very useful. Just about every browser has such features, but some also provide a feature such as IE's Popular Sites dedicated to a one-stop place for accessing your most-often visited sites that may appeal to you.

➡ **Tabs:** Browsers that use *tabs* allow you to open more than one site at a time so you can jump back and forth among them or open an additional site easily. Most of the current browsers use the tab approach, but an older version of a browser may not. Don't worry, you can always update a browser by going to the browser site and downloading the latest version.

Navigate the Web

1. You need to learn how to get around the web using a browser such as the popular Internet Explorer (IE) from Microsoft. Open IE by clicking the Internet Explorer icon in the Windows Taskbar.

2. Enter a web address in the Address bar, as shown in **Figure 19-4,** and then press Enter.

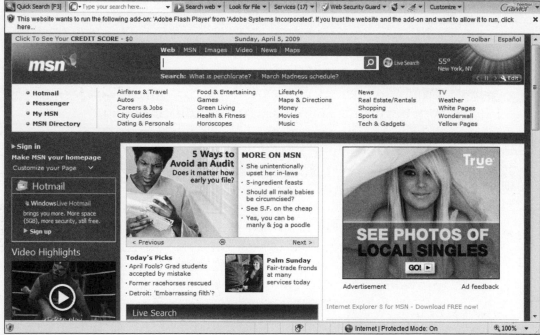

Figure 19-4

3. On the resulting web site, click a link (short for *hyperlink;* a *link* takes you to another online page or document), display another page on the site using navigation tools on the page (such as the Education tab on the page), or enter another address in the address bar to proceed to another page.

 A text link is identifiable by colored text, usually blue. After you click a link, it usually changes to another color (such as purple) to show that it's been followed.

4. Click the Back button to move back to the first page that you visited. Click the Forward button to go forward to the second page that you visited.

5. Click the down-pointing arrow at the far right of the Address bar to display a list of sites that you visited recently, as shown in **Figure 19-5**. Click a site in this list to go there.

Click the arrow

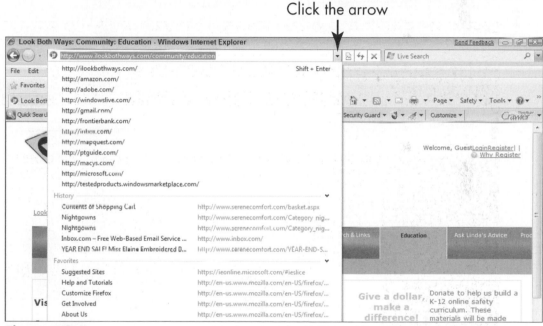

Figure 19-5

The Refresh and Stop buttons on the right end of the Address bar are useful for navigating sites. Clicking the Refresh button redisplays the current page. This is especially useful if a page updates information frequently, such as on a stock market site. You can also use the Refresh button if a page doesn't load correctly; it might load correctly when refreshed. Clicking the Stop button stops a page that's loading. So, if you made a mistake entering the address, or if the page is taking longer than you'd like to load, click the Stop button to halt the process.

Use Tabs in Browsers

1. Tabs allow you to have several web pages open at once and easily switch among them. With Internet Explorer open, click New Tab (the smallest, blank tab on the far right side of the tabs).

2. When the new tab appears, your most popular sites are displayed (see **Figure 19-6**). You can click on a popular site, or enter a URL in the Address bar and press Enter. The URL opens in that tab. You can then click other tabs to switch among sites.

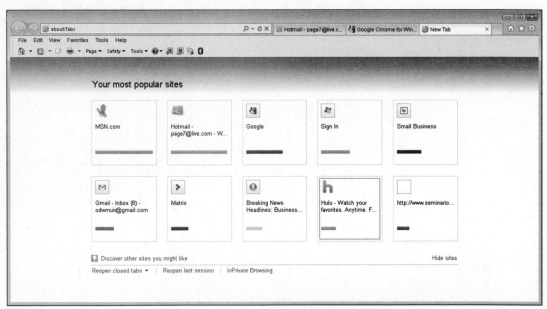

Figure 19-6

3. You can return to a page by clicking that page's tab, thumbnail, or name in the drop-down list (see **Figure 19-7**) that you display by clicking the blue arrow in the Address bar.

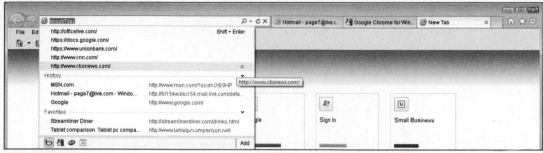

Figure 19-7

4. Close an active tab by clicking the Close button on the right side of the tab.

 A *tab* is a sort of window you can use to view any number of sites. (But you don't have to create a new tab to go to another site. You can navigate to a new site from a page in a tab that you're done looking at.) Having the ability to keep a few tabs open at a time means you can more quickly switch between two or more sites without navigating back and forth either with the Previous or Next buttons or by entering URLs. You can also create more than one Home Page tab that can appear every time you open IE. See the next task "Set Up a Home Page" for more about this.

 You can also press Ctrl+T to open a new tab in Internet Explorer. Also, if you want to keep one tab open and close all others, right-click the tab you want to keep open and choose Close Other Tabs.

Set Up a Home Page

1. Your home page(s) appear automatically every time you log on to the Internet, so choose one or a few sites that you go to often for this setting. Open Internet Explorer and choose Tools⇨Internet Options.

2. In the resulting Internet Options dialog box, on the General tab, enter a web site address to use as your home page, as shown in **Figure 19-8,** and then click OK. Note that you can enter several home pages that will appear on different tabs every time you open IE, as shown in **Figure 19-8.**

Alternatively, click one of the following preset option buttons shown in **Figure 19-8:**

- **Use Current:** Sets whatever page is currently displayed in the browser window as your home page.

- **Use Default:** This setting sends you to the MSN web page.

- **Use Blank:** If you're a minimalist, this setting is for you. No web page displays; you just see a blank area.

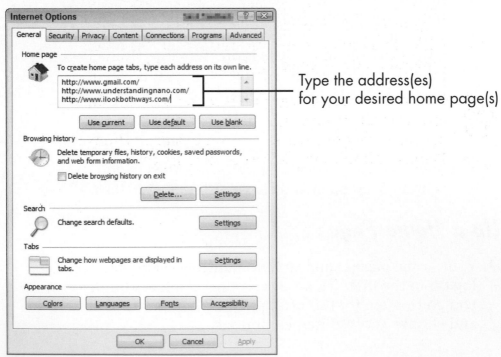

Type the address(es)
for your desired home page(s)

Figure 19-8

3. Click the Home Page icon (see **Figure** 19-9) on the IE toolbar (it looks like a little house) to go to your home page.

The Home Page icon

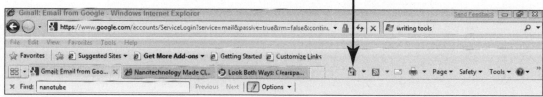

Figure 19-9

 If you want to have more than one home page, you can create multiple home-page tabs that will appear onscreen when you click the Home button. Click the arrow on the Home button and choose Add or Change Home Page. In the Add or Change Home Page dialog box that appears, click the Add This Web Page to Your Home Page Tabs radio button, and then click Yes. Display other sites and repeat this procedure for all the home-page tabs you want.

 To remove a home page you have set up, click the arrow on the Home Page button, choose Remove, and then choose a particular home page or choose Remove All from the submenu that appears.

Browsing the Web with Internet Explorer

Chapter

20

A *browser* is a program that you can use to move from one web page to another. You can also use a browser to search for information, web sites, videos, and images. Most browsers, such as Internet Explorer (IE) and Google Chrome are available for free. Macintosh computers come with a browser called Safari installed, but you can also download and use Safari on Windows-based computers.

Chapter 19 introduces browser basics, such as how to go directly to a site when you know the web address, how to use the Back and Forward buttons to move among sites you've visited, and how to set up the home page that opens automatically when you launch your browser.

In this chapter, you discover more ways of using Internet Explorer. By using IE, you can

➡ **Navigate all around the web.** Use the IE navigation features to go back to places you've been (via the Favorites and History features), and use Google to search for new places to visit.

➡ **Customize your browser.** You can modify what tools are available to you on Internet Explorer toolbars to make your work online easier.

➡ **Work with RSS feeds.** On the Internet, you can use RSS feeds to get content from sites sent to you to keep you up to date on news or opinions from various sources.

➡ **Print content from web pages.** When you find what you want online, such as a graphic image or article, just use Print to generate a hard copy.

➡ **Play podcasts.** You can listen to *podcasts*, which are audio programs you find on many web sites covering a variety of topics.

➡ **Manage your finances.** You can get financial advice, bank, and even manage your investments online.

Search the Web

1. You can use words and phrases to search for information on the web using a search engine. In this example, you'll use Google, a popular search engine. Enter www.google.com in your browser Address bar.

2. Enter a search term in the text box and then click the Search button.

3. In the search results that appear (see **Figure 20-1**), you can click a link to go to that web page. If you don't see the link that you need, click and drag the scroll bar to view more results.

 You can use the Internet Explorer (IE) search feature to perform your searches (it's in the upper-right corner of IE, with a little magnifying glass button on the right edge). Change the search engine by clicking the arrow to the right of the Search field and choosing another provider listed there, or click the Find More Providers link to see a more comprehensive list.

Click a link in the results list

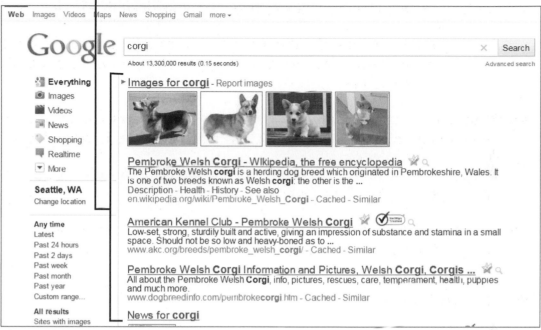

Figure 20-1

4. If you didn't find what you need in Steps 1-3, click the Advanced Search link on the Google home page to change Search parameters and narrow the search.

5. In the resulting Advanced Search page, as shown in **Figure 20-2**, modify any of the following parameters as necessary:

- **Find Web Pages That Have:** These options let you narrow the way words or phrases are searched; for example, you can find matches for the exact wording you enter.

- **But Don't Show Pages That Have:** Enter words that you want to exclude from your results. For example, you could search *countertops* and specify you don't want results that involve *laminate*.

- **Need More Tools:** Here you can control how many results are shown on a page, what language to search for, and specific file types or domains to search.

- **Date, Usage Rights, Numeric Range, and More:** Click here for even more advanced search parameters.

Type the word(s) you want to find

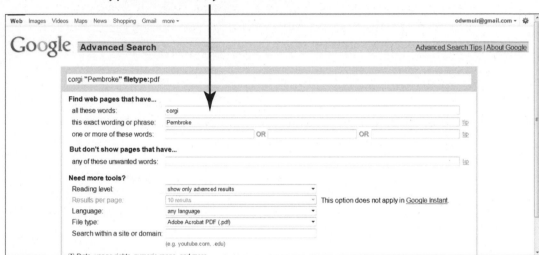

Figure 20-2

 Knowing how search engines work can save you time. For example, if you search by entering *golden retriever*, you typically get sites that contain both words or either word. If you put a plus sign between these two keywords *(golden+retriever)*, you get only sites that contain both words.

 Many search engines allow you to specify the media to search for. For example, you can search for maps, images, videos, or sound files related to your search term. In Google, for example, these options are listed across the top-left corner of the search engine screen. Enter your search term and then click the type of results you want to find.

Find Content on a Web Page

1. With Internet Explorer open and the web page that you want to search displayed, click the Edit menu and choose Find on This Page.

2. In the resulting Find toolbar that appears on the active tab, as shown in **Figure 20-3,** enter the word that you want to search for. As you type, all instances of the word on the page are highlighted. Click the Options button and use the following options to narrow your results:

- **Match Whole Word Only:** Select this option if you want to find only the whole word. (For example, use this option if you enter *elect* and want to find only *elect* and not *electron* or *electronics.*)

- **Match Case:** Select this option if you want to match the case. (For example, use this option if you enter *Catholic* and want to find only the always-capitalized religion and not the adjective *catholic.*)

3. Click the Next button and you move from one highlighted instance of the word to the next. If you want to move to a previous instance, click the Previous button.

4. When you're done searching, click the Close button on the left side of the Find toolbar.

 Many web sites have a Search This Site feature that allows you to search not only the displayed web page but all web pages on a web site, or search by department or category of item in an online store. Look for a Search text box and make sure that it searches the site — and not the entire Internet.

Enter the word to find

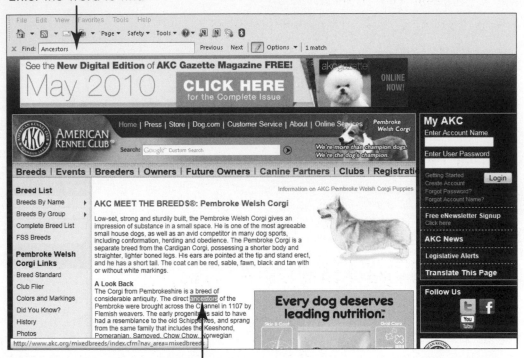

Highlighted instances of the word

Figure 20-3

Add a Web Site to Favorites

1. If there's a site you intend to revisit, you might want to save it to Internet Explorer's Favorite folder so you can easily go there again. Open IE, enter the URL of a web site that you want to add to your Favorites list, and then click Go (the button with two blue arrows on it to the right of the Address bar.

2. Click the Favorites button on the left side of Internet Explorer to display the Favorites pane, and then click the Add to Favorites button.

3. In the resulting Add a Favorite dialog box, as shown in **Figure 20-4,** modify the name of the Favorite listing to something easily recognizable. If you wish, choose another folder or create a folder to store the Favorite in.

Change the favorite name here

Figure 20-4

4. Click Add to add the site.

5. To use your Favorites list, click the Favorites button and then click the name of the site from the list that's displayed (see **Figure 20-5**) to go to that site.

Click Favorites

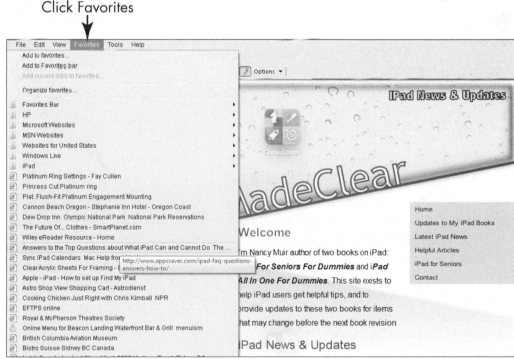

Figure 20-5

Regularly cleaning out your Favorites list is a good idea — after all, do you really need the sites that you used to plan last year's vacation? With the Favorites Center displayed (just click the Favorites button), right-click any item and then choose Delete or Rename to modify the favorite listing.

 Because you might travel with your laptop and encounter all kinds of folks and risk it being stolen, be careful about setting up your browser to remember passwords and then saving those sites as favorites. For example, say you have an account at Amazon.com, save Amazon as a favorite, and have set up Internet Explorer to remember your password at Amazon. Somebody could check your favorites for such sites, and then use your laptop to log on and purchase items using your account. See Chapter 21 for more about staying safe when using your laptop.

Organize Favorites

1. You can organize favorites into folders to make them easier to find. With Internet Explorer open, click the Favorites button to open the Favorites pane. Click the arrow on the right end of the Add to Favorites button and then choose Organize Favorites.

2. In the resulting Organize Favorites dialog box (see **Figure 20-6**), click the New Folder, Move, Rename, or Delete buttons to organize your favorites.

3. When you finish organizing your Favorites, click Close.

Select a favorite...

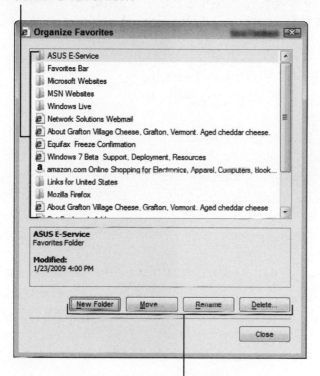

Then click an action

Figure 20-6

 These steps provide a handy way to manage several sites or folders, but you can also organize favorite sites one by one by using the Favorites pane. (You display the Favorites pane by clicking the Favorites button.) Right-click any favorite site listed in the pane and choose a command: Sort by Name, Rename, or Delete, for example.

 You can create new folders to organize your favorites by choosing Organize Favorites from the Favorites menu and then clicking the New Folder button.

View Your Browsing History

1. If you went to a site recently and want to return there again but can't remember the name, you might check your browsing history to find it. Click View⇨ Explorer Bars⇨History to display the History pane. (See **Figure 20-7**.)

The History pane

Figure 20-7

2. Click the down arrow on the History button (see **Figure 20-8**) and select a sort method:

- **View By Date:** Sort favorites by date visited.

- **View By Site:** Sort alphabetically by site name.

- **View By Most Visited:** Sort with the sites visited most on top and those visited least at the bottom of the list.

- **View By Order Visited Today:** Sort by the order in which you visited sites today.

Click this arrow to change the sort method

Figure 20-8

3. In the History pane, you can click a site to go to it.

 You can also choose the arrow on the right of the Address bar to display sites you've visited.

Customize the Internet Explorer Toolbar

1. You can customize the toolbars that offer common commands in Internet Explorer so that the commands you use most often are included. Open IE.

2. Right-click just below the tools on the right side of the toolbar area and choose Customize and then Add or Remove Commands from the submenu that appears. The Customize Toolbar dialog box (as shown in **Figure 20-9**) appears.

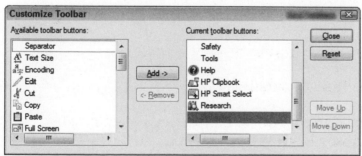

Figure 20-9

3. Click a tool on the left and then click the Add button to add it to the toolbar.

4. Click a tool on the right and then click the Remove button to remove it from the toolbar.

5. When you're finished, click Close to save your new toolbar settings. The new tools appear (see **Figure 20-10**); click the double-arrow button on the right of the toolbar to display any tools that IE can't fit onscreen.

Find new tools here

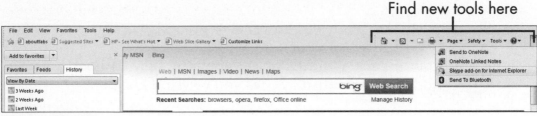

Figure 20-10

You can click to select a tool and then use the Move Up and Move Down buttons in the Customize Toolbar dialog box to rearrange the order in which tools appear on the toolbar. To reset the toolbar to defaults, click the Reset button in that same dialog box.

If you want to add some space between tools on the toolbar so that they're easier to see, click the Separator item in the Available Toolbar Buttons list and add it before or after a tool button.

Add RSS Feeds

1. If you have a site that provides content you'd like to subscribe to, you can add it to the Web Slices Gallery in Favorites. First, display the Favorites bar in IE by right-clicking in the toolbar area and choosing Favorites, and then navigate to the web site you want to add.

2. Click the Feeds button on the Favorites toolbar to display a list of available RSS feeds in the web site.

(See **Figure 20-11**.) IE features a feed technology called
Web Slices that allows you to subscribe to a portion of a
web page; note that if Web Slices are available on a site,
the Feeds button changes to a Web Slices button.

The list of feeds

Figure 20-11

3. Click a Subscribe to this Feed link somewhere on the displayed web page. (See **Figure 20-12**.) In the dialog box
that appears, click the Subscribe button.

Click this link

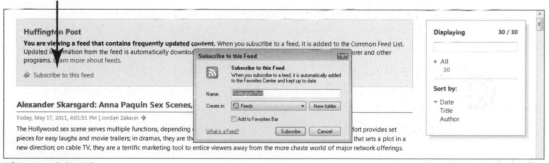

Figure 20-12

4. To view all feeds, click the View menu and choose
Explorer Bars⊅Feeds.

 The View Feeds on This Page button is grayed out
when there are no RSS feeds on the current page, and
it turns red when feeds are present.

Though Internet Explorer has an RSS feed reader built in, you can explore other feed readers. Just type **RSS feeds** into Internet Explorer's Address bar to find more information and listings of readers and RSS feed sites.

Print a Web Page

1. If a web page includes a link or button to print or display a print version of a page, click that item and follow the instructions.

2. If the page doesn't include a link for printing, click the Print button on the Internet Explorer toolbar.

3. In the resulting Print dialog box, decide how much of the document you want to print and then select one of the options in the Page Range area, as shown in **Figure 20-13**.

Choose a page range option

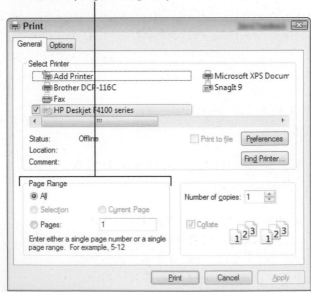

Figure 20-13

Note that choosing Current Page or entering page numbers in the Pages text box of the Print dialog box doesn't mean much when printing a web page — the whole document might print because web pages aren't divided into pages as word-processing documents are.

4. Click the up arrow in the Number of Copies text box to print multiple copies. If you want multiple copies collated, select the Collate check box.

5. After you adjust all settings you need, click Print.

Play Podcasts

Many sites offer *podcasts*, which are audio recordings of interviews, opinions, or informative oral articles. To check this out, go to The New York Times site by entering this address in your browser address bar: `www.nytimes.com/ref/multimedia/podcasts.html`.

Click the little arrow on the right of any podcast, as shown in **Figure 20-14**. The podcast begins playing. (In some cases, a podcast opens a new window with an animated display that plays during the podcast, though that doesn't happen at The New York Times site.) Use the controls to do any of the following:

➡ Click the Pause button (it has two little vertical bars on it) to stop playback.

➡ Click and drag the wedge-shaped volume control to increase or decrease the volume.

➡ Click the diamond-shaped object on the bar that shows the podcast's progress to move forward or backward in the program. Note that the time point where you are in the podcast is displayed to the right of this bar.

Click the arrow to play the podcast

Figure 20-14

Get Advice about Finances Online

You can use the Internet to access a wealth of financial information online. You can read current news stories, get advice about how to invest, and connect with others to share information. Keep in mind that the quality of information online can vary drastically, and you can't always believe everything you read. Try to find sites of reputable financial companies you might know from your offline financial dealings, such as Merrill Lynch or *Forbes* magazine. Also, never give out financial account numbers to anybody via e-mail, even if they claim to be with a reputable company.

Here are some of the resources available to you for planning and monitoring your finances. (See Chapter 19 for details about how to go to any web site.)

➥ Visit sites such as www.money.cnn.com/magazines/moneymag/money101 for simple financial lessons about topics such as setting a budget and planning your retirement, from CNN Money.

➥ Visit www.financialplan.about.com for financial planning advice by age.

➠ Search for online publications such as The Wall Street Journal (www.wallstreetjournal.com), Forbes (www.forbes.com), as shown in **Figure 20-15,** or Kiplinger (www.kiplinger.com) for articles about the latest financial and investing trends.

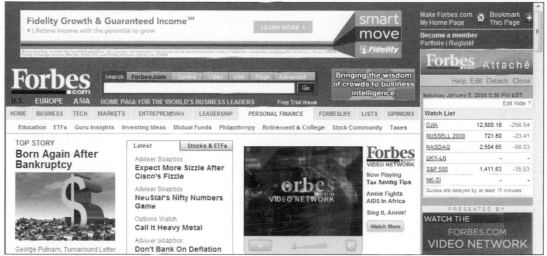

Figure 20-15

➠ Check out online discussion forums such as www. money.MSN.com to connect with others who are interested in learning more about finances. However, be very careful not to reveal too much personal information to anybody you meet online, especially about your specific finances and accounts.

In the U.S., you're entitled to order a free credit report from the three major credit reporting organizations every year, and you can order those reports online. Visit www.annualcreditreport.com to get started.

Windows 7 lets you display *gadgets* (little programs, such as a calculator, that do handy things) on your desktop. Add the Stocks gadget to check stock quotes at a glance. See Chapter 13 for details on adding gadgets.

Bank Online

Many people today are banking online because it's convenient. You can typically make account transfers, check your balance, and even download your account activity to a program such as Quicken to manage your financial records or work with your taxes.

Consider this information when banking online:

➠ Most online banks, such as Barclay's in the United Kingdom (see **Figure 20-16**), have very strong security measures in place; however, you should be sure that you're using a secure Internet connection to go online. If you use a wireless hotspot in a hotel or airport that isn't protected, for example, it's possible for someone to tap in to your online transactions. If you work on a home network, you should have whoever sets up your network enable security features and a firewall. (See Chapter 25 for an introduction to basic online security.) Also, if you use a public wireless network such as those in airports or hotels, don't log on to any financial accounts.

Figure 20-16

➠ You might need to set things up with your bank so that you can access your account online and make transfers among your different accounts. Talk to your bank about what it requires.

➠ Be careful to choose strong passwords (random combinations of letters, numbers, and punctuation are best) for accessing your bank accounts. If you write the passwords down, put them someplace safe. See Chapter 21 for advice about strong passwords.

➠ Be aware of your financial rights, such as how credit cards and bank accounts are protected by law. The FDIC web site offers lots of information about your banking and financial life at www.fdic.gov. It's specific to the United States, but some of the advice about online financial dangers is pertinent no matter where you live.

Invest Online

Every major broker has an online presence. Investing online is convenient, and online brokers enable you to place buy or sell orders very quickly and inexpensively. In addition, you can manage investment accounts online.

Here are some tips for online investing:

➠ **Understand the fees.** Online brokerage fees are typically lower than working with a full-service broker. However, online broker fees can vary widely. Shop around for a broker you trust with reasonable fees.

➠ **Buyer beware.** Though online banking is protected by most federal governments — including that of the United States — online investment accounts don't always share similar protections, depending on what country you live in. Consider asking your investment counselor for advice about how protections work in your country.

➡ **Handle various types of investments.** Beyond buying and selling stocks, you can invest in bonds, deposit to your IRA or other retirement accounts, and more. Companies such as Fidelity (www.fidelity.com) give you lots of investment choices.

➡ **Retain offline access to your account.** Remember that one downside to online investing is that if your laptop connection is down or your broker's server is down, you can't get to your online brokerage to invest. Keep a phone number handy so you can reach your broker by an alternative method in the case of technical glitches.

➡ **Check what others have to say.** Visit sites such as www.MotleyFool.com (see **Figure 20-17**) for articles and advice on investing.

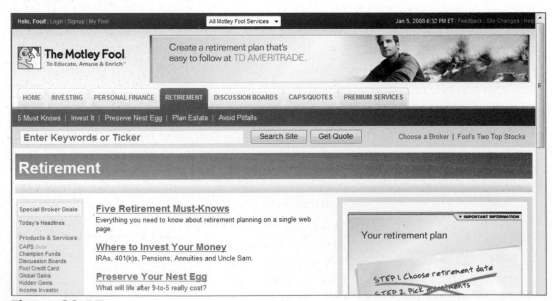

Figure 20-17

Staying Safe While Online

*f you're using your laptop to go online,
you're probably enjoying all the Internet has
to offer. But going online also brings with it
some risks. If you understand those risks, you
can learn to avoid most of them and stay relatively safe online.

In this chapter, you discover some of the risks
and safety nets that you can take advantage of
to avoid risk, starting with these points:

➥ **Understand what risks exist.** Some risks
are human, in the form of online predators wanting to steal your money or abuse
you emotionally; other risks come from
technology, such as computer viruses. For
the former, you can use the common
sense you use when interacting offline to
stay much safer. For the latter, there are
tools and browser settings to protect you.

➥ **Be aware of what information you
share.** Abuses such as identity theft occur
most often when you or somebody you
know shares information about you that's
nobody's business. Find out how to spot
who is exposing information (including
you) and what information to keep private, and you'll become much safer
online.

➠ **Avoid scams and undesirable content.** You can use the Content Advisor to limit the online locations that you can visit so that you don't encounter sites you consider undesirable. You can also find out how to spot various e-mail scams and fraud so that you don't become a victim.

➠ **Create safe passwords.** Passwords don't have to be hard to remember — just hard to guess. I provide some guidance in this chapter about creating passwords that are hard to crack.

Understand Technology Risks on the Internet

When you buy a car, it has certain safety features built in, though you may have go to the dealer's service department to have a faulty part replaced now and then. Your laptop is similar to your car in terms of the need for safety. It comes with an operating system (such as Microsoft Windows) built in, and that operating system has security features. Sometimes that operating system has flaws that have to be repaired, or new threats emerge after it's installed. You need to get regular updates to keep your computer secure.

As you use your laptop, you're exposing it to dangerous conditions and situations that you have to guard against. Threats to your laptop security can come from a file you copy from a disc you insert into your laptop, but most of the time, the danger is that you'll download a harmful program from the Internet. These downloads can happen when you click a link, open an attachment in an e-mail, or download one piece of software without realizing that *malware* (malicious software) is attached to it.

You need to be aware of these three main types of malware:

➠ A *virus* is a little program that some nasty person thought up to spread around the Internet and infect computers. A virus can do a variety of things, but typically, it attacks your data, deleting files, scrambling data, or making changes to your system settings that cause your laptop to grind to a halt.

➠ *Spyware* consists of programs that help somebody track what you do with your laptop. Some spyware simply helps companies you do business with track your activities so that they can figure out how to sell you things; other spyware is used for more insidious purposes, such as stealing your passwords.

➠ *Adware* is the computer equivalent of telemarketing phone calls at dinner time. After adware is downloaded onto your laptop, you'll get annoying pop-up windows trying to sell you things all day long. Beyond the annoyance, adware can quickly clog up your laptop. Its performance slows down, and it's hard to get anything done at all.

To protect your information and your laptop from these various types of malware, you can do several things:

➠ **You can buy and install an antivirus, anti-spyware, or anti-adware program.** It's critical that you install an antivirus program, such as those from McAfee, Symantec (see **Figure 21-1**), or Trend Micro, or the freely downloadable AVG Free. People are coming up with new viruses every day, so it's also important that you update the software regularly with the latest virus definitions. Many antivirus programs are purchased by yearly subscription, which gives you access to updated virus definitions that the company constantly gathers throughout the year with the click of a button. Also, be sure to run a scan of your laptop on a regular basis. For convenience, you can use settings in the software to set up automatic updates and scans. Consult your program's Help tool for instructions on how to use these features.

Figure 21-1

→ **Install a program that combines tools for detecting adware and spyware.** Windows 7 has a built-in program, Windows Defender, which includes an anti-spyware feature. (I cover Windows Defender tools later in this chapter.) If you don't have Windows 7, you can purchase programs such as Spyware Doctor from PC Tools (www.pctools.com) or download free tools such as Spybot (http://spybot-download.net) or Spyware Terminator (www.spyware terminator.com).

→ **Use Windows tools to keep Windows up-to-date with security features and fixes to security problems.** You can also turn on a *firewall*, which is a feature that stops other people or programs from accessing your laptop without your permission. I cover Windows Defender and firewalls in Chapter 25.

➡ **Use privacy and security features of your browser,** such as the SmartScreen Filter and InPrivate Browsing features in Internet Explorer 8 and 9.

 Laptop users who travel with their laptops face another type of security concern. Because you carry your laptop with you, it is exposed to potential theft or loss. See Chapter 25 for more about protecting laptops while travelling.

Download Files Safely

1. Open a web site that contains downloadable files (such as www.adobe.com, which offers its Adobe Reader program for free). Typically, web sites offer a Download button or link that initiates a file download

2. Click the appropriate link to proceed. Windows might display a dialog box asking your permission to proceed with the download; click Yes.

3. In the resulting File Download dialog box, as shown in **Figure 21-2,** choose either option:

   • **Click Run to download to a temporary folder.** You can run an installation program for software, for example. However, beware: If you run a program directly from the Internet, you could be introducing dangerous viruses to your system. You might want to set up an antivirus program to scan files before downloading them.

   • **Click Save to save the file to your hard drive.** In the Save As dialog box, select the folder on your laptop or removable storage media (a USB flash drive, for example) where you want to save the file. If you're downloading software, you need to locate the downloaded file and click it to run the installation.

Figure 21-2

 If you're worried that a particular file might be unsafe to download — for example, if it's from an unknown source and, being an executable (.exe) file type, could contain a virus — click Cancel in the File Download dialog box.

 If a particular file will take a long time to download (some can take 20 minutes or more) you may have to babysit it. If your laptop goes into standby mode, it could pause the download. If your laptop automatically downloads Windows updates, it may cause your laptop to restart automatically as well, cancelling or halting your download. Check in periodically to keep things moving along.

Turn on InPrivate Browsing and Filtering

1. InPrivate Browsing is a feature that stops Internet Explorer version 8 or 9 from saving information about your browsing session, such as cookies and your browsing history. InPrivate Filtering allows you to block or allow activity from sites that are automatically collecting information about your browsing habits. To activate InPrivate for your browsing session, open IE.

2. Click Safety on the toolbar and choose InPrivate Browsing to turn that feature on. The tab shown in **Figure 21-3** appears.

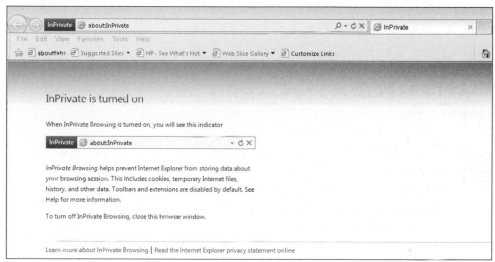

Figure 21-3

3. Browse to a site within the window that opened in the previous step. If a site is dangerous, InPrivate Browsing will offer you the option of blocking access to the site. Note that this protection lasts only as long as you are using the window that InPrivate Browsing opened (though you can open any number of tabs in that window and still be protected).

 If you don't want to use InPrivate Browsing but would like to clear your browsing history manually from time to time, with IE open you can press Ctrl+Shift+Delete to do so.

Use SmartScreen Filtering

1. SmartScreen Filter lets you check web sites that have been reported to Microsoft as generating phishing scams or downloading malware to your laptop. To turn

SmartScreen Filter on, click the Safety button on the Internet Explorer toolbar and then choose SmartScreen Filter⇨Turn On SmartScreen Filter. In the confirmation dialog box that appears (shown in **Figure 21-4**), click OK.

Figure 21-4

2. To use SmartScreen Filter, go to a web site you want to check. Click the Safety button and choose SmartScreen Filter⇨Check This Website.

3. The SmartScreen Filter window appears (see **Figure 21-5**), indicating whether it found any threats. Click the OK button to close the message.

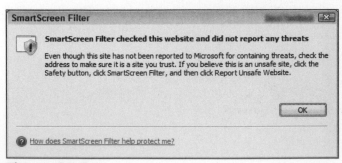

Figure 21-5

Once turned on, SmartScreen Filter checks web sites automatically — and will generate a message if you visit one that has reported problems. Keep in mind, however, that this information is updated only periodically; if you have concerns about a particular site, use the procedure given here to check the latest information about the web site.

Change Privacy Settings

1. You can modify how Internet Explorer deals with privacy settings to keep information about your browsing habits or identity safer. With IE open, choose Tools⇨Internet Options and click the Privacy tab, as shown in **Figure 21-6** and then click the Default button.

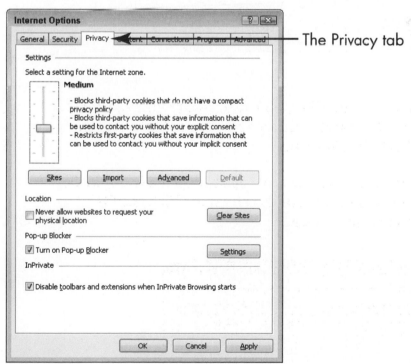

The Privacy tab

Figure 21-6

2. Click the slider and drag it up or down to make different levels of security settings.

3. Read the choices and select a setting that suits you.

4. Click the Sites button to specify sites to always or never allow the use of cookies. In the resulting Per Site Privacy Actions dialog box (as shown in **Figure** 21-7), enter a site in the Address of Website field and click either Block or Allow.

Enter a web site here

Figure 21-7

5. Click OK twice to save your new settings.

The default setting, Medium, is probably a good bet for most people. To restore the default setting, click the Default button on the Internet Options dialog box's Privacy tab or use the slider to move back to Medium.

There's a lot of news today about sites and devices that pinpoint your physical location. If you don't want to allow the location of your laptop to be tracked, click the Never Allow Websites to Request Your Physical Location check box in the dialog box shown in Figure 21-6.

 You can also use pop-up blocker settings on the Privacy tab to specify which pop-up windows to allow or block. Just click the Settings button, enter a web site name, and then click Add to allow pop-ups.

Enable the Content Advisor

1. Use Content Advisor to alert you when you visit sites with certain types of content that you or your family might find objectionable. With Internet Explorer open, choose Tools⇨Internet Options.

2. In the resulting Internet Options dialog box, click the Content tab to display it.

3. Click the Enable button; if a confirmation dialog box appears, click Yes to proceed. (*Note:* If there is no Enable button but Disable and Settings buttons instead, Content Advisor is already enabled. Click the Settings button to see the options and make changes if you wish.)

4. On the Ratings tab of the Content Advisor dialog box (see **Figure 21-8**), click one of the categories (such as Depiction of Drug Use) and then move the slider to use one of three site screening settings: None, Limited, or Unrestricted.

5. Repeat Step 4 for each of the categories.

Figure 21-8

6. Click the Approved Sites tab (see **Figure 21-9**) and enter the name of a specific site that you want to control access to. Then click Always or Never.

- **Always:** Allows users to view the site, even if it's included in the Content Advisor screening level you've set.

- **Never:** Means that nobody can visit the site, even if it's acceptable to Content Advisor.

7. When you finish making your settings, click OK. If prompted to create a supervisor password, do so. Click Apply to save your settings, and then OK to close the dialog box.

Enter a web site here

Figure 21-9

 If you want to view sites that you don't want others to see, you can do that, too. On the General tab of the Content Advisor dialog box, make sure that the Supervisor Can Type a Password to Allow Viewers to View Restricted Content check box is selected, and then click Create Password. In the dialog box that appears, enter the password, confirm it, and then enter a hint and click OK. Now if you're logged on as the system administrator, you can get to any restricted site by using this password.

 To find rating systems that various organizations have created and apply them to Internet Explorer, click the Rating Systems button on the General tab. Here you can chose a system already shown there. Or click Add; then, in the resulting Open Ratings System File dialog box, choose another system to apply.

Understand Information Exposure

Many people think that if they aren't active online, their information isn't exposed. But you aren't the only one sharing your information. Consider these relationships in your life:

➡ **Employers:** Many employers share information about employees. Consider carefully how much information you're comfortable with sharing through an employee bio posted on your company web site. How much should be visible to other employees on your intranet? When you attend a conference, is the attendee list shown in online conference documents? And even if you're retired, there may still be information about you on your former employer's web site. Review the site to determine if it reveals more than you'd like it to — and ask your employer to take down or alter the information if needed.

➡ **Government agencies:** Some agencies post personal information, such as documents concerning your home purchase and property tax (see **Figure 21-10**), on publicly available web sites. Government agencies may also post birth, marriage, and death certificates, and these documents may contain your Social Security Number, loan number, copies of your signature, and so on. You should check government records carefully to see if private information is posted — and demand that it be removed.

➡ **Family members and friends:** They may write about you in their blogs or mention you on special-interest sites, such as those focused on genealogy.

➡ **Clubs and organizations:** Organizations with whom you volunteer, the church you attend, and professional associations may reveal facts such as your address, age, income bracket, and how much money you've donated.

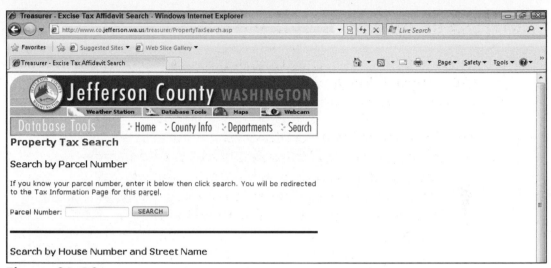

Figure 21-10

➡ **Newspapers:** If you've been featured in a newspaper article, you may be surprised to find the story, along with a picture of you or information about your work, activities, or family, by doing a simple online search. If you're interviewed, ask for the chance to review the information that the newspaper will include, and be sure that you're comfortable with exposing that information.

➡ **Online directories:** Services such as www.white pages.com, shown in **Figure 21-11**, or www. anywho.com list your phone number and address, unless you specifically request that these be removed. You may be charged a small fee associated with removing your information — a so-called privacy tax — but you may find the cost worthwhile. Online directories often include the names of members of your family, your e-mail address, the value of your home, your neighbors' names and the values of their homes, an online mapping tool to provide a view of your home, driving directions to your home, and your age. The record may also include previous addresses, schools you've attended, and links for people to run background checks on you.

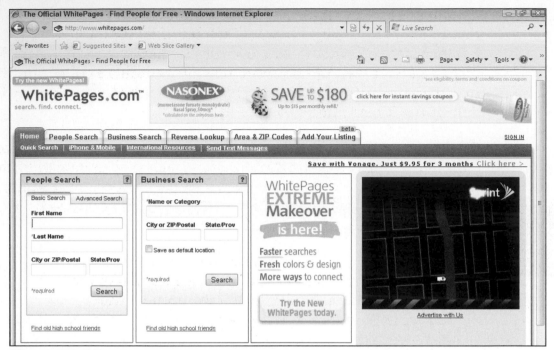

Figure 21-11

Because services get new information from many sources, you'll need to check back periodically to see if your information has again been put online — if it has, contact the company or go through their removal process again.

Try entering your home phone number in any browser's address line; chances are that you'll get an online directory listing with your address and phone number (although this doesn't work for cellphone numbers).

Keep Your Information Private

Sharing personal information with friends and family enriches your relationships and helps you build new ones. The key is to avoid sharing information with the wrong people and shady companies — because exposing your personal information online is one of your biggest risks, just as it is in the real world.

Criminals come in all flavors, but the more savvy ones collect information in a very systematic way. Each bit of information is like another piece of a puzzle that, over time, collects to form a very clear picture of your life. And be aware that after criminals collect and organize the information, they never throw it away because they may be able to use it many times over.

Fortunately, information exposure is a risk you have a great deal of control over. Before sharing information such as your date of birth, make sure that you're comfortable with how the recipient will use it. Consider the following points regarding the types of information you might be asked for:

➡ **Address and phone number:** Abuse of this information results in you receiving increased telemarketing calls and junk mail. Although less common, this information may also increase a scammer's ability to steal your identity and make your home a more interesting target for break-ins.

➡ **Names of husband/wife, father, and mother (including mother's maiden name), siblings, children, and grandchildren:** This information is very interesting to criminals, who can use it to gain your confidence and then scam you, or use it to guess your passwords or secret question answers, which often include family members' names. This information may also expose additional family members to ID theft, fraud, and personal harm.

➡ **Information about your car:** Limit access to license plate numbers; VINs (vehicle identification numbers); registration information; make, model, and title number of car; your insurance carrier's name, coverage limits, loan information, and driver's license number. The key criminal abuse of this information includes car theft (or theft of parts of the car) and insurance fraud. The type of car you drive may also indicate your financial status, and that adds one more piece of information to the pool of data criminals collect about you.

➡ **Information about work history:** In the hands of criminals, your work history can be very useful for "authenticating" the fraudsters and convincing people and organizations to provide them with more of your financial records or identity.

➡ **Information about your credit status:** This information can be abused in so many ways that any time you're asked to provide this online, your answer should be no. Don't fall for the temptation to check your credit scores for free through sites that aren't guaranteed reputable. Another frequent abuse of credit information is found in free mortgage calculators that ask you to put in all kinds of personal information in order for them to determine what credit you qualify for.

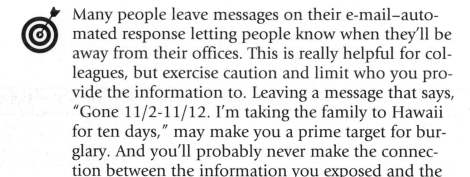 Many people leave messages on their e-mail–automated response letting people know when they'll be away from their offices. This is really helpful for colleagues, but exercise caution and limit who you provide the information to. Leaving a message that says, "Gone 11/2-11/12. I'm taking the family to Hawaii for ten days," may make you a prime target for burglary. And you'll probably never make the connection between the information you exposed and the offline crime.

You may need to show your work history, and so may post your résumé on Internet job or business networking sites. Be selective about where you post this information, create a separate e-mail account to list on the résumé, and tell what kinds of work you've done rather than give specifics about which companies and what dates. Interested, legitimate employers can then contact you privately, and you won't have given away your life history to the world. After you've landed the job, **take down** your résumé.

Think of it as risk management — when you need a job, the risk of information exposure is less vital than the need to get the job, but make that info private again when it's served its purpose.

Spot Phishing Scams and Other E-mail Fraud

As in the offline world, the Internet has a criminal element. These cybercriminals use Internet tools to commit the same crimes they've always committed, from robbing you to misusing your good name and financial information. Know how to spot the types of scams that occur online, and you'll go a long way toward steering clear of Internet crime.

Before you click a link that comes in a forwarded e-mail message or forward a message to others, ask yourself:

➡ **Is the information legitimate?** Sites such as www. truthorfiction.com, www.snopes.com (see **Figure 21-12**), or http://urbanlegends.about. com can help you discover if an e-mail is a scam.

Figure 21-12

➡️ **Does a message ask you to click links in the e-mail (see Figure 21-13) or instant message?** If you're unsure whether a message is genuinely from a company or bank that you use, call them, using the number from a past statement or the phone book. *Remember:* Don't call a phone number in the e-mail; it could be fake. To visit a company's or bank's web site, type the address in yourself if you know it or use your own bookmark rather than clicking a link. If the web site is new to you, search for the company using your browser and use that link to visit its site. Don't click the link in an e-mail, or you may land on a site that looks right — but is just a good fake.

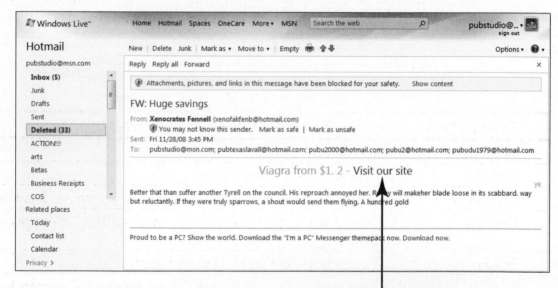

Link within an e-mail

Figure 21-13

➡️ **Does the e-mail have a photo or video to download?** If so, exercise caution. If you know the person who sent the photo or video, it's probably fine to download, but if the photo or video has been forwarded several times and you don't know the person who sent it originally, be careful. It may deliver a virus or other type of malware to your laptop.

In addition to these questions, also remember the following:

➠ **If you decide to forward (or send) e-mail to a group, always put their e-mail addresses on the Bcc: (or Blind Carbon Copy) line.** This keeps everyone's e-mail safe from fraud and scams.

➠ **Think *before* you click.** Doing so will help save you and others from scams, fraud, hoaxes, and malware.

Create Strong Passwords

A strong password can be one of your best friends in protecting your information in online accounts and sites. Never give your password to others, and change passwords on particularly sensitive accounts, such as banks and investment accounts, regularly.

Table 21-1 outlines five principles for creating strong passwords.

Table 21-1	Principles for Strong Passwords
Principle	**How to Do It**
Length	Use at least ten characters.
Strength	Mix it up with upper- and lowercase letters, characters, and numbers.
Obscure	Use nothing that's associated with you, your family, your company, and so on.
Protect	Don't place paper reminders near your laptop.
Change	The more sensitive the information, the more frequently you should change your password.

Look at **Table 21-2** for examples of password patterns that are safe but also easy to remember. Keep in mind: Just use these examples for inspiration; don't use *any* of them as your real password. (You never know who else might be reading this book.)

Table 21-2	Examples of Strong Passwords
Logic	*Password*
Use a familiar phrase typed with a variation of capitalization and numbers instead of words (text message shorthand).	L8r_L8rNot2day = Later, later, not today 2BorNot2B_ThatIsThe? = To be or not to be, that is the question.
Incorporate shortcut codes or acronyms.	CSThnknAU2day = Can't Stop Thinking About You today 2Hot2Hndle = Too hot to handle
Create a password from an easy-to-remember phrase that describes what you're doing, with key letters replaced by numbers or symbols.	1mlook1ngatyahoo = I'm looking at Yahoo (We replaced the Is with 1s.) MyWork@HomeNeverEnds
Spell a word backwards with at least one letter representing a character or number.	$lidoffaD = Daffodils (The $ replaces the s.) y1frettuB = Butterfly (The 1 replaces the l.) QWERTY7654321 = This is the six letters from left to right in the top row of your keyboard, plus the numbers from right to left across the top going backwards.
Use patterns from your keyboard. Make your keyboard a palette and make any shape you want.	Typing 1QAZSDRFBHU8 is really just making a W on your keyboard.

 It's a good idea to password-protect your laptop. That way, if it's left running in a public place, or lost or stolen, nobody else can log on to access the information on it. See Chapter 25 for information about setting up a Windows password.

Keeping In Touch with E-Mail

To use e-mail, you have to have an Internet connection through an Internet service provider, such as your phone or cable company. If you use a wireless-enabled laptop or tablet, you can also connect through public wireless networks called hotspots or with some tablets through a 3G cellular connection. Once you are online, you can use an *e-mail program*, which is a tool you that allows you to send e-mails (text messages that you send to others over the Internet). These messages are delivered to e-mail *inboxes*, usually within seconds.

You can attach files to e-mail messages and even put photos or other images within the message body. You can get an e-mail account through your Internet provider or through sites such as Yahoo! or Microsoft Live. These accounts are typically free of charge.

When you have an e-mail account, you can send and receive e-mail through the account provider's e-mail program online, or you can set up a program on your laptop — such as Microsoft Outlook, which comes with Microsoft Office — or you can use a service such as Windows Live Hotmail, which is built in to the Internet Explorer browser to access your account.

Get ready to . . .

To make your e-mailing life easy, this chapter takes a look at how to perform these tasks:

➠ **Choose an e-mail provider.** Find out how to locate e-mail providers and what types of features they offer.

➠ **Manage your e-mail account.** Make settings so you can send and receive messages for different e-mail addresses from one e-mail account. This ability to check all your messages in one place can be useful if you use both a work and a home e-mail account, for example.

➠ **Receive, send, and forward messages.** Deal with the ins and outs of receiving and sending e-mail. Use the formatting tools that Windows Live Hotmail provides to make your messages more attractive and readable.

➠ **Add information into Contacts.** You can quickly and easily manage your contacts as well as organize the messages you save in e-mail folders.

➠ **Set up the layout of all Windows Live features.** Use the Folder bar and Layout features to create the most efficient e-mail workspace.

Set Up an Internet-Based E-Mail Account

Your Internet service provider (ISP), whether that's your cable or phone company or a satellite provider, probably offers you a free e-mail account along with your service. You can also get free accounts from many online sources, such as Yahoo!, AOL, Gmail, and Windows Live Hotmail.

Here are some tips for getting your own e-mail account:

➠ **Using e-mail accounts provided by an ISP:** Check with your ISP to see whether an e-mail account comes with your connection service. If it does, your ISP should provide instructions on how to choose an *e-mail alias* (that is, the name on your account, such as `SusieXYZ@att.com`) and password and sign in.

➠ **Searching for an e-mail provider:** If your ISP doesn't offer e-mail, or you prefer to use another service because of the features it offers, use your browser's search engine (see Chapter 20 for more about how to search online) to look for what's available. Don't use the search term *free e-mail* because results for any search with the word *free* included are much more likely to return sites that will download bad programs like viruses to your laptop. Alternatively, you can go directly to services such as Yahoo!, AOL, or Gmail by entering their addresses in your browser address box (for example, www.gmail.com).

➡ **Finding out about features:** E-mail accounts come with certain features that you should be aware of. For example, they each provide a certain amount of storage for your saved messages. (Today services often offer 25 gigabytes or more — or even unlimited storage — for free.) The account should also include an easy-to-use Address Book or Contacts feature to save your e-mail contacts' information. Some services also provide better formatting tools for text, a calendar, and a to-do list feature. Whatever service you use, make sure it has good junk-mail features to protect you from unwanted e-mails. You should be able to control junk-mail filters to place messages from certain senders or with certain types of content in a junk-mail folder, where you can review or delete them.

➡ **Signing up for an e-mail account:** When you find an e-mail account you want to use, sign up (usually there will be a Sign Up or Get An Account button or link to click) by providing your name and other contact information and selecting a username and password. The username is your e-mail address, in the form of UserName@*service*.com, where service is, for example, Yahoo!, Windows Live Hotmail, or AOL. Some usernames might be taken, so have a few options in mind or select one of the options the service presents you with.

➡ **Choosing a safe username:** Don't use your full name, your location, age, or other identifiers if possible. Such personal identifiers might help scam artists or predators to find out more about you than you want them to know. A username such as `GolfFan@aol.com` tells little about you that someone could use to find you. On the other hand, `Joan75Phoenix@gmail.com` reveals your name, age, and location.

Manage Accounts in Windows Live

In addition to providing your Windows Live e-mail address so that others can send you mail directly, you can use settings in various e-mail programs to forward your mail to your Windows Live address so that you can receive all your e-mail messages in one place. You can then make settings in Windows Live Hotmail to use other e-mail addresses when responding to messages so that your recipients assume the messages are coming from the originating account.

1. In the tasks in this chapter, I use Windows Live Hotmail as an example of an e-mail service, but most tasks work similarly in any e-mail program. The first step is to set up an e-mail account in Windows Live. Open your browser and type **www.windowslive.com** in the address field and press Enter.

2. Your browser displays the Windows Live Hotmail Sign-In page shown in **Figure 22-1**. If you need to start a new account at this point, click the Sign Up button and go through the sign-up procedure. If you already have an account, click the Sign In to Windows Live button, click the account you want to sign in to if you have multiple accounts, enter your password in the field that appears, and then click the Sign In button.

3. After signing in, click the Hotmail link to go to the Hotmail portion of Windows Live.

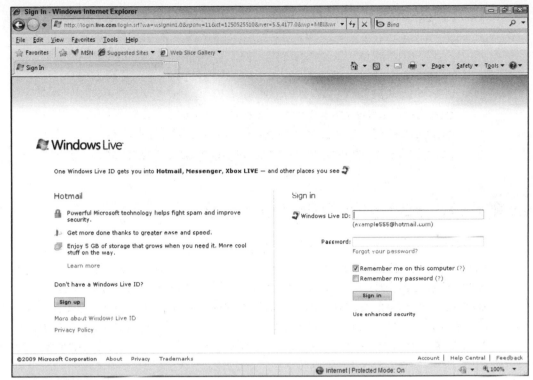

Figure 22-1

4. Choose Options⇨More Options. In the resulting Options window, as shown in **Figure 22-2,** click the Sending/Receiving Email from Other Accounts link.

Click this link

Figure 22-2

5. In the resulting window, click the Add an E-mail Account link.

6. In the following screen, enter an e-mail address and password and click Next.

7. In the Add an E-Mail Account window that appears, choose whether to place mail from this account into your Inbox or into a separate folder. If you like, you can choose to have messages for this account to appear in a unique color; click one of the radio buttons in the How Would You Like Unread Messages for *xxx@xxx.com* to Appear section. Click Save.

8. Once you're set up to send out messages with that account name, messages from that account will be delivered to the folder you selected in Step 7. When you create a new e-mail form, simply click the account name above the To: field and select the account you want the message to go from.

Get to Know Windows Live Hotmail

Windows Live Hotmail (see **Figure 22-3**) is typical of many e-mail programs: It includes both menus and tools to take actions, such as deleting an e-mail, creating a new e-mail, and so on. There's also a list of folders on the left. Some typical folders are your Inbox, where most incoming mail appears; your Outbox or Drafts folder, where saved drafts of e-mails are saved ready to be sent; and your Sent folder, where copies of e-mails you've sent to other people are stored.

Finally, the central area of the screen may display folder contents or, if you are creating or viewing a message, a preview pane that shows the contents of the selected message. (**Figure 22-3** displays the contents of a message being composed.)

Folders   Preview pane

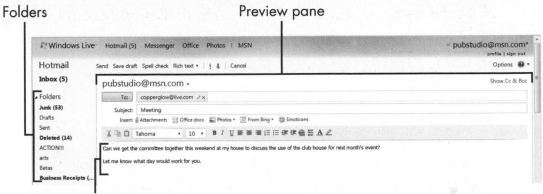

Contents of the message

Figure 22-3

To organize messages in the Inbox, click any of the items in the horizontal Show list above the message list, such as From Contacts (to sort the messages alphabetically by sender), Unread (to sort by the messages you haven't yet opened), and so on and then click Arrange by.

When you access Windows Live Hotmail and many other online e-mail services, you are using a program that is hosted online, rather than software on your laptop. That makes it easy to access your mail from any computer because your messages and folders are kept online. If you use an e-mail program such as Outlook, the software and your messages are stored on your laptop.

Open and Receive Windows Live Hotmail

1. Use your browser to go to Windows Live at www.mail. live.com.

2. Your browser displays the Windows Live Sign-In page shown in **Figure 22-4**.

Figure 22-4

3. If you're signing in from a computer that Windows Live recognizes, your e-mail account may be listed and if so, click it; if it's not, click the Sign In to Windows Live button. Enter your password in the field that appears, and then click the Sign In button to sign in. Windows Live then sends and receives all messages automatically.

4. New messages are displayed in your Inbox (you can see what my Inbox looks like in **Figure** 22-5). Unread messages sport a small closed-envelope icon; those with attachments have a paperclip icon as well.

Messages in the Inbox

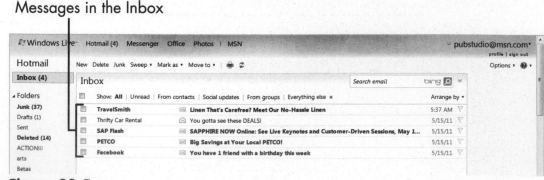

Figure 22-5

If your mail doesn't come through, it's probably because your e-mail provider's servers are experiencing technical problems. Just wait a little while. If you still can't get mail, make sure your connection to the Internet is active. Your browser may show you your Inbox, but if you've lost your connection, you won't receive new messages.

 Note that if an e-mail has a little exclamation point next to it in your Inbox, somebody has flagged it as urgent. It's usually best to check out those e-mails first — but before you do, make sure they're from senders you know!

Create and Send E-Mail

1. Creating e-mail is as simple as filling out a few fields in a form. Open Windows Live Hotmail in your browser by going to www.mail.live.com.

2. Sign in, and then click the Hotmail button on the Windows Live Hotmail screen if needed to go to your Inbox.

3. Click the New button to create a new blank e-mail form. (See **Figure 22-6.**)

A new, blank e-mail

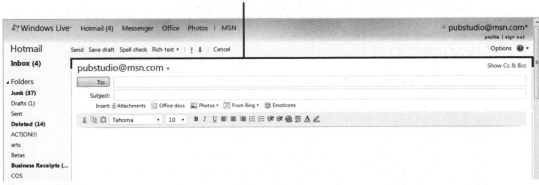

Figure 22-6

4. Type the e-mail address of the recipient(s) in the To field text box. If you want to send a copy of the message, click the Show Cc & Bcc link and enter the address(es) in the Cc: or Bcc: field text boxes.

5. Click the Subject text box and type a concise yet descriptive subject.

6. Click the message window and type your message. (See Figure 22-7.)

Enter your message here

Figure 22-7

 Don't press Enter at the end of a line when typing a message. Windows Live Hotmail has an automatic text wrap feature that does this for you. Do be concise. If you have lots to say, consider sending a letter by snail-mail or attach a printable document to the e-mail. Most people tire of reading text onscreen after a short while.

 Keep e-mail etiquette in mind as you type. For example, don't type in ALL CAPITAL LETTERS. This is called *shouting*, which is considered rude. Do be polite even if you're really, really angry. Your message could be forwarded to just about anybody, just about anywhere, and you don't want to get a reputation as a hothead.

7. When you finish typing your message, you should check your spelling (unless you're the regional state spelling champ). Click the Spell Check button, and Windows Live automatically checks spelling and places a red, wavy line under questionable words. (See **Figure 22-8.**) Click the word and select the correct spelling from the drop-down list that appears. If you add more text to your message and want to check the new text for spelling, click the Spell Check button again.

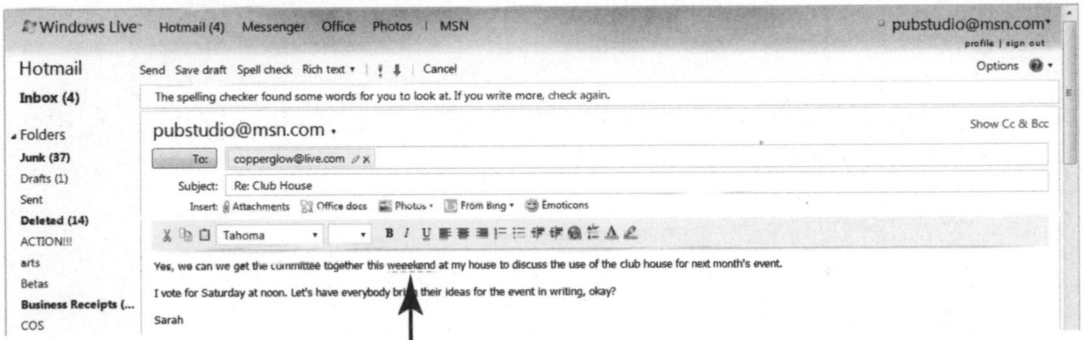

A questionable word

Figure 22-8

8. Click the Send button. A message appears, like the one in **Figure 22-9,** telling you the e-mail is on its way!

Confirmation of a sent message

Figure 22-9

If the message is really urgent, you might also click the High Importance button (it looks like a red exclamation point) to add a bright-red exclamation mark to the message header to alert the recipient. Click the Low Importance button (it looks like a blue, downward-pointing arrow) to return the priority to Low.

 Remember that when creating an e-mail, you can address it to a stored address by using the Contacts feature. Click the To button, and your Contacts list appears. (Check out the "Add People to the Contact List" task later in the chapter to find out how to populate your e-mail Contact files with specific information.) You can then select a name(s) from there. Windows Live Hotmail also allows you to just begin to type a stored contact in an address field (To, Bcc:, or Cc:), and it provides a list of likely options while you type. Just click the correct name when it appears in the list, and Windows Live enters it.

Send an Attachment

1. It's very convenient to be able to attach a document or image file to an e-mail that the recipient can open and view on his end. To do this, log on to your Windows Live e-mail account and click New to create a new e-mail message.

2. Address it, enter a subject, and type a message.

3. Click the Attachments button.

4. The Open dialog box appears. (See **Figure 22-10.**) Locate the file that you want and then click Open.

5. The name of the attached file appears in the Attach field (see **Figure 22-11**), indicating that it's uploading. When the first attachment finishes uploading, you can click the Attachments button again and repeat Step 4 as many times as you like to add more attachments.

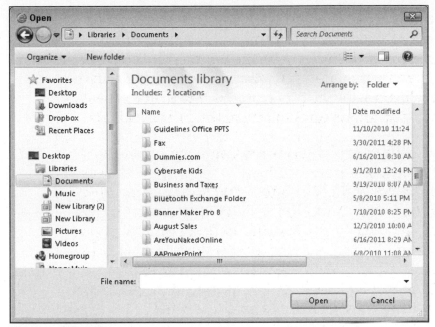

Figure 22-10

An attached file

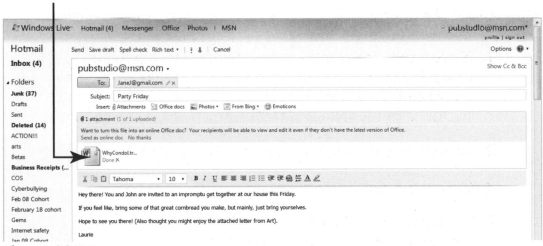

Figure 22-11

6. Click the Send button to send the message and attachment.

You can attach as many files as you like to a single e-mail. Your only limitation is size. Various e-mail programs have different limits on the size of attachments, and some prevent you from attaching certain types of files for security reasons. If you attach several documents and your e-mail fails to go through, it might be too large; just send a few e-mails and spread the attachments out among them.

Read a Message

1. When you receive an e-mail, your next step is to read it. Click an e-mail message in your Inbox or double-click it to open it in a larger window. Unread messages sport an icon of an unopened envelope to the left of the message subject.

2. Use the scroll bars in the message window to scroll down through the message and read it. (See **Figure 22-12**.)

3. If the message has an attachment, it shows a paper clip symbol next to the message in your Inbox; attachments are listed in the open message. To open an attachment, click it.

Scrollbar

Figure 22-12

4. In the File Download dialog box (see **Figure 22-13**), click the Open button to open the file with the suggested program. The attachment opens in whatever program is associated with it (such as the Windows Media Center for a video file) or the program it was created in (such as Microsoft Word).

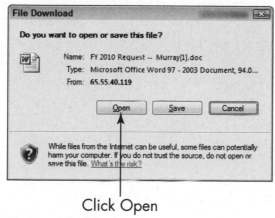

Click Open

Figure 22-13

 If you'd rather save an attachment to a storage disk or your hard drive, click the Save button in Step 4, choose the location to save the file to, and then click Save.

Reply to a Message

1. If you receive an e-mail and want to send a message back, use the Reply feature. Open the message you want to reply to, and then select one of the following reply options, as shown in **Figure 22-14**:

• **Reply:** Send the reply to only the author.

• **Reply All:** Send a reply to the author as well as everyone who received the original message.

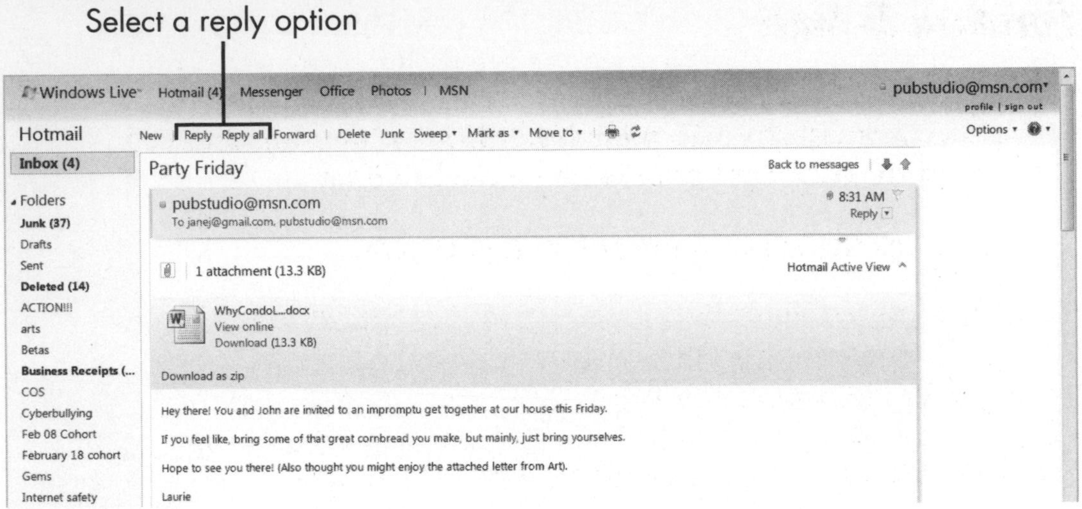

Select a reply option

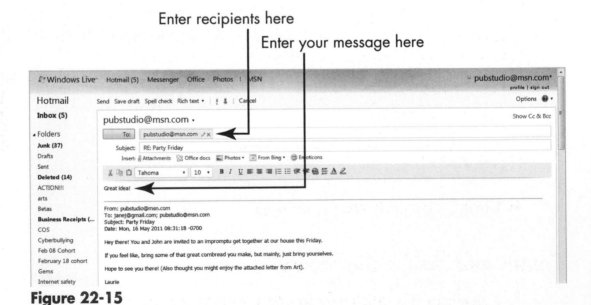

Figure 22-14

2. In the resulting e-mail form (see **Figure 22-15**), enter any additional recipient(s) in the To: and/or Cc: or Bcc: text boxes and type your message in the message window area.

Enter recipients here

Enter your message here

Figure 22-15

3. Click the Send button to send the reply.

Forward E-Mail

1. To share an e-mail you receive with others, use the Forward feature. In the Inbox, click the message that you want to forward or open the e-mail message.

2. Click the Forward button on the toolbar.

3. In the message that appears with FW: added to the beginning of the subject line, enter a new recipient(s) in the To: and/or Cc: and Bcc: fields, and then enter any message that you want to include in the message window area, as shown in the example in **Figure 22-16.**

Enter your message here

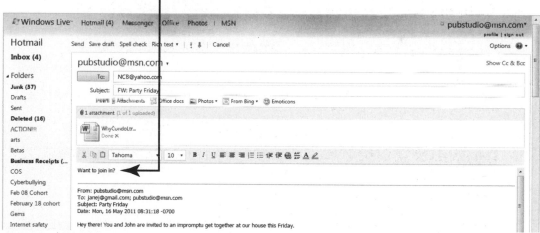

Figure 22-16

4. Click Send to forward the message.

Create and Add a Signature

1. A *signature* is a quick way to add some closing information, such as your name and organization, to the end of every message. Choose Options⇨More Options to open the Options page. Click the Personal Email Signature link (under Writing Email). (See **Figure 22-17.**)

Click this link

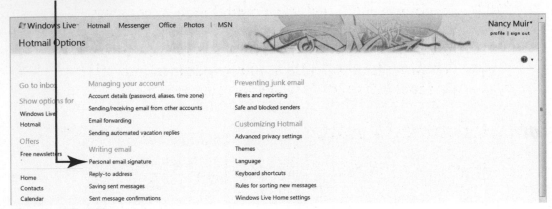

Figure 22-17

2. In the Personal EMail Signature form that opens (see **Figure 22-18**), type your signature. If you'd like, you can use the formatting tools on the toolbar to change the look of the text, including the font, font size, or effects such as bold or italic.

3. Click Save to save the signature.

 If you have a web site and want to include a link to it in your signature, click the Insert Hyperlink button on the toolbar shown in **Figure 22-18**. Enter the address in the text box that appears and then click OK.

Enter your signature here

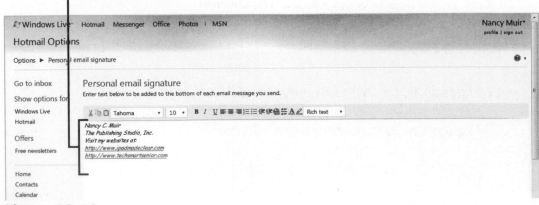

Figure 22-18

Remember that if you attach your signature to every outgoing e-mail, including e-mail replies, whoever you communicate with will get the information provided there. Consider issues of identity theft before you provide your address, phone number, and other personal information to all and sundry.

Format E-Mail Messages

1. Windows Live Hotmail provides tools to format the text in your message to change fonts, add color, and more, just as you would in a word-processed document. Create a new e-mail message (or open an existing message and click Reply or Forward).

2. Enter text, and then click and drag with your mouse or touchpad to select the text you want to format. (See Figure 22-19.)

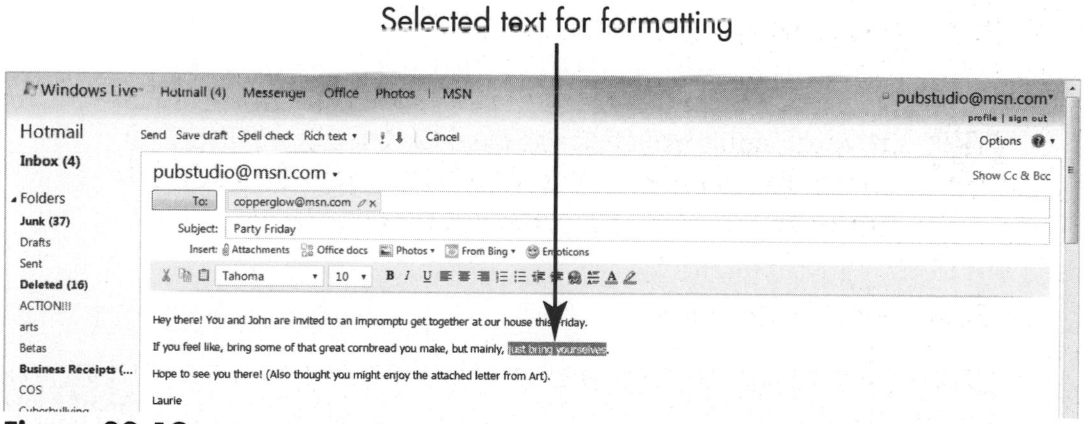

Selected text for formatting

Figure 22-19

3. Use any of the following options to make changes to the font. (See the toolbar containing these tools in Figure 22-20.)

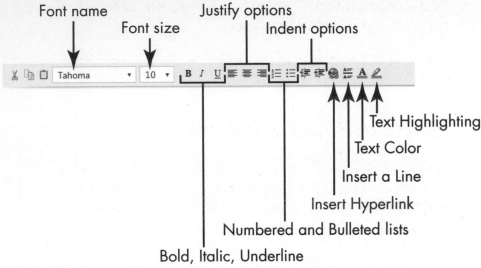

Figure 22-20

- **Font Name drop-down list:** Choose an option from the drop-down list to apply it to the text.

- **Font Size drop-down list:** Change the font size here.

- **Bold, Italic, and Underline buttons:** Apply styles to selected text.

- **Justify Left, Justify Center, and Justify Right buttons:** Adjust the alignment.

- **Insert Numbered List and Insert Bulleted List buttons:** Apply numbering order to lists or precede each item with a round bullet point.

- **Decrease Indent and Increase Indent button:** Indent that paragraph to the right or move it (decrease the indent) to the left.

- **Insert Hyperlink button:** Use this to insert a hyperlink to a web site or online document.

- **Insert A Line button:** Inserts a line dividing the signature from the message body.

- **Text Color button:** Display a color palette and click a color to apply it to selected text.

- **Text Highlight button:** Add color to the background of the message.

Apply a Theme and Add a Picture

1. You can modify the appearance of Windows Live Hotmail by applying a theme, which contains preset designs and colors, to the window. Choose Options➪More Options.

2. In the Hotmail Options page that appears, under Customizing Hotmail, click Themes.

3. In the Themes page that appears (see **Figure 22-21**), click a theme from the list.

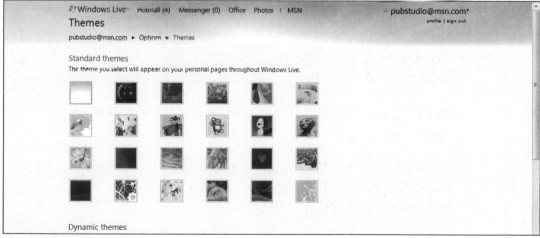

Figure 22-21

4. Click Save to apply the theme to Windows Live Hotmail, and click the Mail link to return to your Inbox sporting the new look. (See **Figure 22-22**.)

If you're the visual type, you should know that you can also insert a picture into an e-mail message. With the e-mail form open, click the Photos item in the Insert list under the Subject text box and choose Web Images or Clip Art, depending on the type of image you want. In the pane that appears for clip or web art, enter a search term in the Search field text box to find an image online, and then click any image result to insert it in your e-mail. You can also use the Insert list to add an Office document, item from Bing, or an emoticon.

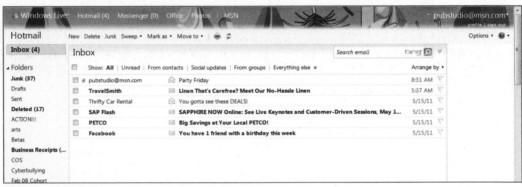

Figure 22-22

Add People to the Contact List

1. To make addressing e-mails faster, you can save people's e-mail addresses and more in the Contacts List. In the Windows Live Hotmail main window, click the Contacts link in the lower-left pane to open the Contacts page shown in **Figure 22-23**.

2. To create a new contact, click the New button.

3. In the resulting New Contact dialog box, as shown in **Figure 22-24**, enter the contact information that you want to save in your Contacts.

- **Name and E-Mail:** Enter the person's first and last name. (This is the only information you must enter to create a contact.)

- **Contact info:** Enter the person's nickname, birthday, e-mail address, home and mobile phone numbers, home addresses and any other information you wish.

- **Work Info:** Enter information about the company that the person works for, as well as his or her work e-mail, phone, fax, address, and so on.

Figure 22-23

Figure 22-24

4. Click Save to save your new contact information, and then click Hotmail to return to your Inbox.

 You can search contacts by clicking Contacts in any Windows Live Hotmail window and entering search text in the Search Your Contact List field. You can also click the letters listed across the top of the Contacts window to look for people whose last names begin with that letter.

Customize the Reading Pane Layout

1. You can modify the layout of elements in the Windows Live Hotmail main page to suit you. In the Hotmail portion of Windows Live, choose Options⇨More Options to open the Options window. Click the Hotmail link in the left pane.

2. Click Reading Pane Settings (under Reading Email). Select various options in the Reading Pane Settings, as shown in **Figure 22-25,** to modify where the Reading Pane appears and when to show messages in the Reading Pane.

Choose the location for the Reading Pane

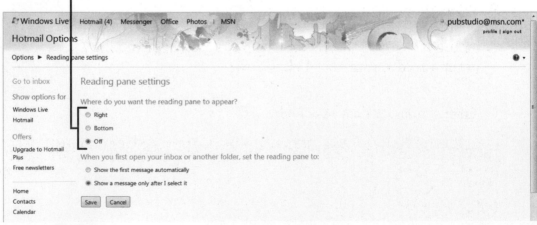

Figure 22-25

3. Click Save to save your Reading Pane settings.

Create Message Folders

1. Message folders are a way to organize your incoming messages so that you can find them easily. You can create folders with a few simple steps. Click the icon on the right side of the Folders item in the left pane and choose Manage Folders in the drop-down menu that appears to display the list of folders shown in **Figure 22-26.**

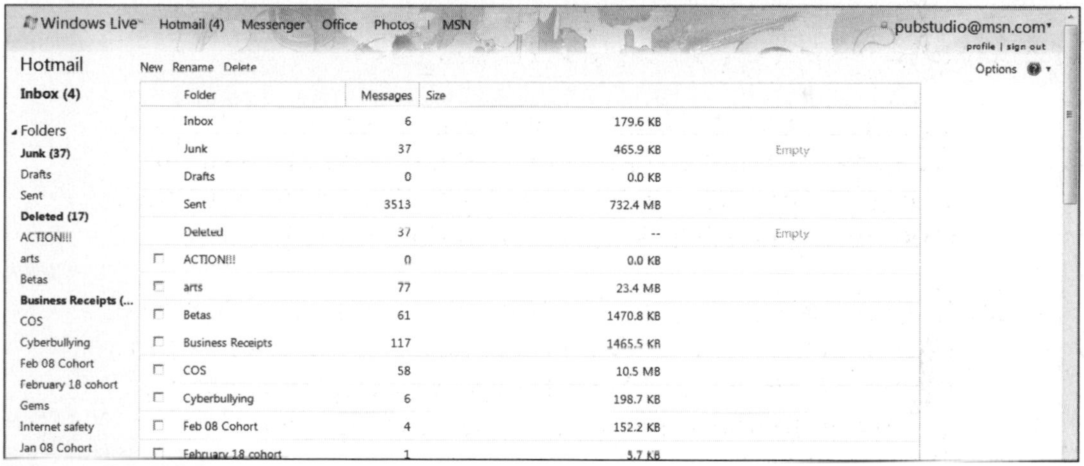

Figure 22-26

2. Click New.

3. In the New Folder form that appears (see **Figure 22-27**), enter a folder name and click Save.

Enter a name for the new folder

Figure 22-27

4. Click Hotmail to return to your Inbox.

 If you want to remove or rename a folder, you can use the Rename and Delete buttons in the Manage Folders window shown in **Figure 22-26** to do so.

Organize Messages in Folders

1. To move a message from your Inbox into a folder, select the check box to the left of the message and then click Move To⇨*folder name*, as shown in **Figure 22-28**.

The message being moved

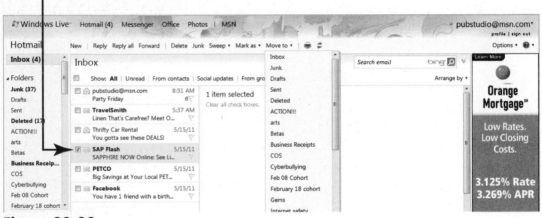

Figure 22-28

2. To move a message between folders, with a folder (such as the Inbox) displayed, click a message and then drag it into another folder in the Folders list.

3. To delete a message in a folder, click the folder name to open it, and click the check box in front of the message. Click Delete.

 If you want to mark a message as junk mail so that Windows Live Mail puts any message from that sender in the Junk folder from now on, click the check box in front of the message and then click Junk.

Connecting with People Online

*T*he Internet is a great place to find people with similar interests and share information.

You'll find discussion boards and chat features on a wide variety of sites, with people sharing information from news to recipes. There are some great senior chat rooms for making friends, and many sites allow you to create new chat rooms on topics that interest you at any time.

Instant messaging (IM), on the other hand, isn't a web site but a service. Using software such as Windows Live Messenger, IM allows you to chat in real time with your contacts. You can access instant messaging programs via your computer or your cellphone.

Another great way to use the Internet to communicate is by making calls using services such as Skype, and even using your laptop's web camera (called a *webcam*) to make video calls where you and the other person can see each other as you talk.

You can use handy event planning sites to schedule your next meeting, send greeting cards in electronic form, and more.

In this chapter, I look at some ways you can share information with others online, and I tell you how to do so safely.

Use Discussion Boards

A *discussion board*, also sometimes referred to as a *forum*, is a place where you can post written messages, pictures, and videos on a topic. Others can reply to you, and you can reply to their postings.

Discussion boards are *asynchronous*, which means that you post a message (just as you might on a bulletin board at the grocery store) and wait for a response. Somebody might read it that hour — or ten days or several weeks after you make the posting. In other words, the response isn't instantaneous, and the message isn't usually directed to a specific individual.

You can find a discussion board about darn near every topic under the sun, and the information on them can be tremendously helpful when you're looking for answers. They're also a great way to share your expertise — whether you chime in on how to remove an ink stain, provide history trivia about button styles on military uniforms, or announce the latest breakthroughs in your given field. Postings are likely to stay on the site for years for people to reference, so be aware that what you read there may be up to date or not that current.

1. To try out a discussion board, enter this URL in your browser address field: **http://boards.fool.com/**. (Note that some discussion boards require that you become a member with a username and that you sign in before you can post comments. If you want to post a reply in Step 4 below you will first have to join the site.)

2. In the topic list that appears (see **Figure 23-1**), click a topic, such as Great Movies, to see a list of discussions. Click a discussion to view the original posting and any responses.

3. When you click a posting that has replies, you'll see that they are organized in the middle of the page in easy-to-follow *threads*, which list comments on the original posting in chronological order (see **Figure 23-2**). You can review the various participants' comments as they add their ideas to the entire conversation.

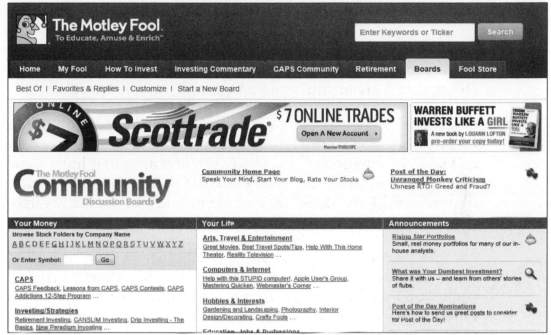

Figure 23-1

4. To reply to a posting yourself which requires that you be a member, first click the posting, and then enter your member information. Fill in your comments and post the reply.

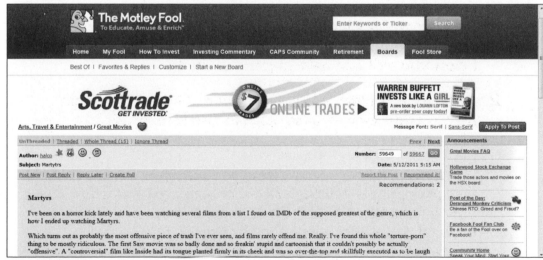

Figure 23-2

With any site where users share information, you can stay safer if you know how to sidestep some abuses, including *data mining* (gathering your personal information for commercial or criminal intent), *social engineering* ploys that try to gain your trust and access to your money, ID theft scams, and so forth. Throughout this chapter, I provide safety tips, but remember that if you're careful to protect your privacy, you can enjoy socializing online with little worry.

Participate in Chat

A *chat room* is an online space where groups of people can talk back and forth via text, audio, web camera, or a combination of media. (See **Figure 23-3,** which shows a web site that links to hundreds of chat rooms.) In chat, you're having a conversation with one or more people in real time (without delay, as with a discussion board), and your entire conversation appears in the chat window. Here are some characteristics of chat you should know:

➡ When the chat is over, unless you save a copy, the conversation is typically gone.

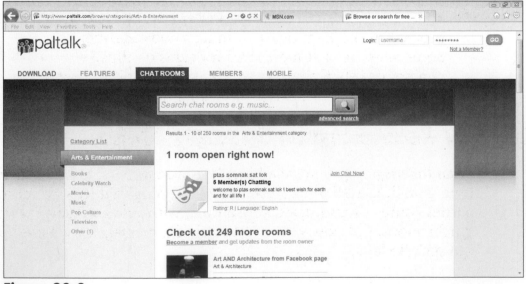

Figure 23-3

➡ Several people can interact at once, although this can take getting used to as you try to follow what others are saying and jump in with your own messages.

➡ When you find a chat you want to participate in, sign up to get a screen name, and then you simply enter the chat room, enter your message, and submit it. It shows up in the stream of comments, and others may — or may not — reply to it.

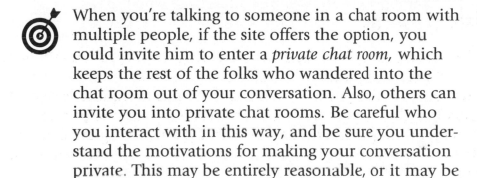 When you're talking to someone in a chat room with multiple people, if the site offers the option, you could invite him to enter a *private chat room*, which keeps the rest of the folks who wandered into the chat room out of your conversation. Also, others can invite you into private chat rooms. Be careful who you interact with in this way, and be sure you understand the motivations for making your conversation private. This may be entirely reasonable, or it may be that you're dealing with someone with suspect motivations.

Warning: Before you get started, check out the web site's Terms of Use, privacy, and monitoring and abuse reporting procedures to understand the safety protections in place before joining a conversation. Some sites are well monitored for signs of abusive content or interactions; others have no monitoring at all. If you don't like the terms, find a different site.

Send and Receive Instant Messages (IMs)

Instant messaging (often called just *IM*) used to be referred to as real-time e-mail. It used to be *synchronous*, meaning that two (or more) parties could communicate in real time, without any delay. It's still synchronous, but now you can also leave a message that the recipient can pick up later.

Instant messaging is a great way to stay in touch with the younger generations, who rarely use e-mail. IM is ideal for quick little messages where you just want an answer without writing a formal e-mail, as well as for touching base and saying hi. Texting on cellphones, which you see kids doing on every street corner, is largely the same phenomenon: This isn't a tool you'd typically use for a long, meaningful conversation, but it's great for quick exchanges.

Depending on the IM service you use, you can do the following:

➡ Write notes to friends, grandchildren, or whoever, as long as they've installed the same IM service that you're using.

➡ Type in your comments as if you were talking on the phone.

➡ Send photos, videos, and other files.

➡ Use little graphical images, called *emoticons* (such as smilies or winks) and *avatars*, to add fun to your IM messages.

➡ See participants via web cameras.

➡ Get and send e-mail.

➡ Search the web, find others using Global Positioning System (GPS) technology, listen to music, watch videos, play games, bid on auctions, find dates, and more.

➡ Track the history of conversations and even save transcripts of them to review later.

Instant messaging programs vary somewhat, and you have several to choose from, including Windows Live Messenger (available at `http://download.live.com/?sku=messenger`), Yahoo! Messenger (available at `http://messenger.yahoo.com`), and AOL Instant Messenger, also know as AIM, (available at `www.aim.com`). Google mail (`www.gmail.com`) has a built-in IM feature.

To get started with a new messaging program, you need to follow the general steps in the upcoming list. But as with any software, if you aren't sure how to use its features, consult its Help documentation for specific instructions.

1. Download and install the messaging program according to the instructions on the provider's web site.

2. Set up an account and sign in; this may simply involve entering your e-mail address and a password.

> In the Windows Live Messenger IM program shown in **Figure 23-4,** you see the dialog box where you can choose your overall privacy settings when you set up your account.

> **Warning:** You can send IMs from a computer to a mobile phone (and vice versa) and from one mobile phone to another. If you include your mobile phone number as part of your IM profile, anyone who can see your profile can view it. This is useful information for friends *and* criminals, so it's important to consider whether you want your number exposed — especially if you have many people on your contact list who you don't personally know.

3. Double-click a contact to initiate chat. (You can import contacts from your e-mail contacts when you sign up, or you can add them yourself.)

4. Click the phone button or other call icon to initiate a phone call.

> IM programs let your contacts see when you're online, unless you change your settings to hide this information — something that's good to know when you're busy and don't have time to chat. You can choose availability settings such as Online, Busy, Be Right Back, Out to Lunch, or even display your status as Offline, even when you aren't.

Figure 23-4

 IM is one place where people use shortcut text. Some of this will be familiar to you, such as FYI (for your information) and ASAP (as soon as possible). Other short text may be less familiar, such as LOL (laughing out loud). Visit www.swalk.com for a table of common shortcut text terms. Knowing these will make communicating with younger folks more fun.

 Warning: Consider what you're saying and sharing in IM and how you'd feel if the information was made public. IM allows you to store your conversation history, which is super useful if you need to go back and check something that was said. But it has its downside. Anything you include in IM can be forwarded to others. If you're at work, keep in mind that many employers monitor IM (and e-mail) conversations.

 Warning: If you run across illegal content — such as child pornography — downloading or continuing to view this for any reason is illegal. Report the incident to law enforcement immediately.

Use Webcams

Webcams are small video cameras you can use to transmit your picture to somebody in an online conversation or meeting. They are relatively inexpensive, and most laptops now come with webcams embedded in their lids. (See **Figure 23-5**.) Each computer manufacturer includes a software program to use with your built-in webcam or you can find another online, such as CyberLink YouCam. Some software even allows you to record, edit, and post video to video sharing sites such as YouTube.

When you use instant messaging software or join an online meeting, your webcam is likely to begin displaying video automatically. Use the tools in that program to control your webcam.

A webcam can be a great way to communicate with friends and family, but it can quickly become risky when you use it for conversations with strangers.

➠ Giving your image away, especially one that may show your emotional reactions to a stranger's statements in real time, simply reveals too much information that can put you at risk.

➠ If you use a webcam to meet with someone you don't know online, they may expose you to behavior you'd rather not see.

➠ Note that webcams can also be high-jacked and turned on remotely. This allows predators to view and listen to individuals without their knowledge. When you aren't using them, consider turning your webcam off — or disconnecting it, if it isn't a built-in model.

Figure 23-5

 Warning: Teens in particular struggle to use good judgment when using webcams. If you have grandchildren or other children in your care, realize that normal inhibitions seem to fall away when they aren't physically present with the person they're speaking to — and many expose themselves, figuratively and literally. In addition to having a conversation about appropriate webcam use with children and teens, it may be wise to limit access to webcams.

Use Skype to Make Calls Online

Skype is a popular site for making phone calls using your Internet connection and a technology called VoiP (Voice over Internet Protocol). There are several benefits to using Skype to make phone calls, including:

➡ Calls to other users of Skype are absolutely free, even it the other person is located around the world from you. If you call landlines or mobile phones, you still get low rates for your calls using credits that you purchase.

➡ You can use the video feature of Skype along with a webcam to make video calls to others. This is an awesome way to keep in touch with the grandkids or other friends in distant places.

➡ You can store contact information for others and call them with a click.

➡ If you're not at your computer when a call comes in, you can set up a voicemail feature to take messages.

To get set up to use Skype, follow these steps:

1. Go to `http://skype.com` and click Get Skype.

2. Click the appropriate Device and operating system in the drop-down list that appears.

For example, you might choose Windows under the Computer heading to download Skype to a Windows-based laptop.

3. On the following screen, to get Skype Free click the Download Skype button (see **Figure 23-6**) and follow the instructions to run the Skype installation program.

4. Once Skype has downloaded, open it from the Windows Start menu.

5. In the Skype window shown in **Figure 23-7,** click Add a Contact to add people to your Contact list.

6. Fill in the form that appears with the person's e-mail, phone number, full name, and Skype name (the name they used when registering their Skype account) and then click the Add button.

Click this button

Figure 23-6

Click this option

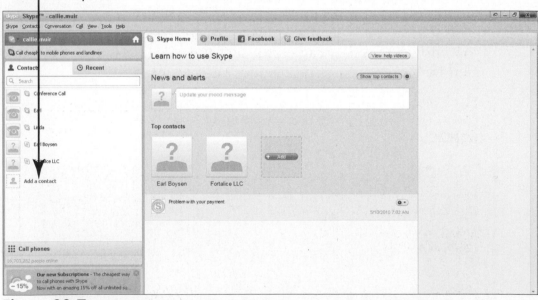

Figure 23-7

7. Now you can make phone calls by simply clicking a contact name in the Skype window and then clicking the Call Phone button.

Though using Skype is relatively simple, there is much more you can discover such as how to purchase credit to call non-Skype members, how to make video calls, and more. For help with these tasks consider buying a book such as *Skype For Dummies* by Loren Abdulezar, Susan Abdulezar, and Howard Dammond (John Wiley & Sons, Inc.).

Schedule Events

You know what an annoyance it can be to schedule a meeting or party? You e-mail or call a few people to see if they're available. One person can make it, but another can't. You leave phone messages for two other people who you don't hear back from. Then you reschedule the event only to find that two people you never heard back from are out of town that day.

Today you can use online event planning sites such as Evite (www. evite.com) or Doodle (http://doodle.com/main.html) shown in **Figure 23-8** to plan events by sending out electronic invitations that offer recipients a range of dates and times. The invitees let you know when they can come, and the service helps you to easily identify the best time and date for your event.

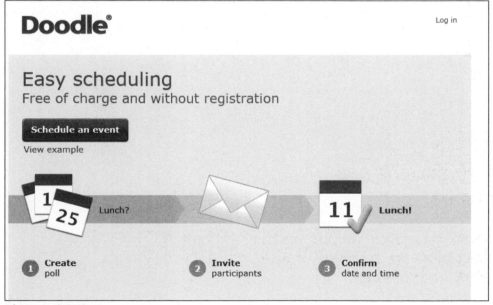

Figure 23-8

Most of these services are free, and you can use handy views such as calendars and tables to help you organize your various events.

Send E-greeting Cards

Who among us hasn't had the experience of suddenly realizing a dear friend or relative's birthday is tomorrow and we forgot to get and mail a card? The Internet to the rescue: You can now use online greeting card services to send fun e-cards with animation and music. The convenient part is that your greeting can get to recipients at the very last minute.

Visit sites such as www.hallmark.com (shown in **Figure 23-9**) and www.123greetings.com to check out what they have to offer. Some of these sites are free; some offer a few free cards but charge you a yearly fee to access their full range of cards.

 When you use some sites that are entirely free, you run a greater risk of downloading viruses or having advertising placed on your cards. The yearly subscriptions to legitimate sites are very low, allowing you to send out as many greetings as you like for the entire year, so you might consider spending the money to use one.

When you use an online greeting card site it will give you easy instructions, but you typically follow these steps in some order:

1. Search the site to find a card.

2. Personalize the card with a greeting and select certain formatting for text.

3. Preview the card.

4. Enter the recipient's e-mail address.

5. Send the card on its way. The recipient gets an e-mail notification with a link to click to view the card.

Figure 23-9

Recommend a Site to Others

A phenomenon called *social bookmarking* allows you to share your likes and dislikes for online sites and content with others. Web sites that sport icons from services such as Digg, StumbleUpon, Delicious, and Diigo provide a way for you to report your opinion about articles, videos, and more. **Figure 23-10** shows one site with several social bookmarking icons on display. Services such as Facebook and Twitter also allow you to rate content by posting a comment on their sites. Google buzz is another way to publicly or privately share your opinion.

When you click any of these icons, you're taken to a web page where you can sign in to an account or open a new account with a service. You can then type your comment in to whatever form that service provides, such as the one from Google buzz shown in **Figure 23-11.** With social sites such as Facebook and Twitter, you can share a comment and link with your Facebook friends or those following you on Twitter.

Social bookmarking icons

Figure 23-10

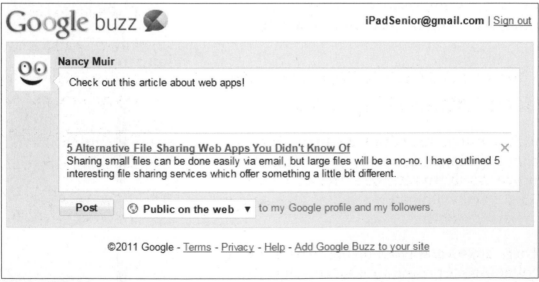

Figure 23-11

Getting Involved in the Social Net

*I*n this chapter, I look at the world of the social net. Social networking sites such as Facebook are a great way for you to connect with others and share your thoughts, your images, and your activities.

If you're new to social networking, this chapter gives you an overview of what it's all about, shows you the different types of services available, and even takes you through the signup process on one popular site for seniors. In addition, I provide some advice on online dating services and image-sharing sites (which are discussed in more detail in Chapter 18).

Overview of Collaborative and Social Networking Sites

Although you may think kids are the most active group using social networking, statistics prove that it isn't the case. In fact, people 35–54 years old make up a large segment of social networkers.

There are several types of sites where people collaborate or communicate socially. The following definitions may be useful:

➡ **Wiki:** A web site that allows anyone visiting to contribute (add, edit, or remove) content. Wikipedia, for example, is a virtual encyclopedia built by users providing information in their areas of expertise. Because of the ease of collaboration, wikis are often used when developing group projects or sharing information collaboratively. One such site, Wikipedia (`http://en.wikipedia.org`), is shown in **Figure 24-1**.

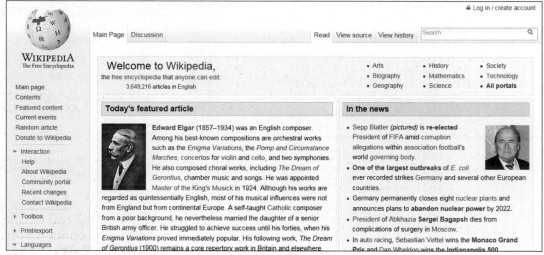

Figure 24-1

➡ **Blog:** An online journal (*blog* is short for *web log*) that may be entirely private, open to select friends or family, or available to the general public. You can usually adjust your blog settings to restrict visitors from commenting on your blog entries, if you'd like.

➡ **Social networking site:** This type of web site (see **Figure 24-2**) allows people to build and maintain an online web page and create networks of people that they're somehow connected to — their friends, work associates, and/or other members with similar interests. Most social networking sites also host blogs and

have social networking functions that allow people
to view information about others (in the form of
member profiles) and contact each other.

Figure 24-2

⟶ **Social journaling sites:** Sites such as Twitter
(http://twitter.com) allow people to go online
with short notes which are typically about what
they're doing or thinking at the moment. Many companies and celebrities are now *tweeting,* as posting
comments on Twitter is referred to. You can follow
individuals on Twitter so you're always informed if
somebody you're a fan of makes a post.

Compare Popular Services

Many social networking sites are general in nature and attract a wide variety of users, such as Facebook, Bebo, or Myspace. Facebook, which was begun by some students at Harvard as a college student–only site, has become today's most popular general site, and many seniors use its features to blog, exchange virtual "gifts," and post photos. Other social networking sites revolve around particular interests or age groups. For example, LinkedIn (www.linkedin.com) is aimed at those who want to network with a focus on their careers, and Eons (www.eons.com) is a social site for seniors.

There are also sites that provide social networking features which are focused around issues such as grief and healthcare, and sites that host politics- or consumer-oriented discussions.

 Visit TopTenReviews for a detailed comparison of social web sites at http://social-networking-websites-review.toptenreviews.com/. You can find out handy information such as which sites have mostly under 18 users, which have stronger privacy settings, and which allow you to share videos, music, and other types of contents with others.

Sign Up for a Social Networking Service

Here's where you can walk through the signup process for Eons, a senior social networking site, to see the kinds of information they ask for. Follow these instructions to do so:

1. Type this URL into your browser address line: **www.eons. com**.

2. Click the Sign Up link near the top of the page.

3. In the signup form that appears (see **Figure 24-3**), enter your name, e-mail address, a password, your birthdate, gender, and zip code and then click Sign Up.

Note that the site requires your birthdate to verify that you are a senior, but you can choose to hide this information from others later if you don't want it displayed.

The Sign Up button

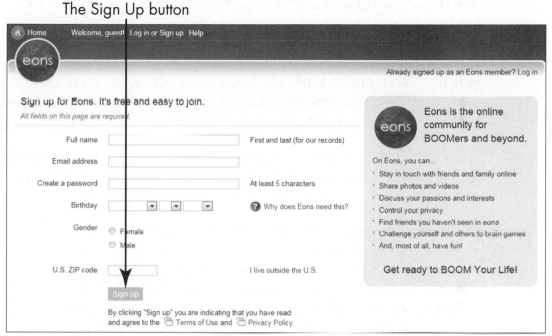

Figure 24-3

4. On the screen that appears (see **Figure** 24-4), you can enter a screen name.

Consider nicknames and the messages they send. Names like `lookin'forlove` or `lonelyinHouston` may send a message that you're lonely and emotionally vulnerable.

5. Click Check Availability to see if the alias you entered is not already in use as a screen name. If the screen name you request is already taken, choose another screen name and try again.

6. Click Sign Up.

Part IV: Exploring the Internet

Enter a screen name here

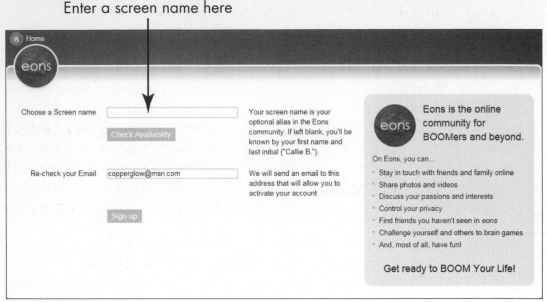

Figure 24-4

7. At this point, you're instructed to check your e-mail
account for a message. When you receive the message,
click the link in it to confirm your e-mail address. When
you do, a page appears saying that your e-mail address
has been confirmed and instructing you what to do next.
Click the Explore the Eons Homepage button on this
page, and your Eons page is displayed (see **Figure 24-5**).

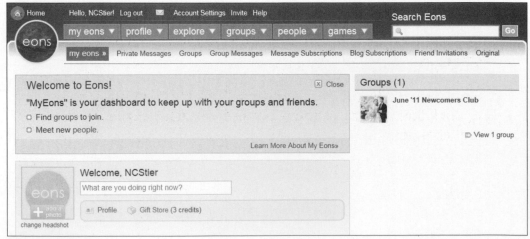

Figure 24-5

Click the Account Settings link at the top of your page and review the privacy setting there to control who can access information you post on your page.

Create a Profile

When signing up for a service, understand what is *required* information and what is optional. You should clearly understand why a web service needs any of your personally identifiable information and how they may use that information — before providing it. Consider carefully the questions that sites ask users to answer in creating a profile.

 Warning: Accepting a social networking service's default settings may expose more information than you intend.

Follow these steps to create a profile in Eons (there are similar steps for adding to your profile in other popular social networking sites):

1. After creating an account (see the previous task), log in to Eons by going to www.eons.com, clicking the Log In link, and entering your screen name or e-mail address and password.

2. Click the arrow on the Profile tab and then choose About from the drop-down list.

3. Click a tab in the About section such as Relationship (see **Figure 24-6**) to modify your profile and click Save Changes.

4. Continue to click tabs and enter information, being sure to click Save Changes at the bottom of each tab to save any changes.

The Save Changes button

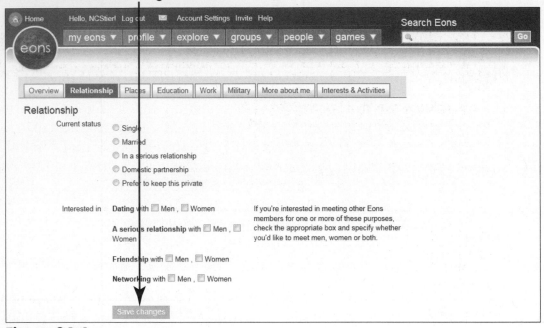

Figure 24-6

Invite Friends

1. Having logged in to your account, with your page displayed, click the People tab and choose Find Real Life Friends.

2. In the form that appears, shown in **Figure 24-7**, enter a name and e-mail address for somebody you know, and then click Find My Contacts to see whether that person has an Eons account.

You can also click the Use Your Email Address Book link to search your saved e-mail contacts.

3. On the screen that appears (see **Figure 24-8**) with a contact selected, click the Invite button.

Your friend receives an invitation in her e-mail inbox; by clicking a link in the invitation, she will become your friend on Eons.

The Find My Contacts button

The Use Your Email Address Book link

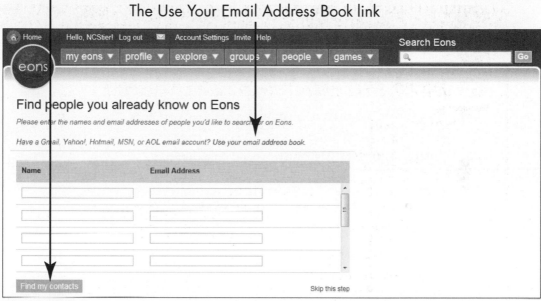

Figure 24-7

Click the Invite button

Figure 24-8

 Display a list of friends by clicking the People tab and choosing My Friends.

See How Online Dating Works

Many seniors are making connections with others via online dating services. In fact, finding a possible partner online can be a good way to gradually get to know somebody (and make sure he or she is right for you) before you meet in person. If you've been wondering if this route could be for you, here's how you can jump into the world of online dating:

➡ Choose a reputable dating site. (See the next task.)

➡ Sign up and provide information about your likes, dislikes, preferences, and so on. This often takes the form of a self-guided interview process.

➡ Create and modify your profile to both avoid exposing too much personal information and ensure that you're sending the right message about yourself to prospective dates.

➡ Use search features on the site (see **Figure 24-9**) to find people who interest you and send them messages or invitations to view your profile.

➡ You'll get messages from other members of the site, to which you can respond (or not). Use the site's chat and e-mail features to interact with potential dates. You may also be able to read comments about the person from others who've dated him or her, if the site has that feature.

➡ When you're comfortable with the person and feel there might be a spark, decide whether you want to meet the person offline.

 Formal dating sites aren't the only places that people meet online, but they typically have the best safeguards in place. If you want to interact with people you meet on other sites, you should provide your own safeguards. Create a separate e-mail account (so you can remain anonymous and abandon the e-mail address if needed). Many dating sites screen participants and provide strong reporting measures that are missing on other types of sites, so be particularly careful. Take your time getting to know someone first before connecting.

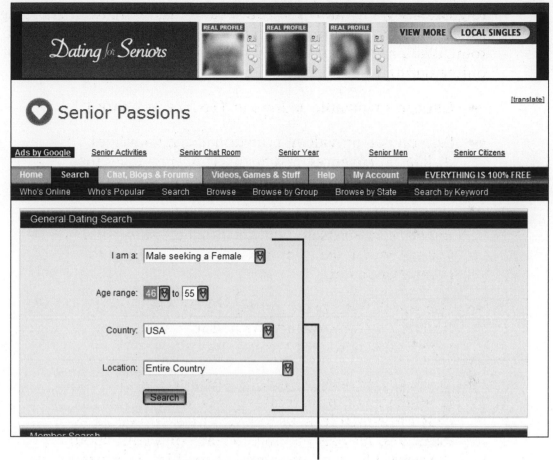

Identify the type of people you'd like to meet

Figure 24-9

Select a Dating Service

Select your online dating service carefully.

➡ Look for an established, popular site with plenty of members and a philosophy that matches your own.

➡ Review the site's policy regarding your privacy and its procedures for screening members. Make sure you're comfortable with them.

➠ Use a service that provides an e-mail system that you use for contacting other members only (sometimes called *private messaging*). By using the site's e-mail rather than your own e-mail address, you can maintain your privacy.

➠ Some sites, such as `http://saferdates.com`, shown in **Figure 24-10,** offer stronger levels of authenticating members. Safer Dates, for example, uses fingerprint identification and screening to make you more confident that you know who you're interacting with.

Figure 24-10

➠ Visit a site such as `www.onlinedatingsites.net` for comparisons of sites. Whether you choose a senior-specific dating site such as DatingForSeniors.com or a general-population site such as Match.com, reading reviews about the sites ahead of time will help you make the best choice.

Most people have good experiences with online dating, but if you try a site and experience an unpleasant incident involving another member, report it and make sure the service follows through to enforce its policies. If it doesn't, find another service.

Explore Twitter

Twitter is a *microblogging* service, which means you can share your thoughts with others, but with a limit of 140 characters. When you join Twitter, you can create a profile and gain followers who can read your postings (see **Figure 24-11**). You can also follow others. It's an interesting way to get quick updates on what your friends or family members are doing, or to follow a public figure or celebrity's activities and thoughts.

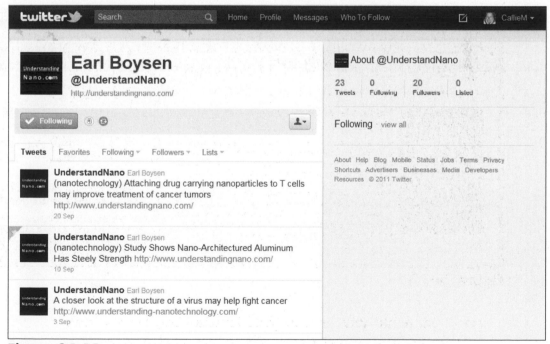

Figure 24-11

You can also set up Twitter on your mobile phone and get notifications when people you're following post new messages, called *tweets*. You can include location information with your tweets, share photos and videos, and include links so your followers can go to another site to read more detailed information than the limited characters allowed in a tweet.

Get Involved in Video and Photo Sharing

The ability to share photos and videos online is a wonderful way to connect to others. You can use services such as YouTube, Clickster, or PhotoBucket, or you can simply share your images on your social networking page.

 See Chapter 18 to read the steps you can follow to join Flickr and post a photo to the site.

Do be cautious about what images you share if your page isn't totally private. It's easy to copy images from the web and distribute them widely, so if you wouldn't want anybody in your life to see a particular image, don't post it.

Part V
Taking Care of Your Laptop

The 5th Wave   By Rich Tennant

" A centralized security management system
sounds fine, but then what would we do
with all the dogs?"

Laptop Security and Safety

*Y*our laptop contains software and files that can be damaged in several different ways.

One major source of damage is from malicious attacks that are delivered via the Internet. Some people create damaging programs called *viruses* that are specifically designed to get onto your laptop's hard drive and destroy or scramble data.

Companies might download *adware* to your laptop, which causes pop-up ads to appear, slowing down your laptop's performance.

Spyware is another form of malicious software that you might inadvertently download by clicking a link or opening a file attachment; *spyware* sits on your laptop and tracks your activities, whether for use by a legitimate company in selling you products or by a criminal element to steal your identity.

Microsoft provides security features within Windows 7 that help to keep your laptop and information safe, whether you're at home or travelling.

In this chapter, I introduce you to the major concepts of laptop security including:

Chapter

Chapter

25

➠ Understand laptop security and why you need it.

➠ Run periodic updates to Windows that install security solutions and patches to the software (*patches* fix security problems).

➠ Enable a *firewall*, which is a security feature that keeps your laptop safe from outsiders and helps you avoid several kinds of attacks on your data.

➠ Set up a password to protect your laptop from others.

➠ Protect yourself against spyware.

➠ Use devices such as a laptop lock or fingerprint reader to keep bad guys away from your laptop.

➠ Protect your laptop from physical damage.

➠ Find your laptop or protect the data on it from thieves if it's lost or stolen.

Understand Laptop Security

When you buy a car, it has certain safety features built in. After you drive it off the lot, you might find that the manufacturer slipped up and either recalls your car or requests that you go to the dealer's service department to get a faulty part replaced. In addition, you need to drive defensively to keep your car from being damaged in daily use.

Your laptop is similar to your car in terms of the need for safety. It comes with an operating system (such as Microsoft Windows) built in, and that operating system has security features. Sometimes that operating system has flaws, and you need to get updates to it to keep it secure. (I tell you more about that in the next two tasks.) And as you use your laptop, you're exposing it to dangerous conditions and situations that you have to guard against.

Some files contain programs that threaten your laptop security. Such files may get transferred to your laptop when you copy them from a disc you insert into your laptop, but most of the time, the danger is from a program that is downloaded from the Internet. These downloads can happen without you knowing it when you click a link or open an attachment in an e-mail; or you may download a legitimate piece of software without realizing that another program is attached to it.

There are three main types of dangerous programs (collectively called *malware*) you should be aware of:

➡ A *virus* is a little program that some nasty person thought up to spread around the Internet and infect computers. A virus can do a variety of things, but typically it attacks your data, deleting files, scrambling data, or making changes to your system settings that cause your laptop to grind to a halt.

➡ *Spyware* consists of programs whose main purpose in life is to track activities on your laptop. Some spyware simply helps companies you do business with to track what you do online so they can figure out how to sell you things; other spyware is used for more insidious purposes, such as stealing your passwords.

➡ *Adware* is the computer equivalent of telemarketing phone calls at dinner time. Once adware is downloaded onto your laptop, you'll get annoying pop-up windows trying to sell you things all day long. Beyond the annoyance, adware can quickly proliferate, slowing down your laptop's performance until it's hard to get anything done at all.

To protect your information and your laptop from these various types of malware, you can do several things:

➡ **Buy and install an antivirus, antispyware, or antiadware program.** Programs such as McAfee Antivirus, Norton Antivirus from Symantec (see **Figure 25-1**), or the freely downloadable AVG Free from Grisoft can help prevent the downloading of malicious files. These types of programs can also detect files that have somehow gotten through and delete them for you. Remember that after you install such a program, you have to download regular updates to it to handle new threats, and you need to run scans on your system to catch items that might have snuck through. Many antivirus programs are purchased by yearly subscription, which gives you access to updated virus definitions that the company constantly gathers throughout the year.

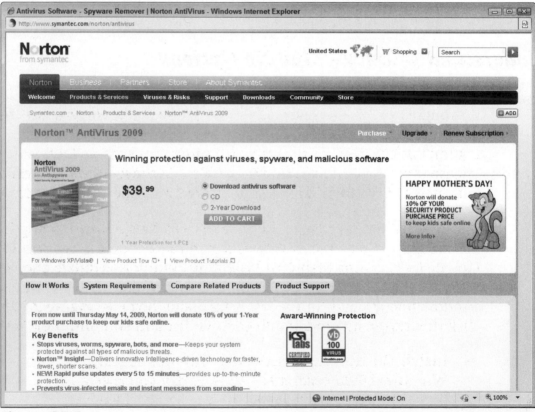

Figure 25-1

➡ **Some other programs, such as Spyware Doctor from PC Tools, combine tools for detecting adware and spyware.** Windows 7 has a built-in program, Windows Defender, that includes an antispyware feature.

➡ **Use Windows tools to keep Windows up to date with security features and fixes to security problems.**

➡ **Turn on a firewall, which is a feature that stops other people or programs from accessing your laptop without your permission.**

The last two features of Windows are covered in this chapter.

Understand Windows Update Options

When a new operating system like Windows 7 is released, it has been thoroughly tested; however, when the product is in general use, the manufacturer begins to find a few problems or security gaps that it couldn't anticipate. For that reason, companies such as Microsoft release updates to their software, both to fix those problems and deal with new threats to laptops that appeared after the software release.

Windows Update is a tool you can use to make sure your laptop has the most up-to-date security measures in place. You can set Windows Update by choosing Start➪All Programs➪Windows Update and clicking the Change Settings link on the left side of the Windows Update window that appears. In the resulting dialog box (see **Figure 25-2**), click the Important Updates drop-down list and you find these settings:

➡ **Install Updates Automatically:** With this setting, Windows Update starts at a time of day you specify, but your laptop must be on for it to work. If you've turned off your laptop, the automatic update will start when you next turn on your laptop, and it might shut down your laptop in the middle of your work to reboot (turn off and then on) and complete the installation.

Click this arrow for drop-down list

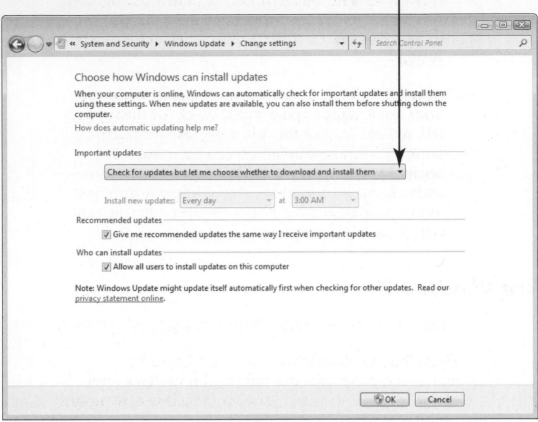

Figure 25-2

➡ **Download Updates But Let Me Choose Whether to Install Them:** You can set up Windows Update to download updates and have Windows notify you (through a little pop-up message on your taskbar) when they're available. You get to decide when the updates are installed and when your laptop reboots to complete the installation. This is my preferred setting because I have control and won't be caught unaware by a sudden laptop reboot.

➠ **Check for Updates But Let Me Choose Whether to Download and Install Them:** With this setting, you neither download nor install updates until you say so, but Windows notifies you that new updates are available.

➠ **Never Check for Updates:** You can stop Windows from checking for updates and check for them yourself, manually. (See the following task for instructions.) This puts your laptop at a bit more risk because you may neglect to download important updates, but it's useful for you to know how to perform a manual update if you discover a new update is available that you need.

Run Windows Update

1. Choose Start⇨All Programs⇨Windows Update.

2. In the Windows Update window, click Check for Updates. Windows goes out hunting for updates for a while, so feel free to check your latest Facebook messages for a minute or two.

3. In the resulting window, as shown in **Figure 25-3,** click the Updates Are Available link to see all optional or important updates.

4. In the following window, which shows the available updates (see **Figure 25-4**), click to select available critical or optional updates that you want to install. Then click the OK button.

Click this link

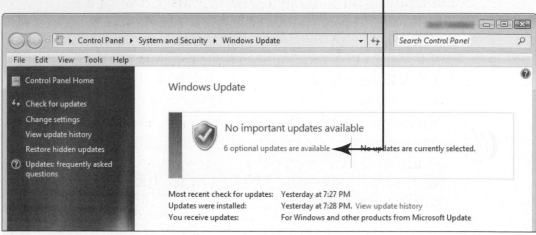

Figure 25-3

Select update to install

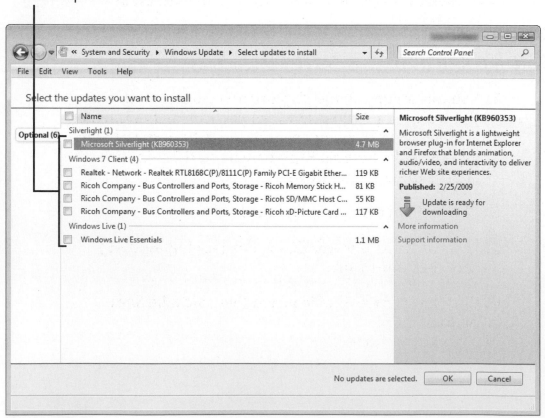

Figure 25-4

5. In the Windows Update window that appears, click the Install Updates button. A window appears, showing the progress of your installation. When the installation is complete, you might get a message telling you that it's a good idea to restart your laptop to complete the installation. Click Restart Now.

You can set up Windows Update to run at the same time every day. Click the Change Settings link in the Windows Update window and choose the frequency (such as every day) and time of day to check for and install updates.

Running Windows Update on a regular basis — either automatically or manually — ensures that you get the latest security updates to the operating system. It's a good idea to stay current with those updates.

Set Up Trusted and Restricted Web Sites

1. You can set up Internet Explorer to recognize web sites you trust — and those to which you don't want Internet Explorer to take you or anybody else who uses your laptop. Click the Internet Explorer icon in the Windows taskbar to start your browser.

2. Choose Tools⇨Internet Options.

3. In the Internet Options dialog box (see **Figure 25-5**), click the Security tab.

4. Click the Trusted Sites icon and then click the Sites button.

Security tab

Figure 25-5

5. In the resulting Trusted Sites dialog box, enter a URL (web site address) in the Add This Web Site to the Zone text box for a web site you want to allow your laptop to access.

If you wish to allow any locations for particular companies, such as Microsoft, you can use a *wildcard* (a character that tells the computer to trust all sites that include that word in the URL). **Figure 25-6** shows the asterisk (*) wildcard in use in the Websites field.

6. Click Add to add the site to the list of web sites, as shown in **Figure 25-6**.

7. Repeat Steps 3–6 to add more sites.

An asterisk serves as a wildcard

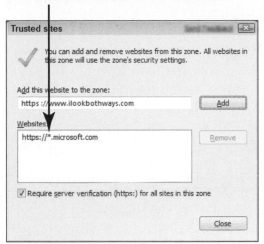

Figure 25-6

8. When you're done, click Close and then click OK to close the dialog boxes.

9. To designate sites that you don't want your laptop to access, repeat Steps 1–8, clicking the Restricted Sites icon rather than Trusted Sites in Step 4 to designate sites that you don't want your laptop to access.

In the Trusted Sites dialog box, if the Require Server Verification (https:) for All Sites In This Zone check box is selected, then any trusted site you add must use the `https` prefix, which indicates that the site has a secure connection.

You can establish a Privacy setting on the Privacy tab of the Internet Options dialog box to control which sites are allowed to download *cookies* to your laptop. *Cookies* are tiny files that a site uses to track your online activity and recognize you when you return to the source site. Some sites need to use cookies to allow you to use your account — and that's fine — but other sites may use cookies to track (and even sell information about) your online activities that could put you at risk. *Trusted sites* are ones that you allow to download cookies to your laptop even though the privacy setting you have made might not allow other sites to do so. *Restricted sites* can never download cookies to your laptop, no matter what your privacy setting is.

Enable the Windows Firewall

1. A firewall keeps outsiders from accessing your laptop via the Internet. Choose Start⇨Control Panel⇨System and Security⇨Windows Firewall.

2. In the Windows Firewall window that appears (see **Figure 25-7**), check that the Windows Firewall is marked as On. If it isn't, click the Turn Windows Firewall On or Off link in the left pane of the window.

Verify the firewall is on

Figure 25-7

3. In the resulting Customize Settings window (see **Figure 25-8**), select the Turn on Windows Firewall radio button for Home or Work (private) Network Location Settings and/or Public Network Location Settings and then click OK.

 It's always a good idea to have the firewall turned on when you go online using a public "hot spot" connection, such as at an Internet café. If you have a home network, you may already have a firewall active in the router (one piece of equipment used to set up the network), so the Windows firewall setting could be optional there.

Select this option

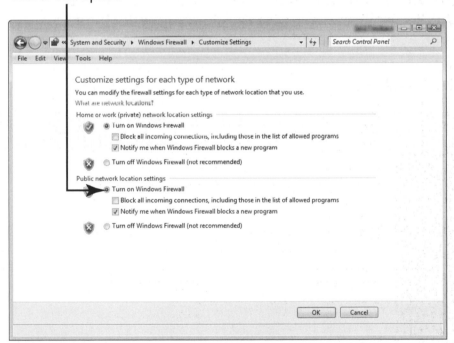

Figure 25-8

4. Click the Close button to close Windows Security Center and the Control Panel.

A *firewall* is a program that protects your laptop from the outside world. This is generally a good thing. If you have set up a Virtual Private Network (VPN) that you connect your laptop to when at home, be aware that using a firewall with a VPN results in you being unable to share files and use some other VPN features.

Antivirus and security software programs may offer their own firewall protection and may display a message asking whether you want to switch. Check their features against Windows and then decide, but usually most firewall features are comparable. The important thing is to have one activated.

Set Up a Password for Your Laptop

1. To set up a password on your user account so others can't get at your laptop and files without entering that password, choose Start⇨Control Panel, and then click User Accounts and Family Safety.

2. In the resulting window (shown in **Figure 25-9**), click the Change Your Windows Password link. Then, if you have more than one user account, click an account to add the password to. Click the Create a Password for Your Account link.

3. In the Create a Password for Your Account screen, shown in **Figure 25-10**, enter a password, confirm it, and add a password hint.

4. Click the Create Password button.

Click this link

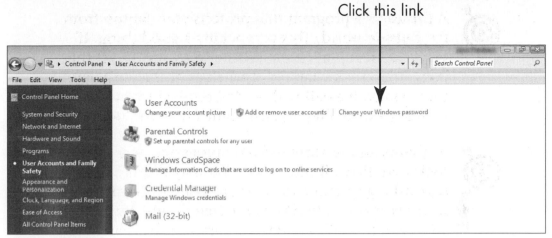

Figure 25-9

Enter and confirm the new password

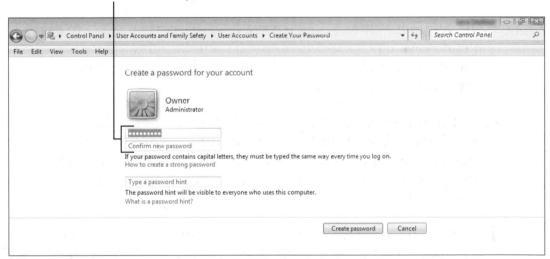

Figure 25-10

5. You return to the Make Changes to Your User Account window. If you wish to remove your password at some point, you can click the Remove Your Password link here.

6. Click the Close button to close the User Accounts window.

If you forget your password, Windows shows the hint you entered to help you remember it, but note that anybody who uses your laptop can see the hint when it's displayed. So if lots of people know that you drive a Ford and your hint is "My car model," your password protection is about as effective as a thin raincoat in a hurricane. Consider using a less known but easy to remember password. If you love Shakespeare, for example, use something like R0me0&Jul1et where you replace the letter Os with zeros and the letter Is with ones. Easy to remember, but hard to guess!

After you create a password, you can go to the User Accounts window and change it at any time by clicking Change Your Password. You can also change the name on your user account by clicking Change Your Account Name.

Check Your Laptop's Security Status

1. Choose Start⇨Control Panel⇨System and Security.

2. In the resulting System and Security window, (see **Figure 25-11**), click the Review Your Computer's Status and Resolve Issues link.

Figure 25-11

3. In the Action Center window that appears (see **Figure 25-12**), check to see if the Security item states whether Windows found any antivirus software on your laptop.

Find out if you have antivirus software

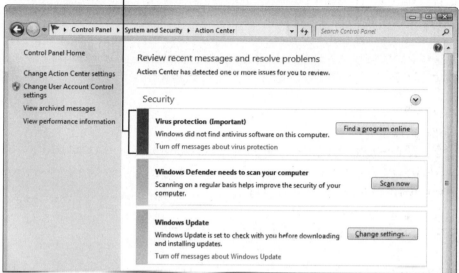

Figure 25-12

4. If Windows did not find such software, click the Find A Program Online button and review the Microsoft recommended security software partners. If you want to purchase one of these software products, click the logo of the company you want to buy from, and you're taken to their site, where you can buy and download the software.

 It's very important that you do have antivirus and antispyware software installed on your laptop — and that you run updates to them on a regular basis. These types of programs help you avoid downloading malware to your laptop that could bother you with advertising pop-ups, slow your laptop's performance, damage computer files, or even track your keystrokes as you type to steal your identity. If you don't want to pay for an antispyware program, consider a free solution such as Spyware Terminator (www.spywareterminator.com).

Use a Lock to Deter Thieves

When you travel with your laptop, you may have to leave it alone for a few moments now and then — perhaps in a cubicle in a branch office or a table at an Internet café while you step away to grab your latte. When that happens, a lock that you clip to your laptop (usually on the back or side, identified by a lock icon) and wrap around a table or desk leg might make you feel more secure. These are similar to the lock you use to keep your bicycle safe as you wander into a store or gym.

Don't count on a laptop lock to keep your laptop safe during a lengthy absence. They are relatively easy to circumvent. But for a short period of time in a non-high-risk area, they can be useful.

Locks are relatively cheap, from about $5 to $30 or so. They're also usually pretty easy to tuck into a laptop case without adding much bulk.

Utilize a Fingerprint Reader

Fingerprint readers use *biometric* technology that identifies you by a unique physical characteristic. Here's what you should know about laptop fingerprint readers:

➡ Many laptops include a built-in fingerprint reader for security. This is useful to keep anybody but you from accessing data on your laptop because your fingerprint is unique. See your manual for instructions on using the reader.

➡ If your laptop doesn't have a built-in fingerprint reader, you can buy an external model such as the Microsoft Fingerprint Reader. These have a wide price range (from about $40 to $200), but they are relatively portable. **Figure 25-13** shows one such device from Eikon.

Figure 25-13

➠ Some fingerprint readers allow you to log in to your laptop by simply swiping your finger over the reader, and some can also store passwords for your online accounts. Laptops or tablets with a touchscreen may allow you to press your finger to the screen to read your fingerprint.

Protect Your Laptop from Damage

Here are a few tips for protecting your laptop from physical damage, or recouping some losses if damage does occur:

➠ A well-made laptop case is really a must when moving about with your laptop. It helps to protect the laptop if you drop it and protect it from things falling on it. Look for one with both good padding and pockets for storing USB sticks and cords and DVDs, a power cord, and possibly a fingerprint reader or lock.

➠ Your laptop screen is one of its biggest vulnerabilities. If it gets scratched or damaged in some way, short of attaching an external monitor (which doesn't do you much good if you're on a plane), your laptop is pretty much a goner. You can buy a fairly low-cost screen protector, a thin sheet of plastic that you place across your monitor that can help prevent scratches and, as a bonus, keep your screen clean.

➡ Because you can't prevent each and every possible disaster, always *back up* your data (copy it to storage other than your laptop's hard drive) so you don't lose it — and consider getting insurance for your laptop. If your homeowner's policy doesn't already cover it, companies such as Safeware offer special laptop insurance against damage and theft. If your laptop is essential to your work or hobby, or if you travel with it a great deal, you might want to get an insurance quote to see whether coverage is within your budget.

Use a Service to Find a Lost Laptop

Laptops are lost or stolen on a frightenly regular basis. The biggest concern, aside from having to buy a new laptop (which may or may not be covered by your insurance), is what a thief might do with the data on the laptop. Stored passwords for financial and retail shopping accounts could be used to steal your identity or run up debt in your name.

Luckily there are software applications such as LapTopCop (see **Figure 25-14**) and CompuTrace, as well as free software such as Adeona or LapTopLock that you can install on your laptop. Adeona, for instance, transmits regular messages as to your laptop's location as long as it's connected to the Internet. Other options offer a central service that tracks your laptop's whereabouts.

Figure 25-14

Using these programs and services, you can do several things, depending on software features — including these:

⟹ Pinpointing where your laptop is whenever it connects to the Internet.

⟹ Remotely disabling the computer, deleting files from it, or locking out any would-be user.

⟹ Issuing a warning to the thief that the computer is now protected and useless.

⟹ Observing what activities the thief is performing on your computer in real time.

Maintaining Windows

Chapter 26

*A*ll the wonderful hardware that you've spent your hard-earned money on doesn't mean a thing if the software driving it encounters problems. If any programs cause your system to *crash* (meaning it stops responding to commands), you can try a variety of measures to fix it. You can also keep your system in good shape to help you avoid those crashes. In this chapter, you find out how to take good care of your programs and operating system in these ways:

➡ When a program crashes, you can simply shut that program down by using the Windows Task Manager. This utility keeps track of all the programs and processes that are running on your laptop.

➡ If you've got problems and Windows isn't responding, sometimes it helps to restart in Safe mode, which requires your system to run only basic files and hardware drivers. Restarting in Safe mode often allows you to troubleshoot what's going on, and you can restart Windows in its regular mode after you solve the problem.

Get ready to . . .

➡ Use the System Restore feature to first create a *system restore point* (a point in time when your settings and programs all seem to be humming along just fine) and then restore Windows to that point when trouble hits.

➡ You can clean up your system to delete unused files, free up disk space, and schedule maintenance tasks.

➡ If you need a little help, you might run a trouble-shooting program to help you figure out a problem you're experiencing with a program.

Shut Down a Nonresponsive Application

1. If your laptop crashes and won't let you proceed with what you were doing, press Ctrl+Alt+Del.

2. In the Windows screen that appears, click Start Task Manager.

3. In the resulting Windows Task Manager dialog box (see **Figure 26-1**), click the Applications tab and select the application that you were using when your system stopped responding.

4. Click the End Task button.

5. In the resulting dialog box, the Windows Task Manager tells you that the application isn't responding and asks whether you want to shut it down now. Click Yes.

If pressing Ctrl+Alt+Del doesn't bring up the Task Manager, you're in bigger trouble than you thought. You might need to press and hold your laptop power button to shut down your computer. Note that some applications use an AutoSave feature that keeps an interim version of the document that you were working in — you might be able to save some of your work by opening that last-saved version. Other programs don't have such a safety net, and you simply lose whatever changes you made to your document since the last time you saved it. The moral? Save, and save often.

 A dialog box may appear when an application shuts down, asking whether you want to report the problem to Microsoft. If you say yes, information is sent to Microsoft to help them provide advice or fix a problem in Windows down the road.

The Applications tab

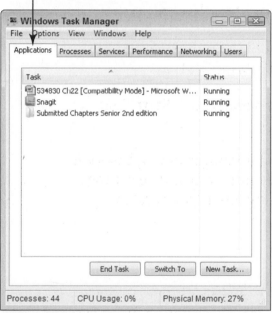

Figure 26-1

Start Windows in Safe Mode

1. To start Windows in a mode that loads only the most vital files, allowing you to get started and fix problems (for example, by performing a system restore to a time before the problems started) remove any CDs or DVDs from your laptop.

2. Choose Start, click the arrow on the right of the Shut Down button, and then choose Restart to reboot your system. (See **Figure 26-2.**)

Figure 26-2

3. When the laptop starts to reboot (the screen goes black), begin pressing F8.

4. If you have more than one operating system, you might see the Windows Boot Manager menu. Use the up- and down-arrow keys to select the Windows 7 operating system. Or type the number of that choice, press Enter, and then continue to press F8.

5. In the resulting Advanced Boot Options (a plain-vanilla, text-based screen), press the up- or down-arrow key to select the Safe Mode option from the list and then press Enter.

6. Log in to your laptop with administrator privileges; a Safe Mode screen appears. (See **Figure 26-3.**) Use the tools in the Control Panel and the Help and Support system to figure out your problem, make changes, and then

restart. When you restart again (repeat Step 2), let your laptop start in the standard Windows 7 mode.

 When you reboot and press F8 in Steps 3 and 4, you're in the old text-based world that users of the DOS operating system will remember. It's scary out there! Your mouse doesn't work a lick, and no fun sounds or cool graphics exist to soothe you. In fact, DOS is the reason the whole *For Dummies* series started because *everybody* felt like a dummy using it, me included. Just use your arrow keys to get around and press Enter to make selections. You're soon back in Windows-land . . .

 When you're troubleshooting and trying things like starting in Safe mode, it's a good idea to plug in your laptop, if possible. Some of these procedures can take some time, and you don't want to run out of battery power while running an important diagnostic and add to your woes!

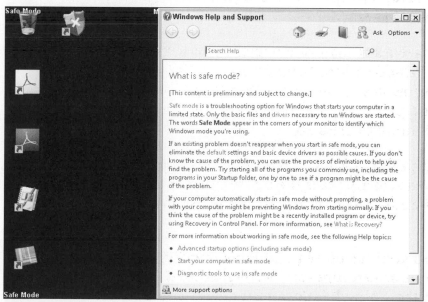

Figure 26-3

Create a System Restore Point

1. You can back up your system files, which creates a restore point you can later use to return your laptop to earlier settings before you began to experience problems. Choose Start⇨Control Panel⇨System and Security, and in the resulting System and Security dialog box, click the System link.

2. In the System dialog box, click the System Protection link in the left panel. In the System Properties dialog box that appears (see **Figure 26-4**), click the Create button.

Click this button

Figure 26-4

3. In the Create A Restore Point dialog box that appears, enter a name to identify the restore point, such as the current date or the name of a program you are about to install, and click Create.

4. Windows displays a progress window. When the restore point is created, the message shown in **Figure 26-5** appears. Click Close to close the message box, and then click Close to close the System Protection dialog box, and Close again to close the Control Panel.

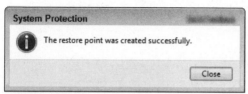

Figure 26-5

 Every once in a while, when you install some software or make some new settings in Windows and things seem to be running just fine, create a system restore point. It's good laptop practice, just like backing up your files, only you're backing up your settings. Once a month or once every couple months works for most people, but if you frequently make changes to Windows settings or install new programs, create a system restore point more often.

 A more drastic option to System Restore is to run the system-recovery disc that probably came with your laptop or that you created using discs you provided. Keep in mind, however, that system recovery essentially puts your laptop right back to the configuration it had when it was carried out of the factory. That means you lose any software you've installed since then, and any documents you've created since you began to use it. (A good argument for creating system restore points on a regular basis, don't you think?)

Restore the Windows System

1. Choose Start⇨Control Panel⇨Back up Your Computer (under System and Security).

2. In the Back Up and Restore window, click the Recover System Settings on Your Computer link. In the Recovery window shown in **Figure 26-6,** click the Open System Restore button.

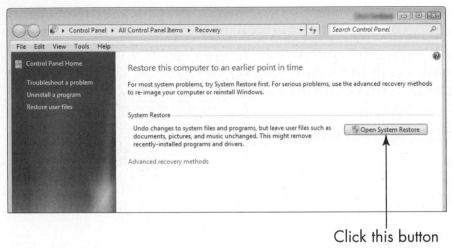

Click this button

Figure 26-6

3. The System Restore feature shows a progress dialog box as it starts. In the resulting System Restore window, click Next.

4. In the System Restore dialog box that appears, click the system restore point to which you want to restore the laptop and then click the Next button.

5. A dialog box asks you to confirm that you want to run System Restore and informs you that your laptop will need to restart to complete the process. Close any open files or programs, and then click Finish to proceed.

6. The system goes through a shutdown-and-restart sequence, and then displays a dialog box that informs you that the System Restore has occurred.

7. Click OK to close it.

System Restore doesn't get rid of files that you've saved, so you don't lose your family genealogy files or holiday card list. System Restore simply reverts to Windows settings as of the restore point. This can help if you or some piece of installed software made a setting that is causing some conflict in your system that makes your laptop sluggish or prone to crashes. If you're concerned about what changes will happen, click the Scan for Affected Programs button shown in the window displayed in **Figure 26-7.**

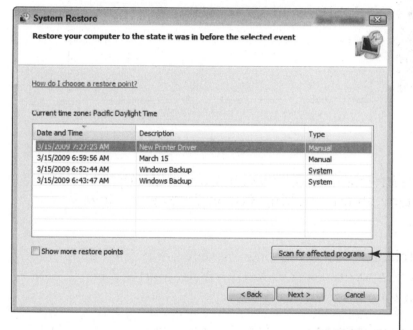

Click this button

Figure 26-7

 System Restore doesn't always solve the problem. Your very best bet is to be sure you create a set of backup discs for your laptop when you buy it. If you didn't do that, and you can't get things running right again, contact your laptop manufacturer. The company may be able to send you a set of recovery discs, though they may charge a small fee. These discs restore your laptop to its state when it left the factory, and you lose applications you installed and documents you created — but you get your laptop running again.

Defragment a Hard Drive

1. To clean up files on your hard drive, choose Start⇨ Control Panel⇨System and Security and then click Defragment Your Hard Drive in the Administrative Tools.

2. In the resulting Disk Defragmenter window (see **Figure 26-8**), to the left of the Defragment Now button is the Analyze Disk button. Use this to check whether your disk requires defragmenting. When the analysis is complete if you want to proceed, click the Defragment Disk button. A notation appears (see **Figure 26-9**) showing the progress of defragmenting your drive.

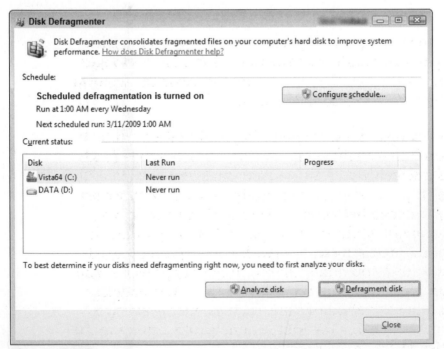

Figure 26-8

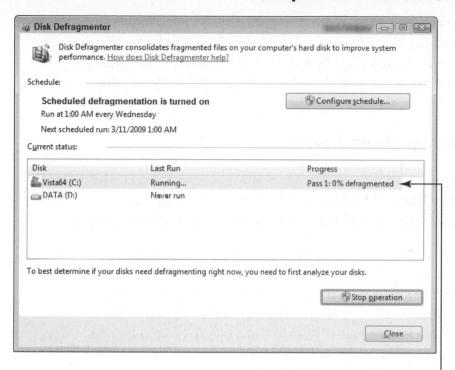

Progress is indicated here

Figure 26-9

3. When the defragmenting process is complete, the Disk
Defragmenter window shows that your drive no longer
requires defragmenting. Click Close to close the window
and then close the Control Panel.

 Warning: Disk defragmenting could take a while. If
you have certain energy-saving features active (such
as a screen saver), they could cause the defragmenter
to stop and start all over again; make sure those are
deactivated beforehand. Try running your defrag
overnight while you're happily dreaming of much
more interesting things (with your laptop plugged
in so that you don't run out of battery power!). You
can also set up the procedure to run automatically
at a preset period of time, such as once every two
weeks, by using the Run Automatically setting in the
Disk Defragmenter window.

Free Your Disk Space

1. To run a process that cleans unused files and fragments of data off of your hard drive to free up space and improve performance, choose Start➪Control Panel➪ System and Security and then click Free Up Disk Space in the Administrative Tools.

2. In the Disk Cleanup dialog box that appears, choose the drive you want to clean up from the drop-down list (typically drive C) and click OK. Disk Cleanup calculates how much space you will be able to free up. (See **Figure 26-10.**)

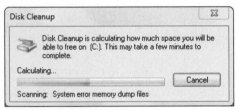

Figure 26-10

3. The resulting dialog box shown in **Figure 26-11** tells you that Disk Cleanup calculated how much space can be cleared on your hard drive and displays the suggested files to delete in a list. (Those to be deleted have a check mark.) If you want to select additional files in the list to delete, click to place a check mark next to each one you want to go away.

4. After you select all the files to delete, click OK. The selected files are deleted. Click the Close button to close the Control Panel.

 Click the View Files button in the Disk Cleanup dialog box to see more details about the files that Windows proposes to delete, including the sizes of the files and when they were created or last accessed.

Figure 26-11

 If you can't free up enough disk space for your needs, you might try using a flash drive (they are available in sizes up to 32GB) to store some of your files. These little storage devices plug in to a USB port on your laptop, are wonderfully portable, and are great for backing up files.

Delete Temporary Internet Files by Using Internet Explorer

1. When you roam the Internet, various files may be downloaded to your laptop to temporarily allow you to access sites or services, but these files can bog down your browsing experience. To clear these away, first open Internet Explorer.

2. Choose Tools⇨Internet Options.

3. On the General tab of the resulting Internet Options dialog box (see **Figure 26-12**), click the Delete button in the Browsing History section.

Click this button

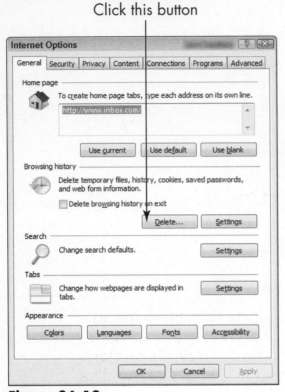

Figure 26-12

4. In the resulting Deleting Browsing History dialog box, as shown in **Figure 26-13,** click the Temporary Internet Files check box to select it, if it's not already selected, and click Delete.

5. A confirmation message asks whether you want to delete the files. Click Yes. Click Close and then click OK to close the open dialog boxes.

Verify this option is selected

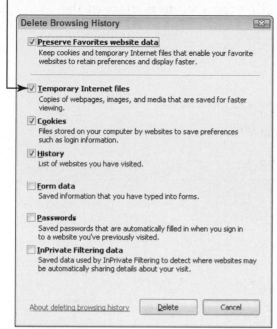

Figure 26-13

 Temporary Internet files can be deleted when you run Disk Cleanup (see the preceding task in this chapter), but the process that I describe here allows you to delete them without having to make choices about deleting other files on your system.

 Windows 7 offers a feature for rating and improving your laptop's performance. From the Control Panel, click System and Security, and then click the Check the Windows Experience Index Base Score link. In the resulting dialog box, click the Rate This Computer button to get a rating of your processor speed, memory operations, and more.

Schedule Maintenance Tasks

1. Choose Start⇨Control Panel⇨System and Security and then click Schedule Tasks in the Administrative Tools.

2. In the resulting Task Scheduler dialog box, as shown in **Figure 26-14**, choose Action⇨Create Task.

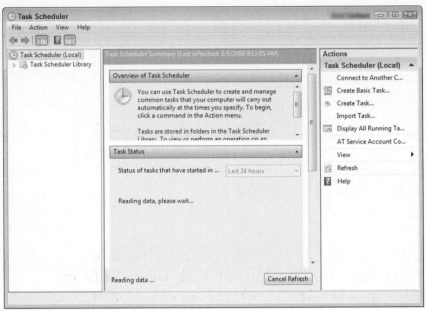

Figure 26-14

3. In the resulting Create Task dialog box (see **Figure 26-15**), enter a task name and description. Choose when to run the task (only when you are logged in, or whether you're logged in or not).

4. Click the Triggers tab and then click New. In the New Trigger dialog box, choose a criterion in the Begin the Task drop-down list and use the settings to specify how often to perform the task, as well as when and at what time of day to begin. Click OK.

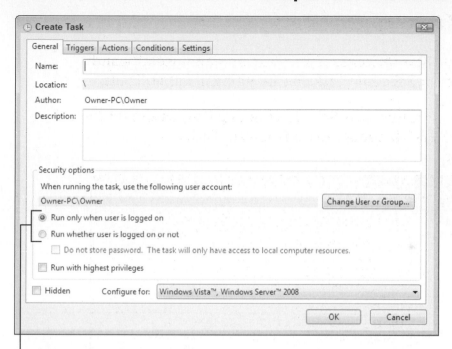

Choose when to run the task

Figure 26-15

5. Click the Actions tab and then click New. In the New Action dialog box, choose the action that will occur from the Action drop-down list. These include starting a program, sending an e-mail, or displaying a message. Depending on what you choose here, different action dialog boxes appear. For example, if you want to send an e-mail, you get an e-mail form to fill in. Click OK.

6. If you want to set conditions in addition to those that trigger the action, click the Conditions tab and enter them.

7. Click the Settings tab and make settings that control how the task runs.

8. After you complete all settings, click OK to save the task.

Troubleshoot Software Problems

1. If you can't figure out why you're having problems with a piece of software, choose Start⇨Control Panel⇨Find and Fix Problems (under System and Security).

2. In the resulting Troubleshooting window (see **Figure 26-16**), click Programs.

Click this link

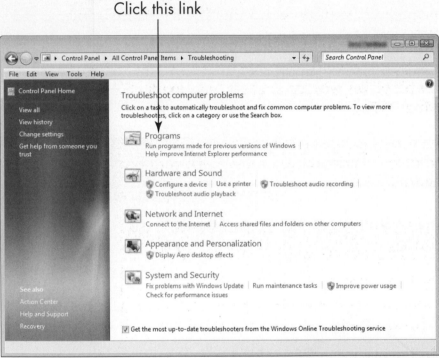

Figure 26-16

3. In the resulting Troubleshooting Problems–Programs window, choose what you want to troubleshoot:

- **Network:** Allows you to troubleshoot a connection to the Internet.

- **Web Browser:** Helps you figure out problems you may be having with the Internet Explorer browser.

- **Program Compatibility:** (Under Programs) This is a good choice if you have an older program that doesn't seem to be functioning well with this version of Windows. Program compatibility is a common cause of problems in running software.

- **Printing:** Allows you to find out why you're having difficulty with your printer, including checking for the correct printer-driver software.

- **Media Player Troubleshooting:** Can be used to pinpoint problems with general settings, media files, or playing DVDs.

4. Follow the sequence of instructions for the item you selected to let Windows help you resolve your problem. (See **Figure 26-17.**)

Figure 26-17

In some cases, you'll be asked for administrator permission for the troubleshooter to perform an action,
so it's a good idea to run the troubleshooting wizard
through an administrator-level account. (See
Chapters 3 and 23 for more about user accounts and
administrators.)

Index

C

M

Apple & Macs

iPad For Dummies
978-0-470-58027-1

iPhone For Dummies,
4th Edition
978-0-470-87870-5

MacBook For Dummies, 3rd
Edition
978-0-470-76918-8

Mac OS X Snow Leopard For
Dummies
978-0-470-43543-4

Business

Bookkeeping For Dummies
978-0-7645-9848-7

Job Interviews
For Dummies,
3rd Edition
978-0-470-17748-8

Resumes For Dummies,
5th Edition
978-0-470-08037-5

Starting an
Online Business
For Dummies,
6th Edition
978-0-470-60210-2

Stock Investing
For Dummies,
3rd Edition
978-0-470-40114-9

Successful
Time Management
For Dummies
978-0-470-29034-7

Computer Hardware

BlackBerry
For Dummies,
4th Edition
978-0-470-60700-8

Computers For Seniors
For Dummies,
2nd Edition
978-0-470-53483-0

PCs For Dummies,
Windows
7 Edition
978-0-470-46542-4

Laptops For Dummies,
4th Edition
978-0-470-57829-2

Cooking & Entertaining

Cooking Basics
For Dummies,
3rd Edition
978-0-7645-7206-7

Wine For Dummies,
4th Edition
978-0-470-04579-4

Diet & Nutrition

Dieting For Dummies,
2nd Edition
978-0-7645-4149-0

Nutrition For Dummies,
4th Edition
978-0-471-79868-2

Weight Training
For Dummies,
3rd Edition
978-0-471-76845-6

Digital Photography

Digital SLR Cameras &
Photography For Dummies,
3rd Edition
978-0-470-46606-3

Photoshop Elements 8
For Dummies
978-0-470-52967-6

Gardening

Gardening Basics
For Dummies
978-0-470-03749-2

Organic Gardening
For Dummies,
2nd Edition
978-0-470-43067-5

Green/Sustainable

Raising Chickens
For Dummies
978-0-470-46544-8

Green Cleaning
For Dummies
978-0-470-39106-8

Health

Diabetes For Dummies,
3rd Edition
978-0-470-27086-8

Food Allergies
For Dummies
978-0-470-09584-3

Living Gluten-Free
For Dummies,
2nd Edition
978-0-470-58589-4

Hobbies/General

Chess For Dummies,
2nd Edition
978-0-7645-8404-6

Drawing
Cartoons & Comics
For Dummies
978-0-470-42683-8

Knitting For Dummies,
2nd Edition
978-0-470-28747-7

Organizing
For Dummies
978-0-7645-5300-4

Su Doku For Dummies
978-0-470-01892-7

Home Improvement

Home Maintenance
For Dummies,
2nd Edition
978-0-470-43063-7

Home Theater
For Dummies,
3rd Edition
978-0-470-41189-6

Living the
Country Lifestyle
All-in-One
For Dummies
978-0-470-43061-3

Solar Power Your Home
For Dummies,
2nd Edition
978-0-470-59678-4

Internet

Blogging For Dummies,
3rd Edition
978-0-470-61996-4

eBay For Dummies,
6th Edition
978-0-470-49741-8

Facebook For Dummies,
3rd Edition
978-0-470-87804-0

Web Marketing
For Dummies,
2nd Edition
978-0-470-37181-7

WordPress
For Dummies,
3rd Edition
978-0-470-59274-8

Language & Foreign Language

French For Dummies
978-0-7645-5193-2

Italian Phrases
For Dummies
978-0-7645-7203-6

Spanish For Dummies,
2nd Edition
978-0-470-87855-2

Spanish
For Dummies,
Audio Set
978-0-470-09585-0

Math & Science

Algebra I
For Dummies,
2nd Edition
978-0-470-55964-2

Biology For Dummies,
2nd Edition
978-0-470-59875-7

Calculus For Dummies
978-0-7645-2498-1

Chemistry For Dummies
978-0-7645-5430-8

Microsoft Office

Excel 2010 For Dummies
978-0-470-48953-6

Office 2010 All-in-One
For Dummies
978-0-470-49748-7

Office 2010 For Dummies,
Book + DVD Bundle
978-0-470-62698-6

Word 2010 For Dummies
978-0-470-48772-3

Music

Guitar For Dummies,
2nd Edition
978-0-7645-9904-0

iPod & iTunes For
Dummies, 8th Edition
978-0-470-87871-2

Piano Exercises
For Dummies
978-0-470-38765-8

Parenting & Education

Parenting For Dummies,
2nd Edition
978-0-7645-5418-6

Type 1 Diabetes
For Dummies
978-0-470-17811-9

Pets

Cats For Dummies,
2nd Edition
978-0-7645-5275-5

Dog Training For Dummies,
3rd Edition
978-0-470-60029-0

Puppies For Dummies,
2nd Edition
978-0-470-03717-1

Religion & Inspiration

The Bible For Dummies
978-0-7645-5296-0

Catholicism For Dummies
978-0-7645-5391-2

Women in the Bible
For Dummies
978-0-7645-8475-6

Self-Help & Relationship

Anger Management
For Dummies
978-0-470-03715-7

Overcoming Anxiety
For Dummies,
2nd Edition
978-0-470-57441-6

Sports

Baseball
For Dummies,
3rd Edition
978-0-7645-7537-2

Basketball
For Dummies,
2nd Edition
978-0-7645-5248-9

Golf For Dummies,
3rd Edition
978-0-471-76871-5

Web Development

Web Design
All-in-One
For Dummies
978-0-470-41796-6

Web Sites
Do-It-Yourself
For Dummies,
2nd Edition
978-0-470-56520-9

Windows 7

Windows 7
For Dummies
978-0-470-49743-2

Windows 7
For Dummies,
Book + DVD Bundle
978-0-470-52398-8

Windows 7 All-in-One
For Dummies
978-0-470-48763-1

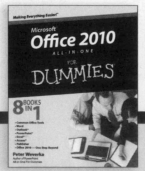

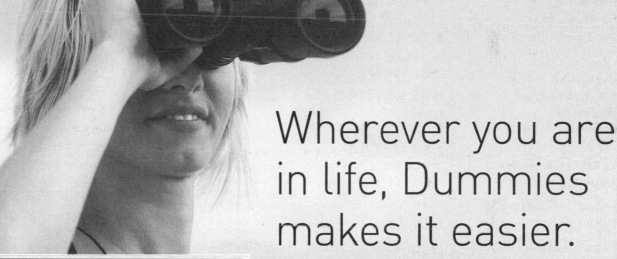

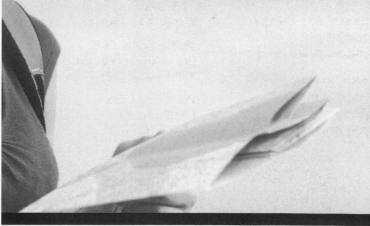

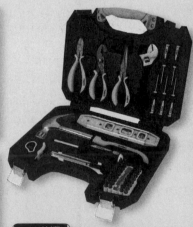